The Cultural Turn

In the second half of the twentieth century the theme of culture has dominated the human sciences. Concepts of culture have generated perspectives and methodologies that have challenged orthodoxies and attracted the energetic enthusiasm of young scholars. More significantly, the forms of contemporary culture demand a radical reappraisal of the terms of description of the modern world. We therefore need to consider our options when culture does not just provide the meaning of experience but is also the terms of that experience. This book reviews these ideas in ways that will be accessible to those new to the field and also stimulating to experts.

Within the three parts of the book, the author reveals his main concerns: first, to review the character and lessons of this 'turn to culture' in a number of academic fields. The author demonstrates the socio-intellectual context within which these themes have been generated and documents the main strengths of the paradigm shift. He also shows why the same developments have sometimes ended in *impasse*. Second, the author explores key themes in contemporary culture. By showing how questions of citizenship and the meaning of places have been colonised under the remit of the culturalist paradigm, a cluster of associated ideas and themes implicit in the paradigm are explicitly tackled. Third, some of the ways in which cultural forms are increasingly seen to dominate social reality are examined. The final chapter explores triumphant culturalism – the postmodern world as the apogee of the turn to culture.

David Chaney is Professor of Sociology at Durham University.

The Cultural Turn

THE S

Scene-setting Essays on
Contemporary Cultural History

David Chaney

London and New York

63093

First published 1994
by Routledge
11 New Fetter Lane, London EC4P 4EE

Simultaneously published in the USA and Canada
by Routledge
29 West 35th Street, New York, NY 10001

© 1994 David Chaney

Typeset in Bembo by
Ponting–Green Publishing Services, Chesham, Bucks
Printed and bound in Great Britain by
Biddles Ltd, Guildford and King's Lynn.

British Library Cataloguing in Publication Data
A catalogue record for this book is available from the
British Library

Library of Congress Cataloging-in-Publication Data
Chaney, David C.
    The cultural turn: scene-setting essays on contemporary
cultural theory / David Chaney.
        p.   cm.
    Includes bibliographical references and index.
    ISBN 0–415–10297–9. – ISBN 0–415–10298–7 (pbk)
    1. Cultural. I. Title. II. Title: Cultural theory.
HM22.F8D776   1994
306–dc20   93–46091
                                                CIP

ISBN 0–415–10297–9 (hbk)
ISBN 0–415–10298–7 (pbk)

306/CHA
7 days

This book is for Sophie

Contents

Acknowledgements

I am grateful to my friends and colleagues at the University of Durham for making it possible for me to take extended research leave which I used to write this book. More generally I have been able to draw upon reserves of intellectual capital that I have accumulated through being able to participate in a caring and stimulating community. Friends who have been particularly important in all sorts of indirect ways over the years include Mike Featherstone, Mike Pickering and Robin Williams.

I appreciate the help that Sarah Busby so willingly gave in reading and correcting a draft version of the early chapters. Chris Rojek's role in relation to this book has been even more important than his usual contribution of constructive support and encouragement. He very neatly enabled me to see the project that I ought to be doing before I could articulate it, and has throughout been a valued and trusted touchstone of what is successful.

Karina has once again worked terribly hard on the unrewarding task of indexing. I am very grateful to her for that and for the gift of all the unnumerable ways in which she cares for and treasures the life we share.

Introduction

The premiss on which this book is based is that the focus of intellectual work in the human sciences in the second half of the twentieth century has been a theme of culture. This may seem unremarkable as culture is obviously one of the foundation concepts of the human sciences and as such has always been central. I believe, however, that culture, and a number of related concepts, have become simultaneously both the dominant topic and most productive intellectual resource in ways that lead us to rewrite our understanding of life in the modern world. In these essays I will attempt to describe what I mean by these claims and illustrate their significance for contemporary social and political theory.

I describe them as essays as each piece of work should be able to be read on its own. There will therefore be a small amount of duplication as common themes are taken up at different points. I have published the essays together because I believe that they constitute a cumulative argument that will be a contribution in its own right to the issues surveyed. The essays have been written so as to be accessible to those who do not have specialist training in social and cultural theory and/or cultural history. Theoretical work on culture is generally difficult to read. I cannot claim to have overcome the problems, since writing about the forms of contemporary knowledge is necessarily abstract, but I have tried hard to avoid the excesses of culturalist jargon.

I have restricted the scope of the discussion to the cultural forms of modernity. (The issue of how modern/ modernity/and thereby the postmodern should be understood has been the trigger for and recurrent theme of the turn to culture, so it will frequently recur in the chapters that follow – for an important summary of some of the most relevant themes see Giddens 1990.) This restriction is not just evidence of laziness or insularity but has seemed appropriate as modern, or what I frequently call post-industrial, societies have been the setting within which certain types of theoretical debate have become possible. The wider relevance of these debates will have to be considered elsewhere. The essays are also specifically focused by work initially published in the English language although reference will be made to influential authors writing in other languages.

The title puns on a phrase, 'the linguistic turn' or 'the turn to language'. This has been used quite widely to describe developments in the philosophy of the human sciences around the beginning of the twentieth century. The phrase obviously signals an extraordinary growth in the range and significance of work concerned with the nature and forms of language. It would not be difficult to put forward a thesis that the more recent focus on culture is a development of this earlier movement. It is not, however, my intention to write a study in the history of the human sciences, but rather to indicate by the pun that the turn to culture is also a significant era of social thought. The title therefore refers to a fundamental movement or era (the term here is necessarily imprecise) in how we as ordinary members of society routinely trade upon and begin to express our sense of meaning, value and significance in everyday experience.

The concept of culture is fascinating but often puzzling because it has been used in several distinctive ways. In different languages and intellectual traditions it carries its own weight of associations, and one of the initial emphases of cultural theory was to show how the meaning of culture and associated words has changed through history (Williams 1976). Although a debate over how culture is to be understood between anthropologists, historians, sociologists and literary theorists among others is much of the stuff of succeeding chapters, we can, I think, get an initial hold on the issue by yielding to the temptation to say that culture has different meanings in different cultural traditions. At first sight this will seem circular, and yet what it is saying is that members of a group have characteristic and persistent forms or patterns of thought and value through which they understand and represent their life-world (culture, in a well-established phrase, is a form of life). Within this set of shared understandings culture (or some equivalent) will be one of the terms they use to describe their own and other groups' symbolically important occasions, practices and objects. Culture is therefore tricky because it uses itself and its own presuppositions in order to become meaningful.

Although the term culture, used in its sense of a way of life as well as the content of libraries, museums, galleries and so on, has become one of the common terms of descriptions of social life, it has retained a quality of privilege. It is the proper subject-matter of people who see themselves as intellectuals (an idea that in Britain is asserted nervously and used derisively by the philistine populists of left and right). It is fitting that a theme that recurs throughout these essays is of a crisis for the intelligentsia (those caught up in or familiar with intellectual discourse). The social changes in the modern world engendered by the power and spread of industries of mass communication and entertainment have posed fundamental problems for the viability of the intelligentsia as a distinctive social fraction. I hope that the basis of this assertion will unfold in the following pages. Exploring the implications of this argument for a rethinking of the sociology of knowledge is a task for future studies.

A major problem for the present book is that the range of material that could be mentioned in this sort of project is necessarily enormous. Rather than attempt a bitty overview in which each published work gets a sentence or two, or swamp each page with thousands of references (although there are still too many), I have used a broad brush to indicate what I take to be the most important features of different areas of work. One possible area of confusion concerns the range of what one means by studies of culture. There has been the development of a school or movement which is identified as cultural studies; broadening out from this rather specific intellectual grouping there are a number of other traditions, perspectives, theorists etc., which together provide a broader discursive framework for the study of culture. While one can make this distinction in principle, I have not found in practice that it is very helpful.

I have therefore used a phrase like cultural studies or the study of culture rather loosely in the following pages, shifting levels as seems necessary, in order to get at the particular intellectual leverage that is being applied in different projects. I have deliberately described them as essays in cultural history rather than cultural theory. This is because I am not concerned with issues in theorising culture, except as it has seemed necessary in the course of other narrative concerns. I am, however, concerned with the ways in which forms of culture have been used in critical accounts of contemporary social change.

This seems to me more properly described as a concern with the process of the institutionalisation of discursive strategies. By the conclusion I hope to have said something useful about the strengths and weaknesses of how culture has been and is being used, and more specifically advance my own understandings and recommendations of the value of turning to culture.

I have written extensively on aspects of the cultural forms of mass society, and specific themes taken up in some of the following essays will look again at ideas I have discussed in the past. Attentive readers may note that I tackle these recurring themes from different perspectives and lock them into different analytic concerns. This is not necessarily a sign of carelessness or inconsistency on my part. It is rather that I feel that the cultural history of modernity is too complex to be encompassed within a single analytic framework.

I deliberately cross and re-cross the same territory, worrying away at familiar issues but hoping by the conjunction of arguments to be accumulating a distinctive account. This does not mean that the ordinary reader is expected to read several publications, I believe that each essay in this collection can be read as sufficient for itself. I do, however, also believe that for me the purpose of writing is to stimulate intrigue, amusement, irritation and fascination rather than annotate all the relevant facets of a particular theme. It is in this sense that these essays are deliberately provisional.

Part I

The study of culture

Chapter 1

The field of cultural studies

THE FIELD

Since the European Renaissance the topic of culture, its forms, values, history and so on, has been specifically, but not exclusively, the province of intellectuals. There have of course been periodic crises when authors or critics have despaired of the sterility or decadence of a particular era or style, but in general the privileges of intellectuals in relation to culture have not been challenged. A theme to which we shall return several times is that the turn to culture in social thought has been occasioned by a crisis in intellectual confidence.

Culture used to refer predominantly to an idea of production or growing as in agriculture. While this sense survives, as when virologists talk about a culture, the predominant sense has shifted to a reference to making meaningful – it is through culture that everyday life is given meaning and significance. The corollary of this shift in reference is, however, that we can imagine circumstances in which there is a crisis in culture. This again could take a variety of forms but two obvious possibilities are: that culture could lose its authority so that people turn away to alternative beliefs and there is a chaos of meaning; and, secondly, that culture could lose its effectiveness so that the institutions and forms through which life is customarily given meaning cease to function.

I do not want to explore the proposal at any length but it is arguable that one of the defining features of the modern world has been a crisis in culture on both these grounds. In particular, following the two great world wars of this century, 1914–18 and 1939–45, there was in Europe a widespread and very profound loss of cultural values. This has been expressed in art movements such as the Dadaists protesting against the mechanisation of slaughter in the European trench war, and, most tellingly, in the horror and angst generated by the revelations of the Holocaust (Bauman 1989). In these art movements we can often detect a profound sense of despair at the meaninglessness of human institutions. This sense of the depths of bestiality at the heart of the most complex civilisation led many European intellectuals into a radical scepticism about the possibility of universal cultural values. A loss of faith in traditional order and values intensified for many intellectuals as it became apparent that new industries of mass communication and entertainment would increasingly threaten traditional forms of stratification between elites and the masses. There have also of course been powerful radical currents of innovation from those who have passionately believed that the people's culture should be taken seriously. Rather than dismissed as crude vulgarity it should be explored as sensitively as more exotic cultures of 'primitive' societies, because. after all, for many the people's culture was expected to provide the basis for a socialist culture that would transcend the apparent failures of capitalism

It has been against this background of crisis that more recently the discussion of culture, especially popular culture, has been dominated by references to postmodernism and postmodern culture. This may suggest that we are engaging with culture in new ways, but I believe that the roots of new theories and styles can be found in the longer history of the social construction of the modern world. In one of his essays considering the role and viability of a concept of postmodernity, Bauman (1992) argues that the central value of the concept lies in the way it has been used to describe how the changing social function of the intelligentsia has been and is being negotiated. A pervasive feeling of crisis, of irrelevance, has led intellectuals to question ever more radically their relationship to the institutions for the production of knowledge.

One of the paradoxes of this crisis has been that an increasing freedom of intellectual debate, rather than strengthening intellectuals' feelings of importance, has actually contributed to a widespread suspicion amongst them that they are superfluous. Worse, Bauman argues, is the realisation for intellectuals that as state power recedes from the management of their privileged territory – culture – it is being taken over by new industries of mass consumption: 'What hurts . . . is not so much an expropriation, but the fact that the intellectuals are not invited to stand at the helm of this breath-taking expansion' (Baumann 1992, p.100).

We are led by these considerations then to consider the idea that the significance of cultural themes in contemporary thought derives from a crisis in intellectuals' confidence in their ability to sustain the status of established styles of knowledge. With the further intriguing thought that the celebrations of the popular amongst the post-modern deconstructionists are in reality a desperate bid to sustain some form of privileged status. I will not offer any further comment at this stage, except by describing in this chapter in very broad outlines the variety of ways in which culture has been formulated as a topic for intellectual concern. In the institutional contexts of intellectual practice the crisis of culture has had to find a distinctive niche from which it could develop.

Intellectual life is conventionally broken into a small number of very broad categories denoting specific types of topic as well as methodology, for example arts, science and social sciences. Similarly, the viability of further sub-divisions of disciplinary programmes such as that between anthropology and sociology is usually only of interest to those working in those fields, university administrators and intellectual historians. This way of mapping the intellectual terrain is, however, often confused by the existence of cross-cutting schools of thought such as Marxism and structuralism and gender studies. Drawing their adherents from a variety of disciplines, these schools are often very influential for a period and then, although unlikely to disappear, they come to seem less significant as a way of characterising contemporary intellectual activity. For this and a number of other important reasons schools are rarely enshrined in the academic bureaucracy with the ultimate accolade of dedicated degree programmes.

In the last four decades of the twentieth century it has become apparent that a new school has come to be a dynamic focus of intellectual excitement. It has become generally known by the vague label of cultural studies, and perhaps the absence of an 'ism' in the title is an adequate indication that there is a no motivating figure or programme providing a core of agreed beliefs or perspectives. I suggest that it might be more appropriate to refer to the newcomer as the *field* of cultural studies. Although a small number of academic departments and centres have been created to facilitate teaching and research, characteristically those working in the field are drawn from a number of disciplinary backgrounds and see their interests as covering a wide range of sub-fields.

A better way of charting intellectual activity, which is more responsive to members' categories than the frequently rigid labels of academic enterprise, is to look at the way new publications are grouped in publishers' catalogues (and, more slowly but for the same reason, booksellers' shelving categories). Using these guides it is apparent that cultural studies is a very active and dynamic field. Professional and teaching associations are springing up under its label and of course an increasing number of journals dedicated to publishing new work. In part, particularly because of the nature of the interests of those working in this field, the history of this coalescence of interests has come to seem one of the topics of the field – critical commentaries on culture, its practice and criticism, are inherently part of the broader discourse of culture. This does not mean, however, that the terrain of the field, its central interests and motivating passions, are broadly agreed (amongst several intro-ductions to the field see Billington et al., 1991).

It has become conventional to take as one of the crucial moments in the innovations of new discourses of culture the publication of two books in Britain in the late 1950s. (I think it is justifiable, for reasons that will become clear in the ensuing discussion, to argue that there were particular factors in British intellectual life that gave this style of culture study international significance. This does not mean that cultural studies has remained exclusively or predominantly British.) The books concerned are *The Uses of Literacy* by Richard Hoggart (1957), and *Culture and Society* by Raymond Williams (1958). Although the books contained very different intellectual projects they had a number of relevant features in common.

The authors were both young men from working-class back-grounds who received their university education in the triumphant years of immediate post-war Labourism. Although both were scholars of English literature, neither was content to be absorbed straightforwardly into the halls of conventional academic discourse. Their books were attempts to come to grips with different aspects of the lack of a common cultural history in British society. They began with the determining conviction that the intellectual culture of Britain masked a diversity of traditions and perspectives in culture as lived experience.

Hoggart's book sprang from his experience of the different meanings of a literate culture. This was based on a contrast between his childhood years as a scholarship boy in a northern industrial city and the processes of cultural change that he saw stemming from developments in mass consumer society. The 'uses' of literacy (the idea of using is itself an importantly active sense of culture as engagement) were therefore ways of staging and enacting culture as the life of a community. Hoggart's book was grounded in a nostalgia for a form of life that was seen to be disappearing; but more importantly it attempted to marry a quasi-ethnographic account of a cultural world with a 'culturalist' account of the social implications of changing forms of entertainment. I have marked the term culturalist because it signals a distinctive concern with meanings and values of culture. Although this is a style of approach that in British terms goes back at least to Leavis, Eliot and Arnold, it was crucially inflected here by the fact that Hoggart wrote from within the working class and showed that it was possible to explore the richly layered meanings of cultural change.

Williams, in contrast, did not write so explicitly from personal experience (to begin with – although his later novels are a crucial counterpoint to his critical theory), but tried instead to show how the concept of culture in the course of industrialisation had been shaped and articulated as an engagement with social change. His book is a form of intellectual history (his second book, published shortly after (1961) is a more directly engaged polemic concerned with the meanings of community), but a form of history that refuses the conventional abstractions of the field. Although Williams charts his history through accounts of significant figures, such as Blake, Morris, Carlyle and Mill, the burden of his concern was with their attempt to formulate the complexities of a social and intellectual culture as it was being made. Williams also makes culture central as a process of, more latterly we might say a site for, struggles over the terms of collective meaning (by which I mean the ways in which we might assess the dignity and value of different forms of life).

While it would be foolish to attach too much importance to two books, one way of summarising why their publication can be seen to have signalled a new set of concerns is to note how their use of culture opened the study of literature and other cultural forms to sociological perspectives (although both had at the time a very limited sense of a sociological perspective). More particularly, it can also be seen that their work made popular culture central to any account of culture in general. Rather than being just ignored and/or deplored and/or despised, popular culture implicitly became an unquestioned part of the syllabus of cultural change. This is not to say that their approach and attitudes to the popular (in these and/or succeeding books) were not subsequently questioned and criticised. It is rather that, although both authors remained deeply uneasy about mass culture in all its forms and were unsympathetic to later work that totally changed the character of their concern with working-class community, they provided a platform from which the arrogance and elitism of previous commentaries on the cultural incorporation of the working class was unmistakable (see also Martin 1981 for a clear account of cultural change from a sociological perspective).

The essence of the innovation of Hoggart and Williams is a sociological insight that any discussion of cultural values in the modern world cannot be left in the abstract realms of traditional liberal elitism. The crisis of culture has to be understood in relation to the structural changes and social turmoil of urbanisation and industrialisation. Although the cultural 'problem' of industrialisation was not discovered in the 1950s but had been there all along, ideological factors had meant that it had only been considered obliquely. The 'problem', put at its simplest, is that the creation of class society had fractured many of the bonds through which the disadvantaged perceived themselves to have some commitments to the sociocultural order. The creation of socially segregated audiences engendered a double (and sometimes painfully appreciated paradoxically incompatible) search for (a) a way of opening up to the working class the civilised consensus of elite culture; and (b) a means of ensuring that the values of that culture could be preserved against the threatening vulgarity of mass access. (A splendidly crisp account of many intellectuals' horror at the threat of mass encroachment is provided by Carey 1992; see also for more general accounts of responses to the promises and threats of mass culture Le Mahieu 1988 on Britain and Ross 1989 on the USA.)

I am not trying to argue that the publication of books by Hoggart and Williams created an awareness of cultural differences within a society such as Britain. After all, Williams' book was a history of the discourse of culture (even if restricted to a peculiarly British focus). Rather, the project of cultural studies was initially provocative and has remained exciting because it has seemed to offer an opportunity to engage more constructively with the values and meanings of popular experience. This was initially a salutary contrast to a broader European quest for cultural authenticity, crucially formulated in the agonising self-consciousness of Romanticism, which had been unquestioningly set in the terms of a series of debates for intellectuals over language, commitment, policy, and so on. Even within Marxism, despite beginning with a self-avowed philosophical attack on established beliefs, there had in practice been a successful evasion of discovering or articulating an indigenous aesthetic in popular culture. Instead of confronting real issues, cultural theorists had too often been hijacked by the intellectual hubris of formulating an 'appropriate' culture for the masses (although this generalisation should be qualified by noting the heroic engagement with themes of a people's culture in the first fifteen years of the Russian Revolution).

When we come to consider in greater detail what we mean by constructive engagement (see in particular Chapter 2), it will be interesting to see how emphases have changed as ideas have spread through English-speaking intellectual communities. In the United States, Canada, Australia and New Zealand (in part carried by a diaspora of intellectuals as well as publications), the theme of culture has tended to be interpreted in terms of the variety of ways in which culture is used, adapted and remade in everyday experience rather than as a theme of ideological indoctrination by ruling groups.

The innovation of cultural studies has meant that the crisis of culture has been firmly placed within the social history of modernity, in particular the impact on traditions of elite and popular culture of the development of industries of mass communication and entertainment. In saying, though, that the turn to culture has transcended some of the limitations of previous intellectual attitudes to modern culture, I do not want to be understood as saying that cultural studies has escaped the incompatibilities of intellectuals legislating for popular culture. This is inappropriate not only because the most common criticism of published work in the field is that it has been characterised by excessive intellectualism and an antagonising use of jargon; but, as I shall also go on to argue in the rest of this chapter, because the issue of the legitimacy of any mode of cultural analysis has remained the central problematic of the field.

MASS ENTERTAINMENT

The development of new forms of mass entertainment in the twentieth century – first the international cinema, then radio, the recording industry and subsequently television, all building on the mass audiences of popular journalism and popular fiction – has cast the cultural problems of industrialisation in a more apocalyptic light. Traditional fears of the unknown urban mob (Pearson 1983) were intensified by the erosion of distinct cultural communities by industries of mass entertainment. In the most forceful version of these concerns it was feared that the new culture industries could be used to so stultify the tastes of mass audiences that not only would they be incapable of appreciating the emancipatory potential of cultural innovation, but that they could also be enslaved by new forms of charismatic leadership.

In the 1930s these ideas were theoretically developed in the canon of Marxist scholarship by a group of thinkers known as the Frankfurt School (Horkheimer and Adorno 1972; Adorno 1991). Their work was generally not translated into English until the 1960s and later (itself helping to stimulate theoretical debate in cultural studies; particularly by the publications of Walter Benjamin – see 1970 – a sometime member of the School). There was, however, some input into American sociology, particularly the new field of communication studies, through the enforced emigration of German scholars fleeing Nazi persecution (Jay 1973).

Although this work was largely unknown in English-speaking societies in the 1930s, they had their own versions of fears of new forms of exploitation. In particular, there was a widespread feeling, especially amongst the intelligentsia, of ideological polarisation. In part a response to the crisis of capitalism engendered by the international slump, and the development of Fascist movements, there was also a pervasive fear, throughout the political spectrum, of the mass mind subject to new forms of ideological domination. It came to seem important to tackle the anonymity of mass society – to show society the multiplicity of its own forms of social life. (There were journeys of exploration, such as Orwell's (1970), which were an important strand in the developing rhetoric of popular life (see also Schwarzbach 1982); and one should mention here the impulse behind and impact of studies of American rural poverty: see Stott 1973.)

The forms and motives of social discovery (what in Britain one group called 'an anthropology of ourselves') followed many paths; their importance in this context is their contribution to an enormous expansion in general appreciation of cultural diversity. This process of turning back and discovering one's own society goes back to the folklorists who recorded the disappearing pre-industrial culture in the early nineteenth century (Boyes 1993). A significant version of the same sort of impulse can be found in the more professional community studies in the 1930s and 1950s, and in the 1960s. The sociological commitment in all these movements was to blow away prejudices and stereotypes by the strong breath of real social knowledge. In Britain the social rhetoric of realism was an essential foundation for the celebratory explosions of working-class culture in the 1950s and 1960s that were the necessary context for rethinking popular culture (Laing 1986).

There was, then, in all the ways people talked about the problems and perils of social change – what we can more briefly call the discourse of modernity – a tension between novelty and tradition: on the one hand the emerging forms of mass society, with the spectacles of entertainment, advertising and consumption, and on the other a common feeling of traditional social forms and communities being forcibly stretched and fractured by new sorts of freedom and prosperity. It has become conventional to see the 1960s as a watershed decade in which there were significant fractures in the traditions of national and regional cultures allowing excited prophets to discern new forms of global culture (McLuhan 1964; Bell 1976).

In Britain the basis of a modern renaissance was both the liberation of confident consumer prosperity (the Conservative slogan in the general election of 1959, 'You've never had it so good' was borrowed from the American election of 1952); and a pervasive perception of the need for change in the management of society. This sense of the necessity of change was fuelled in part by fears of nuclear annihilation, and in part by a generational contempt for the established order – confident of being the clever party, Labour mocked the Conservatives out of office in 1964. This was of course also the first decade of mass television ownership. With comparatively little struggle the BBC monopoly of broadcasting, and all that that meant for cultural paternalism, had been broken by the introduction of commercial television in 1954. There was a palpable sense of cultural change in so many fields that it seemed entirely appropriate for Richard Hoggart, who had by then been appointed to a chair of English at Birmingham University, to use his prestige to support the creation of a new Centre for Contemporary Cultural Studies at the university in 1964.

In North America intellectual responses to the social and cultural changes of mass society had remained more firmly colonised within the remit of academia, in part because sociology was established and respectable; in Britain a significant expansion in the number of chairs in sociology did not happen until the later 1960s. (For a considerably more sophisticated account see Ross 1989.) The 'mass society' debate generated a number of publications concerned with individuality, community and citizenship, which have remained persistent themes (some resurfacing as postmodern insights), but the more embattled political connotations of popular culture were not available in contemporary social discourse. By this I mean that ideological constraints prevented popular culture being theorised as a medium of structural social conflict in contemporary America. It is interesting that a recent and very good collection of papers on popular culture published in the US (Schudson and Mukerji 1991), still has a much broader historical and anthropological frame than a comparable collection would have in Britain.

Those writing on the character of the new mass society clearly had to be concerned with new industries and habits of entertainment, and there were collections on mass culture and popular culture. Unfortunately, the legacy of modified 'Frankfurt' theorising allied with more traditional forms of elitist dismay confronted new modes of rather simplistic populism so that theorising divided unproductively between 'optimists' and 'pessimists' and this early venture into cultural studies was soon exhausted (see for example Rosenberg and White 1957; for more recent writing see Naremore and Brantlinger 1991). Although there had also been a long tradition of research into the effects of mass communication in North America this had generally been trapped within a sterile empiricism. Apart from some major sociological insights (Katz and Lazarsfeld 1956) this tradition had yielded very little of any cultural significance. The general tradition of this work is critically summarised by Gitlin (1978); and for the very different tone of more recent writing see Avery and Eason (1991).

The general sterility of American work on mass culture was made apparent by the failure to anticipate the cultural politics of generational conflict in the later 1960s. There were honourable exceptions such as Gans 1974. Nor do I mean to imply that there has not been a great deal of later American work on mass and popular culture, but this has largely been conducted outside sociology, with only distinguished exceptions, such as Denzin (1992), seeking to bridge divides. In America this was focused on opposition to the waging of an imperialist war in Indo-China, although it was articulated through a rhetoric of subcultural estrangement. Culture, and more forcefully illegitimate popular culture, became the medium through which a sense of historical rupture could be asserted – and thus the explosion into fame of a whole range of counter-cultural icons and texts. Culture was made into an unbridgeable divide that fractured established social structures in ways that orthodox radicalism could not begin to accommodate.

The lack of consensus across generations was seen as self-evident proof of the cultural fragmentation of traditional authority. In Europe this reached its apogee in *les événements* in Paris during May 1968. The significance here lay in its impossibility – a revolution in a mature late capitalist democracy contradicted all the confidence of consumer culture. In the end of course the revolution was dissipated, betrayed as much by the conservative terror of the Communist leadership as by the strength of bourgeois institutions. The symbolic force of 1968 was that despite the brave talk of worker–student alliances it was essentially a cultural interruption. It was not based on the relations of production, or on the working class, but on a cultural intelligentsia, so that the long-term heritage was a transformation of cultural analysis (I am making an oblique reference to the biographies of subsequent culture gurus such as Foucault and Baudrillard).

The cultural revolutions of the late 1960s in late industrial societies created the possibility of combining in a new mode of stardom a popular culture performer who is both a member of an artistic avant-garde and a political – with a very small p – revolutionary (Marcus 1989). Frith and Horne in their study of successive waves of innovation in British popular music (1987) show how art schools were particularly effective breeding grounds for innovating attempts to generate a mode of performance that could claim the integrity of a cultural stance that was in opposition to cultural orthodoxy but that also brought great commercial rewards. Such an initially unlikely transformation of cultural radicalism had in fact been presaged by the mannered ironicising of the artistic image by the Pop Art movement throughout the 1960s. Although the members of this diverse school were rarely any more socially radical than an earlier avant-garde (the Impressionists). British and American innovators in Pop Art had, through their practice, initiated a more serious subversion of the privileges of the

intelligentsia in relation to popular culture than had any previous
avant-garde movement of the century.

ART AND LITERATURE

I have suggested that an essential element of the distinctiveness of
the new forms of engagement with culture was a – largely unacknowledged – turn to (almost an embrace of) a sociological
perspective. In practice I believe we can see now that the embrace
was at best selective, was (rather fittingly) an embrace of an image,
and in its enthusiasm ignored the complexity of the sociological
tradition (and in some variants such as the heyday of the Birmingham Centre was almost wilfully anti-sociological). In this section I
shall spell out what this rather elaborate sentence means. It is
important to say at the beginning that mine is not a sociological
complaint about not being taken sufficiently seriously; it is rather
that it is easier to get a sense of the cultural studies project by
drawing some contrasts between the project as it developed and
what in sociology it was marking itself out from. To do this I shall
briefly describe two contemporary collections.

The first, edited by Albrecht et al. (1970), is rather characteristically American in flavour. A run through the six parts into
which the collection is divided shows: first, a number of papers
giving social, i.e. contextualised, accounts of several forms and
styles of artistic expression; a section on artists subdivided into two
parts on socialisation and careers, then social positions and roles;
a section on distribution and reward systems for artistic production;
followed by a section on tastemakers and publics in relation to art
styles; a section on methodologies appropriate to these types of
study; and a final section on possible historiographic styles and
theories. It is apparent that here a 'sociology of' is being understood
as showing the relevance of the art worlds (as Becker in a later
(1982) book called institutions) that are necessary for any productive activity to become possible. This approach, emphasising the
significance of the ways in which cultural products are made, has
remained a strong theme in American sociology (see for example
Crane 1992).

A later collection edited by Tom and Elizabeth Burns (1974) is
similar although also clearly more European in style. Here the
constituent parts are: first a collection of papers on the interdependence of social institutions and fictional forms (similar to the last

section of the Albrecht book); second a small selection of critical writing that shows some of the same themes; a big third section on different types of interaction in representation between fictional and social forms; followed by a section on conventions of performance bridging the gap between social processes and personal strategies of expression; and a fifth section of papers on readers and audiences in different social contexts. In this collection the understanding of the sociological project can be seen to have shifted from a stress on processes of collective interaction sustaining personal action to a more theoretical interest in how vocabularies of personal expression are based in cultural formations. In some ways this is not a major difference in emphasis, but it does mean engaging with cultural forms as a distinctive level of analysis that would have been difficult in the climate of empiricism that has dominated American conceptions of sociology.

What I have called a theoretical interest in the sociocultural determination of creative practice was, however, being developed from a number of directions. By the time that Janet Wolff published *The Social Production of Art* (1980), which reviews the field and signposts important themes for students, notions of production had advanced quite rapidly. Although Wolff does include a sympathetic discussion of the American post-interactionist relations of production school, her chapter headings indicate a different agenda of interests: social structure and artistic creativity; the social production of art; art as ideology; aesthetic autonomy and cultural politics; interpretation as re-creation; the death of the author; and a conclusion on cultural producers and cultural production.

The emphasis here is on dragging the cultural more clearly into view as an autonomous level of concern. This is carried out through two particularly important lines of argument in this context. The first is that to understand the notion of personal creativity does not just need a grasp of the context of the artists' social world; it is now critically attacked as ideological myth (with all that this means for accounts of cultural history or style – see the discussion in Chapter 2). The second, and closely related, argument is that the work of art should be treated as an instance or example of forms of representation. These forms can then be used as an interpretive resource through which we can study the constitution or production of social knowledge.

Wolff's approach to the study of cultural objects or artefacts or texts is here explicitly drawing upon the Marxist paradigm of the sociology of knowledge. What this means is that the ways of knowing (forms of knowledge) that are available in any historical moment or to any set of actors are determined (to degrees and in ways that we can leave unspecified for the present) by the social organisation and control of the means and relations of production. The significant development of this thesis in the new theorising is that forms of knowledge are now seen to have their specific relations of production. These relations not only determine social knowledge (as should be expected), but, through the power of that knowledge, other modes of production as well (which is a significant innovation for Marxism). It was therefore beginning to become clear in new theories of culture that the mechanisms of determination could be (or even, for some writers, could only be) discoverable through analysis of the practices of knowledge (works of art).

Two further consequences of this reworking of the Marxist tradition that have become characteristic of cultural studies are: first, that works of art which enjoyed a privileged status within bourgeois criticism as 'great' could not in principle be more fruitful for analysis than more vulgar entertainments (a thesis that the traditional intelligentsia of Marxism including Marx himself had never been able to contemplate); and secondly, that the process of how one reads or analyses cultural objects obviously becomes crucial. The further consequence is that the methodology of cultural analysis becomes in itself the primary object of analytic concern. And thus we have that definitive characteristic of contemporary radicalism in the endless recycling of *theoretical*, rather than methodological, debates over the legitimacy of methodological practices.

Further light is thrown on the point that studies of forms of culture provide a privileged means of analysis for contemporary society, if one looks at the edited collection of papers from the British Sociology Association annual conference on culture held in 1978 (Barrett *et al.* 1979a). This was the first time that the theme of the BSA conference had been culture and this itself was a response to the development of a new interdisciplinary field. In their Introduction the editors distance their topic from both anthropological notions of culture and the sociology of literature, and instead see: 'cultural products and practices in terms of the relations between their material conditions of existence and their work as representations *which produce meanings*' (Barrett *et al.* 1979b, p.10; emphasis added).

The latter phrase is confirmed and amplified by the subsequent remark that they see the central issue as: '"culture" defined as the socially and historically situated *process of production of meanings*' (ibid., p.11; emphasis added). In these formulations it begins to become clear that culture, as a productive enterprise, can be analysed through a notion of representation. Or, to put it more precisely, that the nature of the relationships between the 'language' of representation and social life is being invested with a new significance.

My next step in tracing the emergence of a distinctive approach for cultural studies is to look at the paper by Richard Johnson, a member of the staff of the Birmingham Centre for Contemporary Cultural Studies, presented at the conference. Johnson (1979) draws what has become, a familiar opposition in accounts of cultural studies between two theoretical positions in order to answer the question: 'How could we construct more adequate accounts of, say, the culture of a subordinate class' (p. 56; see also the collection from the Birmingham Centre – Clarke *et al.*, 1979).

He labels the opposing positions culturalism and structuralism (see also Hall's (1980) account of the two paradigms of cultural studies). The former is a loose label for the approach of Hoggart and Williams and a number of social historians, principally E.P. Thompson (the significance of social history in cultural studies is discussed more fully in the next chapter). This group is contrasted with a tradition of analysis mainly associated with French theorists, in particular the Marxist theoretician Louis Althusser. In a neat pairing of metaphors Johnson captures the difference between these positions as that between culturalists *listening* for the meaning of culture, while structuralists search for it through a *reading* of appropriate 'texts'.

In retrospect we can see that this was an unnecessary opposition because members of the Birmingham Centre (in its most influential years) had very little interest in the culturalist perspective. What Johnson and his colleagues were in practice more concerned to do was to establish some sort of common ground between their own (Gramscian) version of Marxism and structuralism (these ideological debates are traced very effectively in Harris 1992). This is, however, only marginally relevant here as what we are more interested in is two points Johnson makes. His thesis is that an ethnographic approach to the study of culture suppresses: 'two essential aspects of an adequate social science which are central to

Marx's procedures: the process of systematic and self-conscious abstraction; and the notion that social relations are structured in particular ways and operate in part "behind men's backs"' (Johnson 1979, p. 55) (that is, are determined). It is these aspects that Johnson takes to be central which have influenced so much later cultural theory.

First, the notion of abstraction means a willingness to shift levels of analytic conceptualisation. Secondly, the idea of determination is also a refusal to take the phenomena of experience as given and to insist that the proper object of study is the ways in which these phenomena are constituted: 'groups or individuals as "people" cannot be the be-all and end-all of explanation . . . we can only understand their consciousness and their praxis via a detour that takes as its object the relations in which they stand' (ibid., p. 66). The detection of these relations is an intellectual exercise as they are by definition unavailable to the groups and individuals who are their subjects.

It may seem redundant to make the following point but it is symptomatic of a more general failure of the Centre. When we come to the end of Johnson's theoretical discussion and look to how this might help with the initial project of adequately accounting for the culture of a subordinate class, the actual insights are deeply disappointing. He concludes that the distinctiveness of working-class culture in Britain is: 'that the culture has been built around the task of making fundamentally punishing conditions of existence more or less habitable. The problem, perhaps, is not the *fact* of a powerful relation between class position and culture, but what the precise *forms* of the determinations are' (ibid., p. 77). The first part of this conclusion is so banal it is hard to imagine anyone who would not agree, and the second part merely restates the starting point.

The reason for tracing the two points that Johnson sees as the strengths of the structuralist approach is that they make clearer how the theorists of cultural studies are rewriting the concept of culture. While accepting that culture is a shorthand term for all the ways in which experience is made meaningful, the new theorists deny that 'the ways of making meaningful [are graspable] in their own terms, in their forms of appearance in the world' (Johnson 1979, p. 65). The rejection in cultural studies theorising of this possibility is evident in the central significance of the concept of ideology.

Ideological categories are the relations in which people stand and therefore underlie forms of representation so that they work to produce meanings for human subjects. The tripartite framework of the basic paradigm is now apparent: culture makes the world meaningful but is it itself an articulation of ideology. The mechanisms of connection have typically been rendered by the term 'articulation', a term particularly associated with Stuart Hall. (Hall has subsequently agreed that he uses articulation to mean both expressing and linking as in a type of joint (Grossberg 1986).) Culture is broadened from being (in Marxism) the traditional consequence of social determination to include the processes of determination.

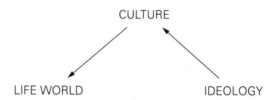

I have set out the steps in these theoretical developments rather carefully as I believe that some form of this tripartite paradigm is used in the great majority of contemporary theories of culture. The sorts of analysis the paradigm has generated and some of their limitations will be discussed in the remaining parts of this chapter and in Chapter 2.

I will now pick out three further aspects of the work of cultural studies and their rationale. It is not so much that they are consequences as that they become more comprehensible in the light of the discussion so far. They are: first, that in this approach to the study of culture the work of analysis is presumed to be intellectual, and fiercely intellectual, analysis; secondly, that the study of language, as the paradigmatic means of representation, will be seen as at least a model for the study of culture more generally; and, thirdly, that the operations of ideology, the terms of knowledge it makes available, are discoverable in cultural practices which can be treated as different types of texts to be read.

The first point has already been made several times and is self-evident in almost any text published in the field. The second point is more complex in that linguistic analysis has come to be a source of ideas in two senses. The first depends upon the theory that language is a system of signs, or what has come to be called a means of signification. If this is so it follows that the study of signifying processes in other means of representation should be able to draw upon insights derived from the study of language. The second sense in which the study of language has been seen to provide a model for cultural studies is structural. Language can be used to express meanings through the use of systematic procedures which are 'invisible' (in that they cannot be specified or described) to the vast majority of competent language users. Language therefore seems to offer a clear example of structural relations which determine social practice. The third point is closely related, in that when language is used to express social rather than personal meanings it has to be read in terms of narrative structure and a host of associated textual features. Neither the naive reader nor the author can claim any authority as to what the text means; the production of meaning becomes a process of creative exegesis.

In this section I have taken what might have seemed to be a long detour through several developments in the sociology of culture. I have had two reasons for doing so. The first is to show the significance of arguing that cultural studies initially offered what might have seemed a development of sociological perspectives rather than the asocial individualism of traditional criticism and critical history. In practice, however, within cultural studies there was from early on a turn towards developing theorisations of culture as a new type of social entity. Although within the discipline of sociology there is a variety of strategies, they can be summarised as a concern with the ways in which the means of experience (knowing how to go on) are embedded in or enacted through the organisation of different forms of collectivity. To treat culture as the body of signifying practices which constitute the terms of knowledge for social actors is to presume that both processes of embedding and forms of collectivity can be inferred from theoretical practice. It seems likely that the new field has been constructed as it has in order to preserve the interpretive scope of literary study.

The second reason for the strategy of this section is to make sensible the theoretical exoticism that has led to cultural triumphalism. A litany of figures from a variety of disciplines and a variety of theoretical perspectives have become the armoury of theoretical debate. Those who would stake out a new contribution to the field need to rehearse the competing nuances and inflections of a symbolic repertoire of figures in order to demonstrate their mastery of an arcane discourse. It is unsurprising in this intense licence of theoretical innovation, and given the autonomy of theoretical practice described in the previous paragraph, to find that the grounding commitment to determination in the social location of cultural texts has come to be seen in certain factions as superfluous. The autonomy of culture is confirmed and celebrated in a triumphalism of discourses and the play of intertextuality (Collins 1989; Connor 1991).

The idea of what I call cultural triumphalism is that theory is enshrined as the determinant of reality (see Chapter 5). In the ultimate revenge of intellectuals for their marginalisation they propose a theory in which the logic of privileging a domain of representations as autonomous is that explanation and analysis necessarily becomes marooned at the level of representation. Culture becomes self-referential and the meaning of representations becomes explicable only through mocking allusions to other modes and styles of representation. It has been argued that in the social formations of communication (post-industrial) economies the process of signification becomes the fundamental means of exchange. In a postmodern culture analysis has to confront the irrelevance of a material basis for representational forms (a thesis particularly associated with Baudrillard: (Gane 1991a; 1991b). In an economy of signs the levels and forms of simulation become endlessly self-reflexive. It can therefore be argued that the study of culture has had to develop new modes of discourse appropriate to the incorporation of social reality in cultural forms (see for example some of the papers in Grossberg 1992).

THE CULTURAL SPHERE

I have traced the development of a distinctive way of conceptualising culture. In order to bring out its distinctiveness I have emphasised how in this perspective culture is being seen as relatively autonomous through acting as a productive agency. There is, however, another social theory of culture within which the relative autonomy of culture has also been emphasised, although with different concerns.

This second perspective has been developed by those scholars interested in histories of modernisation as a process of institutional differentiation. What this phrase means is that in the transition to the modern world, distinct spheres of social organisation have come to be more tightly marked out. These spheres are characterised by their constitutive roles, institutionalised values and distinctive registers of speech and discourse. Examples of such spheres would be the privatised modern family; the public sphere of political institutions; class-segregated occupational organisations; and the spheres of total institutions focusing on various forms of stigma and exclusion such as age, illness, madness and moral turpitude.

Following this general perspective it has been argued that a central characteristic of modernity is the differentiation of a cultural sphere. The creation of this distinctive zone derives from processes of: 'the development of the cultural technologies or means of production commonly known as the media, the specialization of cultural production, and, perhaps most importantly, the attempted *autonomization* of cultural objects' (Lury 1992, p. 368, emphasis is original). Of these three factors I hope the first two are fairly clear while I take the third term to refer specifically to cultural kinds of work which are distinguished by a lack of instrumental function or purpose. Examples of this process might be the creation of markets for memorabilia of deceased cultural celebrities such as Elvis Presley and John Lennon. Indeed, the existence of parasitic industries focusing on celebrities by commenting on, celebrating, recording and generating endless stories is a distinctively modern form of work.

The idea of the cultural sphere directs our attention to the pattern of the processes specified by Lury in each national setting and in relation to different cultural forms. We can also use the idea of the emergence of a distinctive cultural sphere to provide a comprehensible and usable framework to chart the contours of cultural history. For example, it is obviously crucial for our understanding of the values of high or elite culture to have a clear sense of the social circumstances in which the modern category of the artist began to be formulated (Warnke 1993). But to say this assumes that the idea of the artist is not universal in all cultures, with the further possibility that the idea of creative genius is itself an ideological category. More technically, the discourse of creativity centred on notions of artistry has been radically subverted by critiques in contemporary theory which have seen the privileges of authorship to be interdependent with a broader episteme of subjectivity (Sinfield 1992).

Such a rethinking of the conceptual vocabulary of cultural production has gone in tandem with theories of the institutionalisation of new technologies of representation such as print, literacy and photography (Eisenstein 1993 Benjamin 1970). These revisionist histories have in turn been associated with studies of the rise and fall of active processes of reception and appropriation of different types of cultural work (McGregor and White 1986).

As a result of these and other studies we have now a much surer sense of how to relate the differentiation of the institutions of intellectual culture to other aspects of the formations of modernity. What is surprising is that, although there is a very large literature on different aspects of mass communication and popular entertainment, we do not have a more generally agreed theoretical grasp of the institutionalisation of the most important trend in the development of the cultural sphere in the modern world: that is, what Lury called the development of cultural technologies of communication and entertainment. I take this to be the main concern of those who feel that although culture has become more important in postindustrial societies, they do not want to sign up to the theoretical excesses of cultural studies.

In essence, the significance of technologies of communication and entertainment is that it has become possible to produce infinite numbers of identical copies of cultural performances so that audiences no longer have to be local or no longer have to share collective occasions. In mass culture audiences have become national and international anonymous, abstract collectivities. These technologies have created industries of mass communication and mass entertainment which have formed a new landscape for popular culture. My fear is that despite, or perhaps because of, the profusion of studies of different aspects of a culture of mass entertainment, what these studies tell us about the relationships between mass entertainment and a culture of modernity remains confusing.

In following up this issue I will describe the different ways of studying culture from a different perspective, in a way that will complement the account given in the previous section. I will discuss first some general points about the institutions of new cultural technologies, and then consider aspects of the content, and the audience use.

The study of organisations for cultural production can take either an internal focus or a perspective from outside (more generally on the production of culture perspective see Peterson 1976). By the former I mean various types of participant observation where the researcher has sat in on the production process and charted the pressures and constraints which intervene to create organisational goals. The most numerous of these studies have been concerned with the production of news in both broadcasting and newspaper organisations (Tuchman 1974; Fishman 1980; Schlesinger 1978; see also Schudson 1989). There have also been valuable internal studies of documentary production (Elliott 1972; Silverstone 1985) and other types of programming (Espinosa 1982).

Studies taking a more external perspective have been concerned with the structure and organisation of communication industries (see, for example, the overviews in McQuail 1987; Curran and Gurevitch 1991; Avery and Eason 1991). More cultural rather than social studies of new cultural technologies have offered analyses of the forms through which technologies have been used, for example Williams (1974) on television and Neale (1985) on photography and the cinema. Cultural analysis has also generated a considerable amount of work on the characteristic genres of cultural forms (e.g. Corner 1991; Berger 1992).

Other types of work on mass communication which do not fit into the group just described include, for example, more traditionally Marxist work on the political economy of communication industries (see for example Golding and Murdock 1991; Murdock 1993 and papers by Murdock and Golding in Ferguson 1990). The development of multinational media conglomerates has clearly imposed a particular version of global culture with debilitating effects on national cultures, as well as effectively creating a cultural oligopoly in strong cultural economies such as Britain. The unevenness in ownership of cultural technologies and in trade in cultural goods between the United States and other societies has been explored in terms of a theory of cultural imperialism by Schiller amongst others (1992, 1976). These studies are consistent with more conceptual accounts of the intimate interdependence of ideologies and processes of mass communication in the politics of modernity (Gouldner 1976; Thompson 1990. See also Schudson 1993 on the impacts of advertising). Although the concept of ideology is again being placed at the centre of the stage, these studies do not collapse into the arbitrary dystopian theoretical discourse of structuralism.

So the initial idea about how to study the cultural sphere in modern societies is to research the production of culture and communication. But this quickly leads, as we have found, to a concern with the discourses of cultural organisations (that is how they talk about and represent politics and entertainment and everyday patterns of social experience). Moving from the directly social relations of production to a more content-focused study of ideology can lead in three directions.

The first is indicated by a large body of work that has studied types of mass entertainment and mass communication for the ways in which identities are constructed in media discourse; I shall discuss this work shortly below. The second becomes clear in a group of studies which have viewed media content and in particular television content as displaying the characteristics of mythic narratives (see for example Carey 1988 and Wright 1975). In this work a bridge is clearly being constructed between more traditional media studies and some of the concerns of cultural studies. Finally, the third direction can be described as a concern with the public sphere.

This more directly takes up the issue of the significance of processes of mass communication as a constitutive element in the democratic politics of modernity. The concept of public sphere was originally developed by Habermas as a tool with which to describe bourgeois social order (Habermas 1989; Calhoun 1992; see also the fuller discussion of this topic in Chapter 3). It has now been extended to refer to the discourses of public life including explorations of the relationships between media production and organisations representing state power; dominant modes of presentation of public occasions including rituals of exclusion as well as inclusion; and the normal (taken-for-granted) categories of discourse in social politics. The journal *Media, Culture and Society*, founded in 1979, has been one of the more interesting sites for the publication of work bridging common themes in communication and cultural studies. Two collections of papers have been published under its aegis (Collins *et al.* 1986; Scannell *et al.* 1992) both of which have contained a section on the public sphere (see also Inglis 1988).

Closely related to these concerns with political discourses is a body of work which began from an argument that the imaginary communities of modern nations have been dependent on networks of mass communication (most famously formulated in Anderson 1983, although see also Gellner 1983). This has contributed to a broader set of studies of the illusions, ideological closures and mythologies of nationalism (see for example Bhaba 1990; Dodd and Colls 1985). Particularly important in this respect is an emphasis on the ways in which traditions have been invented in order to give the legitimacy of history to modern social order (Hobsbawm and Ranger 1983). Themes from this approach have been productive in a number of ways, including more direct studies of media and popular culture (Hebdige 1992), as well as the nature of citizenship in mass politics (Schlesinger 1991) and a more general interest in the social construction of places and environments as cultural locales.

In the era of mass entertainment it has also become common for ordinary people as well as social science professionals to speak of a loss of community. This is not the place to try to say what this concern means or whether it is well founded, but it seems likely that widespread feelings of social isolation and privatisation are linked to ever more powerful and intrusive industries of mass communication. If there is a connection it is in one sense paradoxical because it seems that the more we share nationally and globally the same diet of news and entertainment the more we feel cut off from each other (Meyrowitz 1985; Sennett 1977). This, it seems to me, is what lies behind the predominance of social research and popular concern with the effects of different sorts of message, for example the consequences of erotic or aggressive stimulation or the conceptual restrictions of stereotypes.

Following this path of linkages and associations we have been moving away from studies which see themselves as directly addressing aspects of the social consequences of processes of mass communication, towards a more wide-ranging set of concerns with affiliations and communities in mass society. The most important trend here has been a steady growth in the perceived significance of leisure as a characteristic of the modern world (Olszewska and Roberts 1989). In social theory, leisure was traditionally disregarded but those attitudes are changing and leisure is now seen, in contrast to work, as the basis for biographies of social identity (that is, the ways people construct versions of themselves through who they mix with and those they aspire to emulate). The aspects of the study of leisure and leisure industries that have directly impinged on popular culture studies have been those in which forms of leisure have been studied as cultural forms – principally sport and tourism as well as forms of entertainment (Rojek 1988; Hargreaves 1986; Wenner 1989).

A more general theorisation of changes in both the socioeconomic structures of late industrial societies and in cultural values relating to status, accomplishment and identity, has been the concept of consumer culture or consumerism as a general label for a range of theoretical concerns (Featherstone 1991; Ewen 1988). The link between leisure studies and consumer culture is that both are essentially concerned with the significance of use by audiences or consumers rather than processes of production. A second line of continuity in their theoretical concerns is an emphasis on the ways that audiences are essentially consuming signs. The activity, objects or entertainment being purchased are images of what are perceived to be desirable styles of life as well of course as being material practices.

This and a number of other changes centrally related to the cultural changes that are the focus of cultural studies have led many of the central themes of consumerism to be incorporated in more wide-ranging accounts of the development of postmodern culture: 'Culture has become all-pervasive and post-modernism has become the "cultural dominant"' (Smart 1993, p.18; see also Harvey 1989; Jameson 1991; Lash 1990a).

There have, of course been many books published under the aegis of explaining or expounding postmodern culture. A journal which has been very influential in creating bridges between sociological theories of culture, theories of postmodern culture and some aspects of cultural studies is *Theory, Culture & Society* (founded in 1980). Particularly important in relation to developing our understanding of modernism and late modern culture has been the work of the journal in making English-language readers more familiar with the theories of continental European thinkers, in particular Norbert Elias, Georg Simmel, Pierre Bourdieu, Ulrich Beck and the English sociologist who has taken up their ideas most directly, Tony Giddens. It would be crass to attempt to summarise the importance of each man; it will have to be sufficient to say that each has been significant in broadening our appreciation of the ways in which forms of life have been institutionalised and changed.

One of the central themes of postmodern discourse has been a radical interrogation of what is held to be the confident belief of modernising social elites that individuality is grounded in a distinctive and unique subjectivity throughout the life-course. In contrast, in post-industrial society the self is more commonly seen to be a fragile process of construction. In everyday life we are aware of a multiplicity of selves and of the ways in which selves are embedded in the symbolic repertoires of institutional contexts (Giddens 1991, 1992; Lash and Friedman 1992). While I think that the crisis of consciousness is inherent in high modernism and obviously must be understood in relation to the perceived signifi-cance of Freudian thought and the psychoanalytic movement in general, there has recently been an enormous increase in the interest expressed in new developments in psychoanalytic theory. In order to fully grasp the relevance of these interests to the field of cultural studies we have to go back to that body of work I referred to earlier which has addressed cultural forms through an interest in the construction of identities.

The most important element missing from my account of the theoretical emphases of cultural studies in the previous section was any reference to the construction of identity through cultural texts. Once culture has been conceptualised as the system that provides (or produces) available meanings, then it follows that individual readers or consumers of a text or performance are in significant ways imprisoned within the cognitive universe of the discourse that the text exemplifies. The key move here is to go from saying that culture is the general name for the available means of expression for any one person, with which presumably everybody would agree, to saying that the forms of culture determine what *can be expressed*. In this way the considerable and unacknowledged debt that cultural studies owes to linguistic relativism becomes clearer.

At its mildest this process may be understood as providing a set of taken-for-granted categories, or what I earlier called the terms of knowledge, through which the subject's world is organised: 'Television confirms the domestic isolation of the viewer, and invites the viewer to regard the world from that position. The viewer is therefore confirmed in a basic division of the world [between public and private spheres]' (Ellis 1982, p. 166, quoted in Lury 1992, p. 394). I have described this as a mild version of the thesis, as the viewer is ostensibly only 'invited' to take up a social position. But it is also clear that a theoretical description of the social situation – the concepts of public and private spheres – is being confirmed through an account of televisual practice. (I have chosen to say televisual practice here because the cultural analysis is likely to include narrative strategies, modes of address and discursive forms, as well as immediately available features of content.)

In stronger versions of this thesis the metaphor of invitation is replaced by more abstract concepts. From Althusser a concept of interpellation, meaning how a subject is addressed or articulated in the flow of discourse, has become influential. The attraction of the concept is that it provides a theoretical bridge between the abstract analysis of what would be claimed to be objective social determinants and the messy imprecisions of subjective lived experience.

There is of course a variety of other formulations but all are essentially engaged in the same project of providing 'positions' for subjects which situate them (the subjects) in ways that determine and thereby explain personal consciousness. At the risk of tediously reiterating the same point let me emphasise again that it is essential to the project of cultural studies that these 'positions' can be extrapolated by textual analysis.

While it will be apparent that this type of account of the nature of constituted subjectivity is essential for Althusserian and other anti-humanist philosophies (Sturrock 1979), the idea of positioning has also proved attractive as a theoretical option even when the broader theory is discarded, as in much of the use of cultural studies by feminist writers (Franklin *et al.* 1992; Long 1991; Bonner *et al.* 1992). Their central concern has been with the representation of gendered categories and the ways in which these representations work to sustain structures of inequality. It is because these structures are all-pervasive in everyday experience that feminist analysis of popular cultural materials has been so wide-ranging (including a lot of valuable work on more traditionally cultural materials such as the Victorian novel).

There have for example been important collections on the representation of the female body (Suleiman 1985; Gallagher and Laquer 1987), the ways in which the gaze of the audience in film and photography has been directed through representations of sexuality (Kuhn 1985), the nature of female audiences' pleasure in certain narrative genres of popular television such as melodramas (Brown 1989; Gledhill 1987; Roman *et al.* 1988; Geraghty 1991), and the punishment and ritual humiliations of the sexualised female body in pornography (Kappeler 1986; Clover 1992). The deconstructionist themes in postmodern theory have been controversial for feminists – while many have welcomed any assault on traditional structures of knowledge and representation, others have been disturbed by the extent to which postmodern writing has seemed to query the distinctiveness of gendered difference (Nicholson 1990; Weedon 1987).

It is natural that if the categories of gender are held to be cultural categories, in that they are articulated through the languages of representation, then the study and analysis of culture will be self-evidently fundamental as a resource for deconstructing structures of oppression. The same arguments will hold for studies of other forms of 'difference' such as the stigmatisation of gay men and lesbian women and the representational constructions of racial and ethnic identities (Gilroy 1987; Van Dijk 1991; Pieterse 1992). Indeed so central have the interrelationships between theories of the construction of subjectivities and languages of representation and cultural studies been that they can often be taken to comprise the essence of the field of cultural studies. Thus an advertisement for the MA in Cultural Studies at the University of Leeds describes the focus of the course as: 'issues in the politics of representation, sexuality and gender, race and ideas of difference' (28 January 1993).

It is also natural (in this context a provocative term) that, with the considerable range of theoretical interests in these issues, the initial groundings in structuralist theory should have been radically inflected, and eventually in certain quarters abandoned. This is not to say that the constitutive processes of subjectivity have ceased to be central, but that with a vastly increased interest in both psychoanalytic theory and the ineluctability of difference there has been a shift in theoretical focus. Rather than see the social organisation of capitalist society as the determining framework much theoretical debate has been oriented towards more pervasive discourses of power.

The dominant theoretical influence on studies of the construction of identities was a commitment to some version of ideology. This tradition of ideology-critique (which Patton 1993, p.82 has wittily referred to as an 'hermeneutics of suspicion') was never as entrenched in North American as in European scholarship and over the last decade has largely been overtaken by interest in how ideological materials are used by different audience fractions. The most important criticism of theories which hold that cultural regimes or texts prescribe or determine spaces for lived experience is that they contradict the most self-evident character of that experience. As consumers of culture we take it for granted that the audience for a particular type of entertainment is not homogeneous.

Thus it is not controversial to imagine the audience for cinema or for jazz as a series of adjacent rings of ripples in a pool. Each galaxy of rings represents a type of film (or music) and within each the closeness to the centre represents the degree of interest, commitment and knowledge. These networks of taste will sometimes overlap for specific films (or performers) and in other cases will remain distinct and unaware of, or possibly even hostile to, each other. It is obviously crucial to the effective marketing of new products, performances and performers to present different sorts of appeal in ways that are appropriate to the tastes and values of different audiences. It is also obvious that the meaning or significance of any one performance will differ as it is appropriated within the discursive framework of each audience.

The logic of this argument is that audiences use cultural texts in ways that cannot be predicted from analysis of the text alone, but this contradicts (or at the least creates problems for) a theoretical paradigm in which audiences are constituted by textual spaces. To raise the possibility of what has been called an active audience is in one sense to turn back to sociological precedents (Chaney 1972, Part 1), and in another sense to effect a form of reconciliation of the culturalist/structuralist paradigm distinction. In practice the impetus for studies which have attempted to engage with some of the issues involved in ideas of audience interpretations of texts has come from two directions.

One is work that falls under the heading of studies of popular television (Morley 1992 reviews both his own work and some of the theoretical issues involved). It has seemed necessary to a number of researchers to undertake more ethnographic studies of audience responses to and interpretations of different types of television material (Scannell 1992, Part 2; see also Lull 1990; Seiter 1989). The other direction from which inspiration for new ideas has been drawn is a dissatisfaction with the implications of dismissive characterisations of formula material. Particularly influential here has been Radway's study of a group of women who are enthusiastic readers of romance literature (1987; see also Press 1991; Hobson 1982; Ang 1985).

Rather than accept a literary characterisation of these books as stereotyped escapism, with the implication that their readers are (to use a phrase from another tradition) cultural dopes, Radway attempts to show that readers create meanings through the ways in which they read romantic books in the context of their own relevancies and interpretive frameworks. There is clearly a political dimension to theorising in which the audience is seen as creative in important ways rather than just as passive subjects (on fan culture see Lewis 1992). While generally welcomed, the current prevalence of 'active audience' concerns is sometimes thought to be carried to controversial conclusions, as for example in two collections of papers by Fiske (1989a, 1989b). Here Fiske takes over a tradition of seeing popular culture as a form of resistance and tries to apply it to a whole range of youth and consumer culture activities.

It will be apparent even from this brief review that a great deal of work is going on in relation to different aspects of the cultural sphere. If we accept the common view that the founding fathers of sociology took as their central theme the character of the modern world, then it is reasonable to argue that this recent explosion of interest in contemporary culture has significantly advanced our understanding of how the discourses of later modernity have developed – to the point of sustaining the view that our world is changing to become postmodern.

Why then did I say that our theoretical grasp of the cultural sphere is still confused? It seems to me that there is a paradox in the treatment of culture, with it being seen as both too strong and too weak. What I mean by this is when the autonomy of culture is interpreted to mean that 'texts' can be analysed as autonomous, generative agents it very quickly leads to absurdly prescriptive theorising. On the other hand to begin from the presupposition that culture is a place on which the struggles for hegemony are enacted (see the further discussion in Chapter 2) is to treat it as too weak, that is as a peg on which we can hang other theoretical interests. There are considerably more active processes of representation continuously in play as we stage and enact social categories to ourselves and others through a variety of modes of performance.

In picking our way through the vital profusion of ways of studying culture we need to be continually alert to the reflexivity of consciousness and representation. We call the social institutions of representational forms culture (and it defines a field of study), but it is processes of institutionalisation we should really be concerned with. I believe that it is these processes that the essays in this book are really addressing.

SUBCULTURES

The development of theories of the active audience, clearly has implications for a concept of culture. This is because the coherence of 'a' culture seems harder to sustain in the face of a multiplicity of forms and styles of cultural involvement. I shall argue that destabilising what we take for granted in using culture as a basis for social theory does not subvert intellectuals' claims to authority, but paradoxically enhances them. But the route to a discussion of contemporary rethinking of cultural theory lies through a consideration of the theme of subcultural analysis in cultural studies.

So far I have stressed the ways in which an effective autonomy of the level or sphere of culture has underlain a number of ways of proposing that culture offers a distinctive opportunity for rethinking political struggles. The concepts of resistance and politicisation in cultural appropriation lead to a third sense of cultural autonomy: concern with studies of subcultures, in particular youth culture.

The basis of this perspective is directly sociological in that the notion of subculture has a long history in studies of deviant behaviour (Downes and Rock 1988). Subcultures have been a distinctive feature of modernity: they are based on an appreciation of the variety of values within a general cultural consensus. The concept of a subculture became particularly attractive in American sociology in the years following the end of the Second World War when a period of unrivalled prosperity did not lead to falling crime rates and greater social integration. Instead, as well as rising rates of more conventional economic crimes, there was also a marked increase in gang-based youth violence, new types of drug use and the emergence of a strong youth culture stressing alienation from established sources of social authority.

I mentioned in the second part of this chapter the significance of generational rebellion and an antagonistic generational culture for the turn to culture in the 1960s. It was in the context of new forms of popular culture that crime and deviance began to be romanticised in important ways (Polsky 1967). The latter term was itself symbolically important, suggesting the glamour of self-conscious and principled difference rather than the furtive nastiness of traditional criminality.

Criminals have always provided a certain type of culture hero (for example the gangster films of Warners' studio in the 1930s: Roddick 1983). It is, however, arguable that in a context of popular existential estrangement, Black Power movements fuelling consciousness of racism in judical systems, and principled civil disobedience by peace movements amongst others, extra-legality could become a central motif of a new rhetoric of cultural revolution. And even if not revolutionaries, bandits from another era, such as those portrayed in films such as *Bonnie and Clyde* or *The Wild Bunch*, could easily be adopted as icons of new cultural consciousness.

It is not surprising that against this background the sociology of crime and deviance became a very productive area for at least two decades, only really losing intellectual impetus in the 1980s. An important location (a travelling biennial conference rather than a particular department) for new ideas and approaches in Britain was the National Deviancy Conference (Cohen and Young 1971; Taylor and Taylor 1973). Amongst ideas fostered in this context was a revitalisation of those theories emphasising the significance of how delinquents are labelled, and now putting greater emphasis on the role of the media of mass communication in amplifying the ascription of deviant identities and in creating moral panics (Cohen 1987). This theme provided an important link to new work in media studies that was more concerned with the exercise of hegemonic power through agenda-setting rather than indoctrination.

It was in this intellectual context that a key development of the theoretical style of the Birmingham Centre for Contemporary Cultural Studies came with publication of a book on street crime (Hall *et al.* 1978). This study of the creation of moral panic over mugging, although not based on conventional primary research, illuminated theoretical debates on the nature of ideology and was a political intervention by cultural studies into the growing concern about the exercise of state power over ethnic minorities.

Another aspect of the style of work of what came to be called 'new deviancy' was a more appreciative approach towards those who had been stigmatised or institutionalised. This marked an important shift because it was more provocative than the precedent of Marxist intellectuals choosing to identify with the proletariat, in two ways. The first was the celebration of the 'other' of respectable morality – those stigmatised for sexual and ethnic deviance. The second mode of provocation was that for the first time the practice of social theory began to see itself as insurrectionary. Once again providing a new dignity and significance for intellectuals, they could see their work to be as directly relevant to the subversion of the social order as more immediately shocking acts of terrorism.

This stance of identifying with the marginal and the oppressed fostered a different type of literature on surviving total institutions (Cohen and Taylor 1974). It also created a receptive intellectual climate for the early work of Foucault on the creation of new disciplinary regimes for the sick, the mad and the bad (1976, 1977; Cohen 1985). These ideas have been very influential in fostering a radical rethinking of the constitution of modernity (and indeed in making modernity the central concept for contemporary theory). Foucault, and related work on the character of power, was also central in helping to highlight the crudities of Marxist accounts of modernisation and the need for new languages of power and oppression.

The appreciative approach stressing the importance of identifying with cultural minorities also generated new ideas in the study of subcultural forms and identities. Rather than seeing youth culture as a problem that has to be reconciled to the social order, new subcultural research was oriented to its subjects – particularly when they were young failures in conventional terms – as inarticulate deconstructionists (Willis 1977; Brake 1985). One of the first collections of such work was published as an issue in the brief series 'Working Papers in Cultural Studies' from the Centre at Birmingham (republished as Hall and Jefferson 1976). Downes and Rock (1988) have aptly pointed out that anomie theory acted as an unacknowledged theoretical source for the Birmingham Centre's more 'radical' theories of subcultures.

This collection is characterised by two themes of a quasi-ethnographic research style allied with a sophisticated theoretical intent in interpretation. The significance of imagery and style in the use of youth cultural fashions was brought out most clearly in Hebdige's book (1979 – possibly the bestselling book so far in the cultural studies field) on the meaning of style in a series of subcultural movements or affiliations. Hebdige's play with the notion of spectacular culture is a deliberate invocation of the influence of the situationist movement of Paris in 1968 (Plant 1992), and is another indication of the politicisation within which subcultural innovation was being framed.

The idea that the culture of the literally vulgar, the marginalised and the excluded could be re-evaluated by being seen as forms of resistance and subversion rather than failure has been centrally important in rewriting the history of modernisation. It has greatly helped to expose the limitations of liberal ideological accounts of culture as something organic, something that springs up naturally in response to specific socioeconomic conditions. A further implication of an engaged notion of popular culture is that theoretical interest cannot be restricted to the youth cultures of commercial entertainment, but must encompass a huge variety of forms of dramatisation of structural conflicts (see for example Rowe and Schelling 1991, and Chafee's rethinking of popular culture forms in South American societies: Chafee 1993).

Once we start dismantling the edifice of conventional cultural knowledge we become more receptive to very different sorts of innovatory thought. I think this lies behind the 'discovery' of a Russian theorist from the early years of the Revolution. Bakhtin's ideas have been used to make important contributions to theories of cultural order, the symbolism of conflict and rethinking low forms of popular vulgarity – in particular the notion of carnival (Bakhtin 1969; Stallybrass and White 1986; Shields 1991). Bakhtin has been particularly influential in deepening concepts of culture as a form of life, so that we can go beyond patterns of lived experience to explore the structures of interdependence of individual and community, order and chaos, the sacred and the profane.

I began this section by claiming that a greater concern with audiences' interpretive practices inevitably subverts the authority of a concept of culture. Conventionally the social-anthropological notion of culture is of the whole way of life of a community, and the ways in which this is inscribed into the places, artefacts and performances of that community. Culture in this sense has been a central resource for theorising in anthropological research but it has not been unproblematic (Wagner 1981). There are, firstly, problems with the idea that there are anywhere distinctively different communities, especially in the modern world. More importantly, the process of inscription – into places artefacts and performances – has come to be fundamentally challenged.

Writing from a lucidly humanistic and interpretivist standpoint, Clifford Geertz has consistently engaged with the nuances of representation (1973, 1983; Silverman 1990). Culture in this perspective is less a set of items to be specified, and more a series of ways of 'telling' which provide some sense of confidence in the consistency of knowing how to go on. The use of a concept of culture is therefore a display of cultural competence, both by members of that culture and by those who would author-ise it – a point I anticipated when I noted that undercutting the solidity and authority of a concept of culture might seem to pose an equivalent attack on intellectual prestige. A further corollary of the ideas that Geertz is opening up is that intellectuals' claimed privilege in the interpretation of culture is thrown into question. If we lose confidence in the systematic authority of culture then perhaps our narratives of different forms of interpretation become equally tentative and provisional (see the collection of essays rethinking 'the poetics and politics of museum display' in Karp and Lavine 1991).

In practice it seems that making culture more open-ended allows greater creativity in interpretation. Chiming with other developments in postmodern social theory, we can see a turn to culture as a way of articulating a reflexive concern with the presuppositions of forms of knowledge in a number of disciplines. Thus in geography (Johnston 1991; Soja 1989), archaeology (Shanks and Tilley 1987), history (Hunt 1989a) and anthropology (Clifford and Marcus 1986; Crapanzo 1992) to name only a few, the theme of the study of culture – that is the study of the modes of the production of knowledge – is providing a stimulating opportunity to reconfigure the terrain of the human sciences. As I noted at the beginning of the chapter, this is characteristic of a *fin de siècle* crisis in intellectual confidence but it is also the promise of a new paradigm of social theory.

Chapter 2

What have we learnt from cultural studies?

SOCIAL DETERMINISM

It is only relatively recently that it has become possible to speak of cultural studies as an established field of interest. There have, however, already been a number of attempts to review important publications and to indicate characteristic strengths of those working in the field (Turner 1990; McGuigan 1992). This process of self-monitoring, which can be seen as a way of establishing traditions, is of course polemical but it does give those working in the field a sense of collective identity, and give new recruits points of reference to make their interests more tangible.

One of the lessons of the sociology of knowledge, of which contemporary studies of culture are a part, has been that traditions institutionalise ideologies and privilege. We could therefore expect that an orthodox history of the cultural turn would similarly work to legitimise intellectual careers and conventional intellectual pre-suppositions. In the previous chapter I tried to circumvent some of these orthodoxies by looking at the field of cultural studies from a number of perspectives. In this chapter I shall point to four themes which have characterised the turn to culture, and use them as an answer to the question of how the intellectual climate of the late twentieth century has been inflected by a concentration on culture.

Before turning to each of those themes I think it necessary to directly address what is involved in the claim that contemporary studies of culture fall (however loosely) under the rubric of the sociology of knowledge. More generally, I can describe this as the troubling issue that is conventionally phrased in terms of the relationship between culture and society. In the previous chapter I spoke of the turn to culture as being based on sociology but then

using notions of culture in ways that transcend conventional sociological perspectives. I attempted to show that culture has come to be
treated as a privileged level for analysis in a variety of ways, and
therefore as one that has to be addressed through a distinctive
methodology and theoretical framework.

I suggested that the – implicit – reasons for the privileges accorded
to the study of culture in contemporary thought are threefold. They
are: that culture is taken to be generative or productive of meanings
for ordinary experience; that these meanings are ideological in that
they serve to sustain forms of socially structured inequality; and
that these meanings are politicised in that they provide a basis for
struggle over terms of collective identity. We can summarise these
points by saying that although culture is privileged as a theoretical
object, it is a complex layering of meanings that can only be
comprehensible as enacted in social practices.

We are thus led to the centrality of the issue of social determinism
(using this as a general heading for a belief that understanding
depends upon a grasp of social uses). It seems to me that the one
thing that provides a watershed between earlier discussions of
culture and the development of the new field is the presupposition
of social determinism for the latter. There had of course been earlier
writers, in particular a tradition of Marxist scholars, who had
stressed the importance of putting art in a social context, but theirs
had been the minority voice and they argued for the relevance of
social interests as a way of recontextualising the character of
individual creativity. The innovation of cultural studies is an
insistence, indeed a presupposition, that culture in all its forms can
only be understood as a mode of social practice.

What this means is that when women and men are making or
engaging with culture they are governed by the same sorts of
consideration as when they are engaged in more immediately
instrumental projects such as familial or occupational relationships.
The cultural 'object' is a social fact much as any other comparable human product (a deliberate reference in this phrasing to
Durkheim's enormously influential approach to the character of
religious symbolism). But the rites of religion and objects of cultural
value are distinctive in that they are commonly held to be meaningful
in ways that other forms of expression are not. The forms of
expression are not directly translatable into other forms of knowledge and are to an important degree mysterious. It follows that the

practices of making and using symbolic objects provide for distinctive types of understanding.

The idea of social determination in this context is then that the practices of engaging with cultural objects will involve themes and ideas which represent social experience in ways that the participants cannot otherwise express. By the same logic, even the author should be understood as the vehicle of collective concerns of which s/he may be ignorant. (This is not to say that author and audience cannot deepen their understanding, but that understanding is not a precondition of appreciation.) From this point the critical or analytic project can be seen as a process of illuminating the collective concerns, bearing in mind the three points that meanings are made, that they are ideological, and that they are political, that are buried in some sense inside cultural objects.

I have been careful to present an initial description of social determination in such general terms that I hope it is non-controversial. I believe it is appropriate, for reasons that will become clearer, to call this perspective constitutive determinism. I shall describe more prescriptive versions, but before doing so I shall illustrate the constitutive approach by reference to a study in the history of art by Meyer Schapiro (1973). In this study Schapiro is concerned with gradual changes in how medieval artists illustrated a scene from scripture when Moses achieved a miraculous intervention in a battle by invoking God's power.

At its simplest his argument is that it is possible to trace a gradual transition from a representation of power in highly stylised symbolic terms to one that is embedded in the dynamics of interpersonal relationships, thus he says of his illustrations: 'These examples and others confirm our belief that the changed illustration of the Moses story is the outcome of more than a change of exegesis. It depends on new norms of representation' (Schapiro 1973, p. 42). Discussing a painting by Giotto in which the new norms he has been tracing are triumphantly celebrated, Schapiro says: 'It is perhaps the first example of painting in which the reciprocal subjective relations of an I and a You have been made visible through the confrontation of two profiles' (ibid., p. 46).

The later mode of representation is commonly seen to be more humane (more lifelike) because a psychologistic frame of reference has become dominant in post-Renaissance European aesthetics. It is this innovation that has provided the basis for the dominant aesthetic view that representations should facilitate sympathetic identification as a criterion of realism. Although it is through the widespread currency of psychologistic dramas of representation that we have come to take for granted a social and moral order based on individualism. Schapiro's study is able not only to show gradual changes in conventions of representation, but also to allow us to relate them to broader changes in norms of individualism that have become defining features of the modern world. Put simply, the premiss of modern social order has been that a society is composed of individual persons each of whom inhabits a unique self, and that their actions and values are fundamentally only comprehensible through the interaction and organisation of self-interests.

The development of a new form of social order requires a language of presentation and representation to give instances of mundane experience form and coherence, and, in its small way, Schapiro's example can be seen as an illustration of such a search for a more appropriate language. We can make this example slightly stronger by linking it to Baxandall's (1972) study of the aesthetics of fourteenth-century Florence. There he argues, that new norms of representation were particularly associated with the development of means for the calculation of value amongst the rising men of trade, accountancy and finance.

Baxandall's development of the argument is more pointed because he links representational conventions with specific social groups, especially social groups who are committed to or involved in new forms of economic organisation. The strengthening of the account of social interests that I have given so far is therefore through tying different types of interest with distinctive social groups. Social formations are, except in certain unusual circumstances, structured by inequalities of access to scarce, desirable resources. A powerful minority will disproportionately control access to the status that these resources sustain (whether it is wealth, land, literacy or some combination of these and other resources). The notion of control here will have to encompass power based upon the command of physical force, as well as the development of means of representation and communication in ways that serve the interests of the powerful. The logic of this argument is that culture is embattled – it is caught up in and indeed shaped and determined by conflicts of interest.

I have so far phrased the idea of social determination in terms of a thesis that cultural objects mean more than they say, and in that sense they are not transparent. The idea of being grounded in conflicts of interest allows us to rephrase this slightly and say that cultural objects are not innocent. That is, culture is inextricably implicated in social conflict.

More prescriptive versions of a theme of social determination have generally taken on the mantle of the Marxist tradition in arguing for three further theses. First, that a loss of cultural innocence is a necessary consequence of a materialist rather than idealist analysis. Secondly, that the fundamental fault-lines under-lying competing interests emerge in social classes as the basis of social identity. And, thirdly, that the forces and relations of production are the generative determinants of social interests that ultimately provide for the meaning of representational agendas. Given the initial clarity of these principles it is surprising that they have not led to greater methodological consistency. Rather, the presupposition of social determination has merely been a starting-point for extraordinarily intense and complex debates about how the mechanisms of determination are to be understood and displayed in concrete instances.

It seems reasonable to ask why the Marxist tradition has remained such a potent source of ideas and has been central to the theoretical development of a new field well over a hundred years after Marx's death (and in relation to the study of forms of representation that Marx would not have recognised as legit-imate). This is all the more surprising because the standard tenets of the Marxist account have proved so singularly inadequate in charting the development of capitalist economies and in explaining the social formations of constitutive classes. (One might add the failure of any movement claiming to be Marxist to produce anything other than a gross dystopian nightmare version of the founding principles of the new society, but it is arguable whether this necessarily indicates deficiencies in the theory.) A combination of the continued authority of the theoretical tradition, allied with its manifest failings, would seem to be an excellent demon-stration of Foucault's (1986) theorem concerning the different functions of authorship.

Foucault argues that authors are an interpretive device. They serve the interests of particular modes of discourse and thereby close off other possibilities in understanding texts. He begins by recognising that the inadequacy of 'an author' as the source or final authority for the meaning of a text should have led to the death of the author (picking up here a phrase from Barthes' earlier essay:

1977). He argues, though, that authorship still serves a number of functions, of which the most interesting is to be able to act as 'a founder of discursivity'. As such authors' names act to author-ise or, more aptly we could say, institutionalise a field of discourse that can encompass innovations within that discourse: 'the work of initiators of discursivity is not situated in the space that science defines; rather, it is the science of discursivity that refers back to their work as primary coordinates' (Foucault 1986, p. 116).

Within this institutionalised space there can develop a possibly infinite number of succeeding authors claiming to be writing within this field, with the consequence that the canonical initial texts are in a constant process of reinterpretation. The productivity of such authored discourses is never explained by reference to effectiveness in empirical settings but by their internal capacity to absorb innovation and to generate further theoretical elaboration, as well as sustain professional careers within institutions and generate an arcane and authoritative distinctive discourse. As discursive fields they share many of the characteristics of other cultural forms, and can therefore be discussed in relation to circumstances of production and occasions for participation as well as specific narrative strategies (as an instance of the sort of reflexive sociology of an intelligentsia that this approach generates see Turner 1992b).

The principal objections to prescriptive determinist accounts of cultural meanings are twofold. First, a feeling that to reduce the complexity of representation in a cultural performance to ideological indoctrination is too narrow a reading; and secondly, that an over-emphasis on ideological prescription misses the complexity of audience responses. Although it would be redundant to attempt to trace the full variety of interpretations of social determinist ideas (a characteristically brave but unsuccessful attempt to wrestle with the issues is Williams 1977); one theme has been particularly influential within the narrower ambit of cultural studies (see Harris 1992 on the Birmingham School and Gramsci). The concept of hegemony, taken from the Italian Marxist, Antonio Gramsci, writing in the 1920s, has been seen by many to transcend the crudities of a thesis of a dominant ideology:

> Gramsci argues that the bourgeoisie can become a hegemonic, leading class only to the degree that bourgeois ideology is able to accommodate, to find some space for, opposing class cultures and values. A bourgeois hegemony is secured not via the obliteration

of working class culture, but via its *articulation* to bourgeois culture and ideology.

(Bennett 1986a, pp. xiv–xv).

Theorists of hegemony are therefore able to preserve a commitment to class cultures, while granting a much greater uncertainty to the meaning that can be read into the variety of mass entertainment. They can recognise a play in the performance of popular culture which: 'consists of those cultural forms and practices – varying in content from one historical period to another – which constitute the terrain on which dominant, subordinate and oppositional cultural values and ideologies meet and intermingle . . . vying . . . to . . . become influential in framing and organising popular experience and consciousness' (Bennett 1986b, p. 19; discussion of hegemony is not restricted to British scholars – see Jackson Lears 1985). I will discuss further aspects of this perspective in the section on cultural reproduction below.

While it may seem that a concept of hegemony allows for a degree of negotiation in the determination of cultural meanings, if it is to retain its ideological edge it has to preserve some notion of constraints on voluntarism even if only in the last instance. There has in practice proved to be an irreconcilable contradiction here between the need to retain a core of prescriptive determinism while recognising the creative use of representational strategies in constituting distinctive social worlds. McGuigan, amongst others, has argued that although lip-service is still frequently paid to the significance of a notion of hegemony, the theory has been exhausted by its attempt to straddle two stools: 'Hegemony theory bracketed off the economics of cultural production in such a way that an exclusively consumptionist perspective could emerge from its internal contradictions: that is one of the reasons why it ceased to be the organising framework it once was' (1992, p. 76).

The problem with theories of hegemony for me, as with all prescriptive versions of social determinism, is that they try to close off the processes of the production of meaning. Such theories cannot allow the free play of irony or reflexivity in cultural discourse. It seems to me that the fundamental mistake is to assume that there are differences in kind between social and cultural concepts. Putting it at its simplest, such theories assume that social entities such as social class exist, one might say in the real world, and then they are talked about, represented and experienced as cultural matters. It follows that the dynamic relations of the former can legitimately be used to explain the character of the latter.

The mistake here is to treat the concept of social class as part of the solution to the problem of cultural meanings, rather than as an instance of that problem. Class and other modes of social identity such as gender and race and age are all versions of the problem. All the ways in which types of collective identity become available to us as social actors are given in cultural forms. Social interests are displayed in cultural objects (however obliquely) because those objects are amongst the resources by means of which those interests become actors on the stage of history.

What we mean then by saying that we can only understand the dynamic intensity of the meaning of cultural practices by reference to social concerns, is that in the performance of those practices we find ways of tackling those concerns. There is of course a necessary interdependence of culture and society but it is not a relationship in which one governs or determines the other, with all that that implies in terms of functionalism or hidden purposes. Participating in and/ or enjoying some cultural object is a form of social action.

It is important to stress that I am not denying what I called earlier the loss of innocence for culture. There is no attempt here to smuggle back in an approach to culture which accepts objects as intrinsically universally meaningful and in which the author is a key focus for critical discourse. That is an approach in which cultural objects are treated somehow as if they are exempt from political – this being used in the very broadest possible way – concerns. What I mean by the loss of innocence is a loss of faith in the idea that cultural practices are personally motivated. But it is just as mistaken to believe that cultural practices are collectively moti-vated – that is by collective subjects such as the bourgeoisie, capital, patriarchy or the play of social fractions within a formation. To believe this may give the illusion of engaging 'objectively' or 'scientifically' with a real world, but it is a world populated by ghosts and demons who may be made to play any role in the theoretical game of their conjuring.

To say that speaking of collective subjects is metaphorical does not mean that one denies the existence of styles of expression which have collective rather than personal import. There are oppressive discourses such as those of sexism and racism, and specific cultural objects or practices can be seen to be grounded in or exemplifying such a discourse. In these ways particular forms of constraint on personal and collective identity are inscribed or sedimented in institutional spheres such as property, discourse and representation. All of us inherit inscribed conventions that give social reality the necessity of objectivity. Struggles against oppression do not, however, need the warrant of an exhausted historiography to subvert the force of necessity.

CULTURAL HISTORY

I promised at the beginning of this chapter to use four themes as a framework with which to characterise the emphases that seem to me to have been the significant contribution of cultural studies. The first theme is a development of the issue of cultural change with which I concluded the previous section. The development of cultural studies has been associated with an enormous shift in the ways we have come to describe the history of modernity – to the extent that the primary significance of modernity is now understood as a change in cultural paradigms. In particular, the turn to culture has greatly stimulated interest in the history of popular experience. This is concerned with how those customarily absent from the historical stage have experienced, participated in and understood social and cultural change.

Any attempt to grasp the culture of subordinate classes has to make central a theme of history being made through the ways in which members of relevant groups struggle over the meanings of rights and duties in relation to other groups: 'the very term "culture", with its cosy invocation of consensus, may serve to distract attention from social and cultural contradictions, from the fractures and oppositions within the whole' (Thompson 1993, p. 6). An important 'moment' in the British history of this type of history came with the publication in 1963 of Thompson's enormously influential book, *The Making of the English Working Class*.

I mentioned the influence of a tradition of social history writing when I described the theoretical opposition that was subsequently constructed between the two paradigms of culturalism structuralism. In Chapter 1 I ignored the distinctiveness of the culturalist approach in order to trace the outlines of a theory of culture that in a variety of forms has effectively dominated later discussion. Within the general influence of notions of ideology there has, however, survived a way of talking about culture as something made in social practice. Thompson's significance, as a key figure for this latter approach, stems from two themes in his work. The first is the twin emphasis in his conceptualisation of the working class as a class culture, of being both a social formation grounded in conflicts of transition, and a form of life with a distinctive culture which was in important ways a self-conscious set of responses to material circumstances.

The second theme is closely related: it is a concern with how customs, in particular the play of communal life, can be read as interventions in the forging and re-forging of social order. The core of Thompson's work is an attempt to excavate another culture, not as a model for ourselves, but in the belief that such critical comparisons will illuminate what is hidden by ideology in more contemporary discourse: 'We shall not ever return to pre-capitalist human nature, yet a reminder of its alternative needs, expectations and codes may renew our sense of our nature's range of possibilities' (1990, p. 15). An important inflection is brought out by noting here that Benjamin's 'pre-history of modernity' through an excavation of nineteenth-century Paris, has also been a very influential attempt to use an account of a prior sensibility to bring out the distinctiveness of modern cultural formations (Benjamin 1973; Frisby 1985; Buck-Morss 1989).

Two examples of Thompson's approach can suffice. The first is a paper on the regulation of time and industrial discipline in late eighteenth-century Britain (Thompson 1967; 1993, Chapter 6). Thompson is concerned here with the process of transition through which the dominant forms of work, which traded upon a particular relationship between a community and its sense of itself as a sufficient lived world, became instrumentalised and disciplined by the abstract routines of a mechanised form of social relations. He seizes upon time, the ways it is owned, measured, lived and managed, as a wonderful symbol of and practical terrain for the interplay of social organisation, economic relationships and communal values: 'In all these ways – by the division of labour; the supervision of labour; fines; bells and clocks; money incentives; preachings and schoolings; the suppression of fairs and sports – new labour habits were formed, and a new time-discipline was imposed' (Thompson 1993, p. 394).

The second paper is again concerned with communal values but this time addresses the nature of crowd disturbances, in particular corn riots in the eighteenth-century countryside (1971; reprinted in 1993 with a critical review of discussion in the intervening years). Rather than see such riots as instances of the breakdown of social order, Thompson argues that they were a dramatisation of a pre-industrial moral order (and indeed more generally that riots, as all other collective activities, are cultural forms – see Harrison 1988). In seeking to regulate the price of corn to an acceptable range the crowd was aspiring not to a revolutionary transformation but to a defence of a form of life that in some ways was seen as being undermined by the values of a new political economy.

The character of Thompson's history is deeply cultural in his concern with forms of life, with the interplay of customs and festivals as representations of community, and with the symbolic rituals of popular experience. Each of these themes has been picked up and developed in subsequent work. The most immediate influence in relation to cultural studies was the critical reconsideration of the impact on established forms of life of the processes of transition called industrialisation and urbanisation (an early but still authoritative account concerned with communal culture is Malcolmson 1973; see also Storch 1982). Conventionally, I suppose, we believe that the history of our society has gradually evolved much as other life forms, so that cultures and customs have changed and adapted in response to new challenges. Thus a commonsense account of British social history would hold that pre-industrial popular culture died out because it was no longer appropriate in the circumstances of metropolitan life. The work of a number of scholars has established a more contested account in which popular culture is seen as the terrain of class conflict (Yeo and Yeo 1981; Donajgrodski 1982).

One of Thompson's most powerful lessons has been the argument that changes in the nature of work must be understood as involving much more than how one labours. This is because if culture itself is seen as a continual process of human labour, then all work, however individual, trades upon versions of communal activity in which people collaborate to sustain a set of shared values and to mark out patterns of mutual reciprocity.

The transformations of work in the shops and factories of the new metropolises meant that traditional communities were ripped apart (see for example Reid 1976 on the significance of the meaning of the loss of Monday as a communally sanctioned day of rest; and Clarke and Critcher 1985), and new more privatised forms of association became standard. In relation to cultural studies the beneficiary of this perspective, almost paradoxically, has been the study of leisure (Cunningham 1980; Golby and Purdue 1984). It is not paradoxical because leisure is not just away-from-work interests but patterns of association that mediate between individuals and different forms of community. Tracing the cultural forms of the new industries of entertainment that sprang up to cater for the urban masses, and the forms of community and association built on the activities of leisure, has enormously enriched our understanding of the social forms of the modern world.

Perhaps because of a stronger Marxist tradition in the social sciences in Britain, this concern with the making of class cultures was initially taken up more enthusiastically in relation to British social history. In recent years, however, a number of studies have pursued similiar themes of the significance of class relationships in relation to popular culture in North America (Couvares 1984; Denning 1987; Levine 1988). Counterbalancing a rather crudely conflictual view of class development, a number of studies, relating to both Britain and America have clarified the social basis of the popular entertainments of new mass publics.

Stedman Jones' early paper on how features of an emergent working-class culture facilitated the consensual politics of citizenship has directed attention to the complexity of interpretations of class culture (1983; see also Barth 1980; Snyder 1986). Indeed, this tradition of cultural history should have meant that the recent emphasis in contemporary culture studies on the power of the 'active audience' to adopt and transform cultural materials would not have been seen as such a radical theoretical innovation

I have argued that a culturalist approach to class formation and development in modern societies has helped to rescue the study of leisure from a previously marginal status in the social sciences (and see Rojek 1985). The reason is that in the making of class cultures – particularly as the old forms of working community based on a single type of employment such as shipyards, or steel mills, or coal mines disappear – the forms of play and entertainment are at least as significant as types of work in creating the tissues of suburban community. Consequently there has been a gradual shift in theoretical attention from class as a social formation based upon relations of production to collectivities focused on leisure, fashion and cultural styles. A further consequence is that tracing the development of new industries of mass entertainment has proved an important element in rewriting the history of modernity.

One aspect of the importance of these industries relates to a reconsideration of ideas of fantasy and pleasure in popular mythology. It has been too easy to dismiss the dramas of illusion and representation as ideological deceptions designed to deflect workers' radical energies (in relation to urban development see Chaney 1993, Chapter 2; R.H. Williams 1982). Particularly important in this respect was the development of the first global medium of mass entertainment, the cinema as a cultural form providing spectacular dramas for working-class entertainment (on America see May 1980; Sklar 1978; on Britain, Chanan 1979). One way of writing the history of cultural forms is through content such as, for the cinema, listing the rise and fall in fashions of genre conventions and stars. In a more production-based alternative authors draw connections between the characteristic products of national centres in particular industries and more general national cultural themes (see for example Roddick 1983 on Warner Brothers' Studio in Hollywood in the 1930s and Barr 1980 on Ealing Studios in post-war Britain).

Critical histories of culture industries are relevant to any reconsideration of the formation of modernity because the products of these industries have constituted, at least in part, the public discourse of mass society. The industries can be argued therefore to have exercised considerable power in providing a language of custom and convention that is distinctive to each national cultural formation: see the comparative discussion of press and broadcasting in Britain by Curran and Seaton (1992); and Curran and Gurevitch (1991, Part 3) on the mediation of cultural meanings; see also Balio (1990) for a collection of papers on the commercial and thematic interaction of cinema and television. Another aspect of the development of interest in cultural history has helped to clarify the arbitrary construction of cultural formations in modern society. In 1983 Hobsbawm and Ranger edited and published a collection of essays on how much of the cultural paraphernalia of nation states, which seems very traditional in the history of those nations, are in fact conscious inventions of the modern world. Hobsbawm's essay in this collection is concerned with the traditions of mass society; one he discusses is the development of sport as a form of mass entertainment.

Modern sport is an interesting cultural form in that it combines the bureaucratic apparatus of modern rationality, with the possibility of mass audiences through mass communication, with the symbolic identification of imagined communities (Wenner 1989; Hargreaves 1986; Holt 1989). Sport is a genre of entertainment which provides a more intensive focus for participation for both performer and spectator than conventional narrative dramas. The history of modern sport is an oblique commentary on the fictions of collective life in three ways: first, through an interest in the invented traditions of spectacular occasions and organisations (MacAloon 1981; Real 1977; Korr 1990); secondly, through distinctive differences in interpretations of norms of appropriate conduct in collective settings (Elias and Dunning 1986; Dunning and Rojek 1992); and thirdly in relation to the ways in which teams and games can provide a tangible focus for popular experience and the sense of community. This type of approach to cultural history obviously pays as much attention to the reported experience of participants, and to the mythologies of communal life, as to the objectively available data of historical record.

I mentioned above that radical British social history focusing on class conflict informing cultural change was active for several years before the same themes were taken up in North America. It is perhaps more appropriate to the explicitly mythical character of nationhood in American political discourse that cultural historians have concentrated more on the invention of national history (see for example Siskind 1991). In particular, they have focused on the myths of the frontier both as a privileged cultural space for free enterprise and masculine autonomy, and as an Edenic wilderness in which nature gradually had to succumb to civilisation (Farrar Hyde 1990).

The deconstruction of frontier mythology has concentrated on the ways in which discourses of economic exploitation and racist notions of savagery and innocence legitimised the destruction of native fauna and the genocide of indigenous inhabitants. The frontier then becomes a very different sort of metaphor for the history of capitalist development. It is fitting that in negotiating history as mythology some of the most potent sources should turn out to be accounts in contemporary popular culture of how the West was being constructed as mythology at the same time as it was being destroyed (Tatum 1982). This is truly cultural history as the culture was constituting the history at the same time as the history was furnishing materials for cultural mythology.

We are touching here on another type of historical methodology; a methodology that is sensitive to the continual interplay in overlapping accounts of modern experience. One aspect of these new methodologies, oral history, has greatly contributed to our understanding of the cultural construction of modern societies. The collection of oral history is clearly committed to sympathetic identification with 'the view from below'. Oral history is in a sense popular history in that listening to the stories of ordinary people's lives provides an ironic commentary on received history (Tonkin 1992). There is in addition a curious interplay of personal experience with what we might call the collective narratives of a community or a culture, for, as Samuel and Thompson point out: 'in order to make meaningful sense of their lives, individuals pillage the resources of tradition' (1990, p. 14; see also Middleton and Edwards 1990).

They suggest that these resources can be understood as myths telling tales about themes and values in community history and about structured differences in how individuals place themselves in relation to the community (thus: 'how women are more likely to speak as "we" or "one", and of relationships or groups, while men use the active "I" and present themselves as the decision-makers' (Samuel and Thompson 1990a, p. 7). The radical import of popular history has been particularly developed by those working on the journal *History Workshop* in Britain, and has led to several publications which have developed the themes, discussed briefly above, of the historical study of the active making of nations and national identities (Samuel 1989).

It will have become clear, in describing the considerable shift in historical perspective that has followed increased attention to cultural themes and matters, that it is impossible to disentangle work which stems directly from the field of cultural studies and that which stems from developments in the study of history. In closing this section it is therefore appropriate to mention three other types of historical work that have greatly influenced our general sense of the formation of the modern world (Hunt 1989a). The first is most directly cultural in that it is specifically concerned with pre-industrial popular culture. It is consistent with other aspects of the study of culture that part of the innovative force of the work of people like Natalie Zemon Davis has come from her familiarity with the theories of cultural anthropologists such as Clifford Geertz and Victor Turner (Zemon Davis 1975; see also Darnton 1984).

It is difficult to draw a clear line between the cultural history of scholars such as those I have just cited and the French *Annales* school of historians which forms the second type of historical tradition that I want to mention. Although the members of this school do have a distinctive concern with levels of historical study, their influence in relation to cultural history clearly stems from their theorisation of *mentalités* as fields of cultural practice and production (LaCapra and Kaplan 1982). The third type of historical work, that associated with the perspectives of Michel Foucault, positions itself as independent and critical of both the Marxist and *Annales* traditions. It has had a major impact because it has been so widely accepted that: 'the very topics of the human sciences – man, madness, punishment, and sexuality for instance – are the product of historically contingent discursive formations' (Hunt 1989b, p. 10). If discourse is culture then the lesson of Foucault's genealogy is that culture encompasses the totality of the human sciences

CULTURAL REPRODUCTION

I believe the work on the making of modernity to have been important for two reasons. The first is more substantive and concerns our better understanding of the social organisation of the modern world. The second is more theoretical in that it concerns the nature of historical knowledge. Increasingly we have come to realise that a narrative of social change can, and I think we can say now must, be told as a number of overlapping accounts; accounts which include the varied narratives of mass entertainment. (By accounts I mean all the ways in which we tell each other stories of change. These include official histories, costume dramas, village festivals, family photo albums and personal reminiscence.)

What these multifarious accounts mean is that although history offers the promise of discovery, any implication of coherence or resolution in what is being discovered is recognised to be misleading. At its simplest the argument here is based on the idea that any story can be told from a number of viewpoints. To attempt to see cultural change from the stance of subordinate classes or oppressed minorities is to throw significant features into a very different perspective. Thus we noted that the practice of oral history can transform the outline of institutional history. (A stress on the multiplicity of accounts in social knowledge is a further recognition that culture is both contested and inextricably implicated in social conflict.)

We can take this argument further by considering the implications of new cultural history for the social fractions of mass society. I have just argued that the industries of mass entertainment including leisure and sub-fields such as fashion, tourism and sport, have been an essential resource for new forms of constituency or audience. New historical perspectives have helped us to appreciate how cultural industries have been implicated in the constitution of social worlds. At its most general the argument here is that the forms of collective experience in mass society are fictions of drama and representation. Performances cannot be contained within the fixed boundaries of theatres or entertainment sites, but spill out in active social processes – the narratives performed being used as an active reference group in the staging of collective identities.

The emphasis of this perspective is on ambiguity and change, which means that the stability of social order is inevitably problematic. How is social order sustained such that it is reproduced through time? The concept of reproduction has become one of the central themes of cultural studies and is the second of my four themes. In human reproduction it is both a gene stock that is recreated as well as the cultural entities of a name, a gender, a family and the ownership of property, status and so on. The concept of social reproduction is exclusively concerned with the recreation of cultural entities and more specifically features of social order – those aspects of collective experience which can be seen to act as stabilising and confirming structural relationships of power, property and privilege.

The maintenance of continuity through generations is a primary requirement of all societies if chaos is to be avoided. Traditionally, social institutions such as the family and religion have been seen as primary media of continuity. More recently, it has been argued that one of the features of mass society is that, as these institutions have lost their centrality, the role of ensuring continuity has increasingly been taken over by cultural forms of communication and entertainment. The idea of cultural reproduction is intimately linked to theories of ideology. I do not, however, want to approach the theme of reproduction from the perspective of ideology. I am more interested in how a variety of authors have attempted to reconcile notions of structured social order with the interplay of the different forms of account just discussed.

One of the most sophisticated contributions is that developed as a theory of structuration by Anthony Giddens, in order to reconcile the fundamental duality in social thought between the creativity of individual actions and the structured continuities of social order (1984). Giddens is writing general social theory that is not confined to themes in the study of culture, but he draws upon a wide range of contemporary theory which has also influenced cultural studies and he has of course been very influential in his own right. The key element of structuration is the process through which social life is recognised to be structured: 'Structure thus refers, in social analysis, to the structuring properties . . . which make it possible for discernibly similar social practices to exist across varying spans of time and space and which lend them "systemic" form' (1984, p. 17).

Structuring properties are characterised by a combination of rules and resources which are both focused in part through codes of signification (that is, genres of representation and languages of social order). I do not want to attempt a trivialising précis of a complex theoretical project, so I shall merely note that the attraction of Giddens' approach is an insistence that the rules and resources of social order are *recursively* implicated in social reproduction: 'By its recursive nature I mean that the structured properties of social activity . . . are constantly recreated out of the very resources which constitute them' (1984, p.xxiii).

Giddens' theory is consistent with my argument that, in studying the forms of cultural reproduction we also need to engage with the practical, everyday use of culture in creating identities. It is also consistent with the approach that in considering the historicity of social consciousness – what I have called a recognition of the multiplicity of accounts – Giddens says that it has been made possible: 'first, by the development of printing and mass literacy and second, by the invention of electronic media of communication' (1984, p. 203).

There are obvious attractions in beginning a review of themes in cultural reproduction with aspects of institutions of education. This is because, although perhaps not directly involved in the production of and participation in cultural forms, the educational process will in any society play a fundamental role in training in cultural expertise. I shall mention three aspects of such training: (a) by providing terms of legitimation for cultural forms (particularly where culture is stratified into high and low forms, part of the practice of education will be to inculcate the values of such distinctions); (b) in providing instruction in critical discourses appropriate to different forms (in the appropriate language to express appreciation of, for example, musical or painterly styles); and (c) in providing historical narratives of the development both of different forms and of specific performers and accomplishments in national contexts (thus providing ways of stratifying the

meaning of culture between ethnic cultures, gendered groups and
'civilisations').

Any attempt to specify those aspects of educational practice
which sustain dominant cultural discourse, while being outside, or
more general than, the specific content of the syllabus in literature
or history for example, also seems to provide an especially effective
opportunity for subversion of that discourse. But as Harris has
made clear (1992, Chapter 3; see also Inglis 1988), challenging
orthodox educational culture involves confronting fundamental
issues in intellectuals' attitudes to popular culture. One way in
which those working in cultural studies have been caught up in
educational concerns has been through a series of interventions
seeking to revise the educational agenda. One example would be the
Open University degree course on Education and Society. (The
Open University is a distance learning institution offering degrees
through teaching methods primarily based on tuition made available through public service broadcasting.) Other modes of intervention have been the creation of study-guides on features of media
culture suitable as the basis of schoolroom teaching under the aegis
of the British Film Institute, as well as other published introductory
guides to media studies. (One of the earliest was a book by Hall and
Whannel, 1964, bridging Leavisite and later more radical concerns
with popular culture.)

Another mode of challenge of cultural orthodoxy can take the
populist form of replacing the 'Great Tradition' in literature and
music, for example, with instances of current popular literature and
music (see some of the discussion in Giroux et al., 1989). While this
approach can help to bridge a cultural divide between educational
institutions and popular experience, it does not necessarily
encourage independent critical thought about the development of
cultural values other than those associated with orthodox tradition.
On another level intellectual privileges can be called into question
by work primarily concerned with the functioning, organisation
and ideologies of educational institutions rather than the more
specifically cultural implications of educational matters. Although
as an illustration of how hard it is to maintain this sort of
distinction, I can point to a tradition of work which has focused on
the language of educational practice. These studies do not share a
common theoretical paradigm but from Bernstein's early work on
language codes (1971), through Hargreaves' (1967; Hargreaves et
al., 1975) work on classroom interaction, one can see a persistent

and important interest in forms of expression acting as a cultural screen pragmatically working to display and reinforce modes of social exclusion and stigmatisation.

I noted that any attempt to critically rethink the mechanisms of cultural transmission through generations inevitably raises questions about appropriate practice for intellectuals when engaging with new audiences. One aspect of these concerns that has been a cause of debate in Britain since at least the Second World War is an educational issue that has been seen as outside conventional educational institutions. This is the extent to which the state should be involved in promoting and disseminating international high culture to popular audiences through schemes of sponsorship and subsidy – in Britain principally through the Arts Council and associated regional bodies (Minihan 1977; Pearson 1982). The political dimensions of the identity of culture are contentious because it can be argued that the state should actively promote its own producers and performers, and because there are always tensions between the nation state and regional identities.

There are broadly four positions in the more general debate over sponsoring culture. The first can be called a welfare state approach; it argues that citizens have a right to culture as much as to any other public good such as health, and that the state should seek to repair deficiencies of conventional education. Intellectuals are here seeking a role of public responsibility. The second position is more concerned with promoting avant-gardist tendencies and argues that the state should support innovations which would otherwise lack popular support; so that intellectuals are here self-consciously leading popular taste.

The third position describes itself as promoting community arts. Here intellectuals seek to abandon their privileges in relation to high cultural forms (often dismissively described as bourgeois culture) and put themselves at the service of popular or people's culture (Braden 1978; an interesting version of this approach is found in Willis' defence of new youth and consumer culture (1990) which is seen as a creative transcendence of an exhausted elite culture). The fourth position denies that intellectuals should have any leading role and that cultural provision should be decided by market forces much as any other leisure product such as tourist entertainments.

While all four positions can be in play simultaneously the history of government policy in Britain over the last fifty years has been roughly a move from the first to the fourth. In these debates culture is clearly politicised, in some ways clearly and self-consciously as an ideological weapon, but more usually as an implicit aspect of more general understandings of citizenship – turning around an often confused sense of culture as the sphere of public life, issues I will take up more fully in the next chapter; I should also note that I would like to take up the developments of this theme of public culture that have focused on the role of museums and galleries in formulating accounts of cultures – see Karp *et al.*, 1992 and Negrin 1993 – but fear it would be an unhelpful digression at this point.

Another type of study that has also taken up the issue of intellectuals' relationship to popular culture comes in research reports on the failure of conventional education to engage with children from socially disadvantaged environments. Studies, such as those by Willis (1977) and Corrigan (1979), link the more clearly established concerns of the sociology of education and cultural studies. Starting from the ethnographic imperative to see social process from the viewpoint of the excluded and the stigmatised, Willis attempts to chart how working-class boys try to reject the educational system. In condemning themselves to educational failure they are also celebrating success in confirming class cultural values of masculine identity.

Willis' account is in two parts combining a sensitive ethnographic report in the first with a more complex theoretical explanation in the second. Willis sets himself a more difficult task than sympathetic acceptance; he also seeks to reclaim the futility of the rejected for a more positive role in the politics of class struggle. He thus has both to frame their actions and values in ways which transcend the distaste his socially progressive readers might feel at the boys' reactionary sexism and racism, and to explain the boys' struggle in ways they are unlikely to accept (unusually and bravely, his concluding section reports that he showed his manuscript to its subjects, and records their amused scepticism).

Willis is concerned with the reproduction of social order: not to show it as fixed and intransigent but as a process of struggle in which there are local victories. (Giddens has interestingly discussed Willis' ethnography at some length as displaying important themes and issues in his theory of structuration: 1984, pp. 288–304.) One of the most frequently cited themes of the study is the lads' derision and contempt for those who conform – 'the ear 'oles' – to the expectations of the educational system. Willis' muted admiration, and that of his readers, at this outrageous refusal is presumably the admiration of those who have succeeded through being 'ear'oles' and yet have always envied the swagger of defiance.

The terrain of struggle here is clearly symbolic rather than instrumental, although this is denied by the way the lads are grooming themselves for the values of a particular occupational community. As such the use of cultural objects here is consistent with reports from other studies which have explored how stylistic choices in music, clothes and life-style combine to constitute distinctive social fractions (see for example Willis 1978). In relation to the theme of reproduction I should note counter-balancing studies to those of Willis which have looked at cultures of femininity amongst adolescent girls and the ways they have worked to negotiate incorporation into the gendered formations of dominant social order. (See in particular McRobbie 1991; McRobbie and Nava 1984 and the feminist critiques discussed in the introduction to Roman *et al.* 1988, which point out that youth culture studies celebrate male opposition even when it is sexist and racist while ignoring patterns of female culture oriented around consumption and media use.)

The theme of cultural reproduction has been productive largely through accounts of the limitations of (and struggles over) incorporation. The notion of struggle takes us on to the central theme of hegemony in cultural accounts of the reproduction of social order. I shall briefly discuss some aspects of how this concept has been used, in particular in relation to political discourse in the mass media. Interestingly, picking up the idea of language acting as a model for accounts of cultural constraint (see the discussion of this theme in Chapter 1), Hall has sought to show both how the objective voice of the news can be used to direct attention, and how the codes of public discourse have to relate to the interpretive strategies of different audience groups (1972; 1980; see also Corner 1986 on the limitations of the language model).

To this end he proposes a variety of forms of reading taken from Parkin's concepts of types of class accommodation while retaining a notion of a preferred reading which underlies and crucially structures the opportunities for other reading strategies. Although these conceptual developments have been extensively discussed, attempts to display their empirical utility have usually remained at a high level of generality. Morley's attempt to find different types of reading of a current affairs television programme, *Nationwide*, amongst a variety of adult education classes ends in an unintelligible welter of special pleading and dubious interpretation, although see his latest thoughts: Morley 1992.

Early studies of the media under the cultural studies umbrella were interested not so much in a lack of objectivity in news reporting as in the grounds of public discourse: 'The process of construction of commonsense is, then, one of the most important ideological (and, of course, ultimately political) processes in which media programmes such as *Nationwide* are engaged as they translate the exotic world of politics into everyday terms' (Morley 1992, p. 9; see also in this context, although not carried under the label of cultural studies, the research associated with Glasgow University Media Group 1976 and 1982).

The same commitment to a study of the constitutive power of media discourse is displayed in the major study of the social problem of mugging and in particular its associations with Black youth (Hall *et al.* 1978). This study built upon earlier work by Stanley Cohen on moral panics (Cohen 1987), but whereas for Cohen the occasional stimulation of moral panics around folk devils was an incidental by-product of media practices, for the Birmingham study (Hall *et al.* 1978) it is a fundamental display of the relationship between the media and the state. The study is concerned to deconstruct the 'facts' of official statistics, and the social theory they imply, in favour of the 'reality' of socio-ideological construction of knowledge. Published a year before the Thatcher government was elected for the first time in Britain, the Birmingham study also seemed propitious in its analysis of the use of social crisis in authoritarian populism, and of new modes of social reproduction in late-capitalist societies.

A study of the creation of a sense of crisis in social order is obviously functional for a more wide-ranging theory of hegemonic power. It does, however, leave important issues unresolved. On the one hand there is a set of empirical concerns which this type of 'reading' of public discourse cannot address. For example: how effective is the language of crisis in creating a climate of crisis amongst ordinary people? and does this climate incline them to support radical conservative policies? and, even if both these questions are answered affirmatively, might not a moral panic in the media be a response to a pre-existing theme of social concern amongst ordinary people? Questions like this raise issues about the character and development of waves of 'public opinion' that cannot be answered by a form of content analysis (see Sparks 1992 for a more sensitive concern with ways of reading moral panics).

There are also, on the other hand, more theoretical doubts about whether it is ever possible to specify the mechanisms, or articulations, that enable the media to function so effectively as an instrument of social order – that is as the hegemonic interests that inform the state as a set of agencies. In the light of these issues it is perhaps not surprising that in more recent years the theme of cultural reproduction has been more fruitfully addressed through a closer concern with the reflexive character of cultural categories (the collection of essays edited by Jenks (1993) is a provocative attempt to bring out more regenerative dimensions of a metaphor of reproduction). It is interesting in this respect that a collection of essays concerned with popular cultural materials and the reproduction of gendered categories is introduced by the editors emphasising that: 'popular cultural forms can be read as texts which produce "warring forces of signification"' (Roman *et al.* 1988, 22).

One source of relevant ideas has been the work of the French philosopher Michel Foucault, whose studies of the epistemic forms of disciplinary regimes concerned with madness, criminal punishment and sexuality have radically transformed notions of the dynamics of social order and power away from the insistence in the Marxist tradition on economic structural determinations. Although Pierre Bourdieu has not broken with Marxism, his more nuanced concern with the reproduction of cultural order through the structural organisation of access to what he calls cultural capital, and his use of a concept of habitus to describe the mediations between the languages of social institutions and the constitutive processes of personal experience (Bourdieu and Passeron 1990; Bourdieu 1991, 1984, 1977), have also been a radical development in theorising cultural reproduction. Neither of these figures works or worked in cultural studies as that field is conventionally understood, but they have been widely adopted and used in different ways so that they have substantially contributed to a reworking of culture as the primary field for the human sciences.

CULTURAL REPRESENTATION

I structured my approach in the previous chapter by the argument that culture has, in at least three distinctive ways, been treated as a privileged level of analysis. One way of grasping what I call its privilege is to appreciate that culture is used as a general term to refer to the processes through which human experience is made meaningful. I hope to explain the significance of this idea by distinguishing three further ideas.

The first is that there is a fundamental distinction between being (living matter) and consciousness (being human). Secondly, the latter is unquestionably, an interpretive activity; and thirdly, the process of interpretation is interpersonal so that individual experience is to some extent dependent upon categories made available through others' interpretive activity. Thus we find that it is common in the literature to talk of social processes of *constructing* meaning; and this theme of constructing or making meaningful runs throughout this chapter.

I am trying to show that there is an underlying framework of ideas shared, despite the variety of schools and perspectives, by those who have been caught up in the turn to culture. To clarify the drift of this framework I need at this point to emphasise one further aspect: that it is necessary to make a distinction between each individual's personal consciousness (which goes on in some way inside each of our heads), and the media or means of consciousness (which are in some ways intersubjectively comprehensible). In practice the two forms of consciousness interpenetrate so that they are only, conceptually, held apart when there is an issue over whether an individual has understood or expressed themselves 'correctly'. I have marked the last word here because its usage reinforces the idea that the media of consciousness or expression can be discussed independently of any particular personal use.

There are objects which serve the function of carrying meaning and which are available to the members of a culture. Another more straightforward way of putting this is to say that they act as means of communication. The objects – or symbols as they are commonly called – may be literally physical, as in a stone or a coin representing value, or an abstract representation, as in speech. It has become common to describe the enormous variety of representational forms as signs, and interdependent clusters of signs as sign-systems or languages.

I have noted at several points how theories of language have provided an essential foundation for cultural studies, in particular structuralist theories, so that it has often seemed attractive to explore an extrapolation from linguistic theory to more loosely cultural matters (Hawkes 1977). It would be a distorting digression from the main lines of my account to go further in these theories. What I have tried to do so far in this section is give the briefest possible review of the reasons why in contemporary theory it has become axiomatic that culture is a shorthand term for all the means and forms of representation characteristic of a community. It follows that issues in representation have been the central theme in cultural studies.

I shall, to begin with, make a couple of points about issues in any theory of representation before going on to consider specific themes in the character of representation in contemporary culture. The first point concerns the relationship between a representation (often called the signifier) and that to which it refers (the signified). Naively we might believe that the latter is more 'real', or more substantial, than the former and that we can check whether something is a good or bad representation by how well it corresponds to material reality. It has become accepted within cultural theory that this approach is inappropriate. On the one hand we clearly quite often represent phenomena or feelings of which we have no independent experience, such as gods and the sacred, while on the other we use representational forms, such as speech, which convey meaning through an arbitrary association between form and content. We can go further then and make a second point that it seems that rather than our means of representation acting as labels or codes for a world we already know, all the aspects of our lived experience are formulated, made manifest, through the constitutive activity of representational resources.

One example of the application of these general theoretical premises is the developments in the study of photography as a cultural form (see Tagg 1988; and more generally Davis and Walton 1983). The photograph is a visual representation which seems to offer a mechanical guarantee of fidelity to objective experience (assuming certain procedural requirements are met, of course). Since photography was invented in the early years of the nineteenth century it has increasingly offered mass audiences the opportunity of memorialising people, places and events in ways that serve to reinforce and symbolise relationships. Photography has also been used as a means of bureaucratic record and thereby control in ways essential to the efficient management of mass transient populations. A very significant aspect of this latter function has been the role of photographs as a medium of news and public discourse in mass society.

It is clear that in several ways photography has been an essential form of social cement in holding together the modern world. The cultural form of photography has not only facilitated new ways of seeing but has also, as argued in the previous section, created new relationships between art and audience (influentially argued by Berger 1972). Cultural theorists, who have criticised the idea that a camera is a machine neutrally representing social phenomena, have not of course been arguing that cameras are inaccurate or distorted, but rather exploring the argument that how a photograph works as a representation is dependent upon cultural and ideological conventions.

As an example I refer to photographs taken by Leni Riefenstahl at the Berlin Olympics in 1936 in connection with the film she made for Nazi propaganda agencies. Most immediately the photographs represent some of the athletes who competed in those Games. More abstractly, the same images also represent ideals of strength and beauty; and they can further be read as representing the themes of physical spirituality and racial essence characteristic of Nazi ideology. Thus we 'read' a photograph much as we read any other text and that which it means is constructed by an interaction of processes of distribution and display with the ways it is appropriated by different audiences. Symbolism is not an abstract mode of representation but the variety of intepretive frameworks through which any form of representation is appreciated (Chaney 1988).

The drift of this approach is to focus attention upon the conventions of representation. While it can be argued that this creates an emphasis on formalism that can lead theory into arcane difficulties, it can more positively allow the deconstruction of symbolic strategies in ways analogous to the reconsideration of the photographic image discussed above. For example, we may well assume that it is just natural to symbolise abstract cultural ideals such as the spirit of the nation or patriotism through the image of a naked or semi-naked female form. In fact when we consider the logic of this tradition of representation we can see cultural categories of gender, power and community as well as their ostensible referents being constituted (Bathrick 1990; Warner 1985).

More generally, we can be led to consider the importance of pictorial imagery in the dominant cultural forms of mass society. In order to understand the social history of mass audiences (Chaney 1993), it is essential to examine the shift towards the centrality of visual images that marks a transition towards the abstract crowd of mass entertainment. More specifically Lash has argued that the social changes of postmodern society have been articulated in a shift from a discursive to a figural sensibility (1990a, Chapter 7). He uses these terms to label complex contrasts between dominant sensibilities, but the first item in the definitional characterisation is an historical shift from the importance of words to images. The recent rapid increase in popularity of computer-based personal games and publicly accessible video arcades has, for example, been taken as evidence of a drift towards a postmodern concern with virtual reality and highly stylised graphic representations rather than the more abstract involvement of narrative prose a sensitivity to the meaning of different media that was anticipated by Marshall McLuhan, 1964.

So far I have discussed conventions of representation as a way of characterising the subject-matter of different cultural forms and the possibility of creating new forms of cultural history through different strategies of representation. But the use of signs or symbols to convey meaning is not just something that happens 'out there', it is inherent in the management of everyday interaction and the manipulation of culture as a form of life. In the paragraphs that follow I shall switch between levels and modes of performance. I shall begin by looking at representation as integral to any adequate account of identity.

The reason for this is that whether we are thinking of personal, social, cultural or some other mode of identity, the relationship between actor and social category is always two-sided. The outsider (you) uses an identity categorisation in relation to the performer (I) based on some set of what seem relevant characteristics. On the other side performers being aware of ascriptive criteria can play more or less willingly and with a variety of degrees of sophistication with others' expectations.

The medium through which this play of similarity and difference is enacted is of course a language of representations which may comprise furnishings, clothing, voice or any other element of social settings. In his study of the multi-faceted ways in which distinctions in social status are sustained through the use of different forms of cultural capital, Bourdieu (1984) can be seen to be broadening our understanding of representations in different cultural forms. Related work can also be found on how the images of women have been fabricated in different modes of performance (Gaines and Herzog 1990).

While it has been conventional to study costume as a way of representing values and attitudes as dimensions of social identity (Davis 1992; Finkelstein 1991), a number of theorists have argued that the body itself is a mode of representation – principally of gender (Turner 1984, 1992a, Suleiman 1985). Gaines has pointed out that in the more complex interplay of insurgency and oppression in which each individual woman confronts cultural expectations of the female body it can become effectively impossible to escape the prescriptions of representation, so that at one extreme: 'The anorexic, at once "supremely defiant" and "supremely obedient", registers precisely what is done to her: she sees her image as not herself, but rather as the projected composite wishes of others' (Gaines 1990, p. 23).

It is through interconnections of representation and identity that psychoanalytic theory, in particular the work of Lacan (see for example Brennan 1989 and Gallop 1982), has become a powerful resource for feminist theory. To the extent that the several forms of the psychoanalytic tradition can be seen as the science of representation in which personal experience is constituted through a complex play of symbol and category, then they provide a challenging counterpoint to structuralist and ethnographic analyses of representation. Clearly here the boundaries between the fields of psychoanalysis, feminism and cultural studies are indecipherable and it would be pointless to try and reserve one sub-set of the domain as more germane to this chapter. At the same time to review the huge body of work implicated under these headings would deserve and demand a completely different type of account.

It is, however, necessary to pursue the politicisation of representation. The complexity of the representation of the body, to self and others, has already indicated that structures of relationships are inscribed in symbolic categories. In practice this has meant that one of the dominant themes of the literature on representation has been the articulation and inscription of cultural categories of gender, sexuality and ethnicity. As with ideology-critiques of structural reproduction through cultural practices, the easiest way of displaying the politics of representation is through analyses of the content of popular culture (see the early articles on the culture and ideology of femininity in Women's Studies Group 1978). One area where a large body of work has accumulated an impressive critique of patriarchal assumptions has been the study of advertising (Goffman 1977; Williamson 1978; and more generally on images of women in the media Tuchman *et al.* 1978). So powerful has been the attack on the inscription of gendered stereotypes that advertisers have become self-conscious and to some extent have treated 'gendered' commodities ironically.

But there is a more powerful argument that the cultural category of gender is essentially, rather than through particular styles, constituted on the terrain of representation: 'Ultimately, the battle for political articulation is fought on the territory of female images and representations' (Mandziuk 1993, p. 169; see also Gammon and Marshment 1988). Making representation fundamental to the culture of femininity rests on theories that oppression necessitates subordinates seeing through the eyes, and categories, of the dominant culture. In negotiating this alienation of identity women are led into simulating appearances through masks in infinite regress, so that, as Schwichtenberg summarises a number of writers, we appreciate: 'the mutable cultural underpinnings of femininity as an exaggeration in which woman "plays" at herself, playing a part' (1993, p. 133; see also Wolff 1990) (a neat reminder of the argument mentioned earlier that social reproduction is enacted through cultural categories).

The theorisations of representations of racial difference have for the same reasons been pitched at more than one level. There have been equivalent critiques to gender studies of ethnic stereotypes not just in advertising but in the news and public discourse generally, and dramatic representations (Gilroy 1987; Van Dijk 1991; Pieterse 1992). Although there is now much greater awareness of the pervasiveness of racial and cultural bias in, for example, the use of humour in cultural forms which have thereby lost their innocence, this has not meant that it has lost its salience and potency (Dundes 1977).

There is, then, a move to a deeper level of theorisation which is concerned with trying to establish some ground for cultural otherness within the totalising representations of 'white culture': 'the notion of society itself is a hypostatic entity, or limp ideological construct of White Culture which ... supersedes and contains white-ethnic interactions in a framework of potential equality' (MacCannell 1992, pp. 144–5). This raises the more alarming prospect that the language of social theory 'mis-represents' as an element in the heterogeneity of representational forms which is integrated through deep structural continuities. Representation, far from being pictures of the social world, is more profoundly understood as the endlessly negotiable ways in which that world is being constituted and articulated.

Clearly the languages of representation for collective identities are used as both taken-for-granted resources, and in ways that are complexly aware of tensions and prohibitions. This has meant that, as part of the realisation of the significance of representation in the turn to culture, conventions of representation have increasingly been emphasised as unstable in popular culture practice. This is in contrast to, or defiance of, theories which have rather tended to stress the function of representation as forms of closure. An early study of subcultural appropriation is in Richard Dyer's book on the stars when discussing the popularity of Judy Garland amongst gay men (1987). Dyer draws revealing parallels between the representational forms of persona-as-star of Garland and its self-conscious theatricality, and certain themes in contemporary gay culture in particular concerning identity, community and estrangement.

More recently, the emergence of Madonna as megastar has generated an enormous academic and popular literature of explanation and comment (see Schwichtenberg 1993 and references therein), much of it explicitly concerned with interpreting the fabrication and representational strategies in the star's persona (see also Gledhill 1991). The problem with Madonna is that as her star persona has shifted and changed and so deliberately flouted a series of 'normal' cultural expectations, a number of readings of the star as representation become possible. Three options are that: she deliberately and particularly through subcultural identifications with gay, lesbian and black styles seeks to defy patriarchal expectations of the feminine; secondly, that these moves are merely a sophisticated commercial generation of publicity through exploitation; and thirdly, that as the acme of postmodernism she tells us that all modes of identity are merely masks and as there can be no reality to be sought behind any mask there is no meaning to any pose.

While each and all of these options could be 'true', to be concerned with truth is irrelevant as the more substantive point concerns the politics of representation. This can be summarised as contesting views on how we should evaluate the meanings of representation. The interesting development in relation to Madonna is that she has become a political icon as a means of representation both for and within subcultural identities:

Madonna is interpreted under different definitions of feminism in different social and discursive formations, and the result is a case study in the ways that popular culture may be articulated to competing social and political practices. There is no way to settle, once and for all, the argument about whether Madonna's texts are feminist.

(Schulze *et al.* 1993, pp. 30–1)

For many political activists, especially those committed to seeing forms of representation as modes of ideology, the more unsettling implication is that Madonna has destabilised fundamental signs of subcultural membership. Even if her stardom is now exhausted, the possibility of her existence and that of figures such as David Bowie is that if all marks of identity are arbitrary, then any form of being becomes pastiche.

Once again the logic of a particular pursuit of the conventions of representation is taking us towards ideas that destabilise the structure of meaning. It seems that the turn to culture involves using culture as a way of opening up the ideological skeleton on which the edifice of reality has been so persuasively erected. And this of course is the same theoretical progression we noted in the first chapter, when I argued that a theoretical emphasis on the autonomy of culture leads to ideology being abandoned in favour of an anarchy of meaning. It is arguable that these ideas are not generally popular with 'ordinary people' possibly because they appear to be celebrating the instability of conventional social order. It seems possible that much of the power of fundamentalist moral movements, in their hostility to what they present as the dangers of mass culture, stems from forms of resentment that cultural representations are not to be trusted (and thereby are imbued with increased power: see Chapter 3.

A thoughtful engagement with some of the issues here has been provided by Sparks' book (1992) on whether the representation of criminality on popular television encourages further law-breaking. In relation to this example we are moving from oppressed minorities' rejection of prejudice to concern expressed by guardians of conventional morality ('the silent majority') that their sense of propriety is being invaded in ways they cannot control. Thus, as Sparks emphasises early in his study, issues of representation of dramatised disorder concern more the grounds of fear than the adequacy of representation, with the further complication that the grounds are themselves a form of representation: 'Fear is not simply a quantity, of which one possesses larger or smaller amounts: rather, it is a mode of perception, even perhaps a constitutive feature of personal identity . . . In this respect the issue of the fear of crime always involves problems of representation and meaning' (Sparks 1992, p. 14).

The paradox of television, as the mass entertainment of private spaces, is that it addresses our ambivalent feelings about public places but in ways that reinforce and reproduce anxieties:

> Rather than by virtue of the 'content' of any individual story television works by placing its stories within routines . . . It is thus inherent that the narratives revolve around a play of anxiety and reassurance and the disruption and restoration of order which is continual and which itself provides the context for any particular story.
>
> (ibid., p. 148)

It seems to me that the logic of Sparks' argument, and indeed the general tenor of my account of studies of representation, is that the concept can easily lead into a quagmire of moral self-righteousness. Here, going back to the first level of concern with the politics of representation mentioned earlier, criticism focuses on the possibly prejudicial effects of misrepresentation in popular culture. (There are some characteristic examples of this approach in Strinati and Wagg 1992; I return to this point in the conclusion to the chapter.)

A great deal of the fear of representation must be due to suspicion that the process of representing is analogous to being given some form of magical powers to conjure into being (and this perhaps harks back to the point that in the culture of mass entertainment images, as the most literal form of representation, have become all-pervasive). While it has been essential that a more active sense of culture as the play of representations has become accepted in the human sciences, the term encourages a comparative contrast between culture and reality. I have always argued that such literalism is inadequate and that it is more fruitful to see representations as embedded in cultural forms. A cultural form does not just consist of a narrative and its means of inscription or performance but also encompasses the social occasion by means of which different audiences participate in it: 'I consider that the interpretation of television viewing, the study of the transactions which take place between institutions, programmes and audiences, is in certain important respects more akin to the study of talk than to the study of texts' (Sparks 1992, p. 49). It is in the realisation of representation that we begin to appreciate the creativity of culture.

CONSUMPTION AND STYLE

The fourth theme that I wish to discuss as a guide to the influence of new studies of culture is concerned with concepts of consumption and style. In everyday speech the idea of consumption usually refers to all aspects of shopping rather than anything specifically cultural. Shopping is a generic term for purchasing commodities and services made available through marketing and, in mass society, advertising. Marketing and advertising are aggressively capitalist in that they are seeking to sell goods for more than they are 'worth'.

It is not surprising that within the Marxist tradition, which has dominated the turn to culture, the idea of social processes of consumption, or worse consumer culture, has been treated with a great deal of suspicion. Marketing has traditionally been seen as by definition exploitative as it promotes 'false' values (in order to generate profits), and unnecessary in that it promotes false needs – consumers are encouraged to want new or more expensive possessions in a competitive spiral that serves only to generate further profits.

These attitudes come from a long puritan tradition and have frequently provided the basis for an austere utopianism. It would be reasonable to expect that they would foster a relative neglect of audience behaviour rather than, as argued here, provide one of the main lessons of increased interest in culture. (Abercrombie has also emphasised an unwillingness to admit the salience of pleasure in the majority of culture critiques, and has argued instead that: 'Popular culture, after all, represents a use of leisure, largely in the home, in which pleasure and consumption have to be centred': 1990 p. 200; see also Mercer 1986.)

While I think it has been true that processes of audience behaviour have been neglected theoretically, compared to the significance claimed for critiques of ideological texts, there are still two good reasons for this section. First, over the last few years we have seen how those positions I have generally labelled ideology-critique have buckled under their own inadequacies and a compensating interest in audience behaviour has developed in their place. McGuigan (1992), for example, has argued that the more theories of hegemony have sought to adapt to the complexities of social fractions and processes of accommodation the more they have been driven towards a consumerist populism.

Secondly, the turn to culture has coincided with, but more importantly been driven by, an enormous interest in the attention being paid to generational culture (recognising of course that fostering generational concerns has been of vast importance to the marketing industry). Youth cultures, and all the ways they have been inseparable from black and female subcultures in particular, have made style central to their dramatisations of identity (well captured by the title of a comparatively early book on youth culture by George Melly: *Revolt into Style*, 1970).

One effect has been that industries of mass entertainment have often been visibly limping after innovations in style by entrepreneurs within audiences rather than fiendishly manipulating cultural dopes. A broader effect has been closer attention to the centrality of style in the ways people, not just youth, create culture through forms of life. I will go on to describe and comment on both of these general positions more fully.

I hope it will now be clearer that in this context consumption will be taken to mean processes of acquisition and appropriation of cultural phenomena. These phenomena range from conventional artworks to any element that is used as signifying material. In order to emphasise continuities across these different types of phenomena I shall refer to all those acquiring and appropriating them as audiences. I have bracketed together both an emphasis upon acquisition to refer to processes of buying, attending, visiting etc., and an idea of appropriation because the latter term is meant to indicate that audiences' consuming is an active process of interpretation and use in relation to audience interests (Shields 1992; Brewer and Porter 1992).

In the process of appropriation audiences are therefore combining and incorporating cultural phenomena in ways that are distinctively different, and thus creating a style of use that stamps those who so do as members of a group, subculture or clan (Tomlinson 1990). This idea of patterns of use and consumption, which provide a basis for social recognition for both insiders and outsiders, has come to be generally known as a life-style or fashionable style. Consumption and style are bracketed together because in combination they refer to the ways in which culture is made through use (these ideas are more fully discussed in Chapter 5).

In the section on cultural history I argued that one of the unexpected benefits to be derived from histories of culture industries is a way of charting changing social formations such as structures of class and gender relations. More generally, we can say that the history and character of leisure in industrial society also offers interesting theoretical challenges. Neither a picture of a gradually increasing commercial utopia of popular choice, nor a picture of inexorable immiseration of the proletariat can be seen to correpond to the record. Instead there is a vastly more complicated story of emergent class cultures in which communal forms have increasingly been serviced by mass industries of commercial entertainment with interweaving discourses of respectability, self-improvement and gendered specificities.

I do not want to try and tell that story here, but rather take from it the lesson that forms of popular culture developed as types of social activity that illuminate several different analytic perspectives simultaneously. What I mean by this is that in seeking to make sense of a cultural form such as popular cinema we have to reconcile accounts of characteristic genres and their limitations with a sympathetic sense of the sorts of pleasure those films could provide in everyday experience (see for example Tudor 1989; and on television Tulloch 1990; on popular fiction Palmer 1991; Bennett 1990; Bennett and Woollacott 1987).

I will develop this line of argument by turning to the example of the history of sport as an interesting form of mass entertainment. I discussed this example in the section on cultural history and I return to it now because sport is germane to any consideration of the interplay between local communities and mass media of communication. Sport is a form of commercial entertainment that displays all the defining features of modernity – for example it is regulated by national and international bureaucracies, and is increasingly governed by the use of quantitative measures of achievement (Guttman 1978).

But sport also provides a focus for class and communal identifications so that it becomes central in sustaining a way of life, and it is also a form of drama which is one of the main staple resources of the media of mass communication. Each of these dimensions is essential for understanding the character of sport in mass society, and none is sufficient in itself to provide an adequate account. (There are of course many further dimensions that can and should be included in any full account such as the nature of professional socialisation, gendered characteristics of types of sports deemed appropriate for women, and the marketing of the Olympics as a mega-national spectacular cultural occasion.)

An aspect of recent theories of sport that is especially relevant to the theme of consumption is the meaning of crowd behaviour. While sports are increasingly being marketed as televisual events so that the majority of the audience are domestic viewers, sport as a focus for communal identification demands a mass crowd that has traditionally posed problems of social order (Guttman 1986). In recent years association football has been associated with violence amongst its supporters, often articulated through radical authoritarian and racist politicisations. There has been controversy amongst commentators on the most appropriate interpretation of behaviour that runs counter to our expectations of strengthening civilisation in mass society (Dunning and Rojek 1992; Williams 1991). What is clear is that any theory has to address the meaning of a specific sport in its cultural context in order to get some sense of the ways in which it is consumed and appropriated by its audiences. (This thesis does not just apply to sport of course; Jenkins has recently published an excellent study of the creative practice of fans of a television drama series: see Jenkins 1992.)

Leisure is particularly germane to a section on consumption because it displays so many of the characteristics of consumer culture. In the discourse of leisure great stress is placed on personal choice, voluntary associations and the use of time as a form of investment as well as expenditure. One of the more significant cultural developments in urban-industrial societies, and one which has conformed to more general features of the discourse of leisure, has been the practice of taking holidays and the emergence of an industry of mass tourism (Ryan 1991). While a great deal of cultural commentary on tourism and tourist entertainments has conformed to a critical style associated with high cultural disdain at the poverty of taste in popular culture, it has also become apparent that the tourist constitutes a distinctive type of consumer.

MacCannell's first book (1977) was important in this respect as he argued that the tourist's visit is a form of production. Anticipating certain themes in postmodern writing, MacCannell stressed the ways in which tourists play with signifiers of place and experience. Whether it is through features of the place being visited, associated accounts and guides, or souvenirs of many types, the tourist actively collaborates in the production of places through their forms of representation. The tourist is therefore an active cultural consumer

– the premiss of tourism is that cultural difference can be appropriated as resource for touristic culture. It follows from this approach that the tourist is primarily concerned with the signs or markers that constitute the distinctiveness of 'a place' (these ideas are further developed in Chapter 4). As we saw in the discussion of representation in general, signs need not be governed by the 'reality' of what they represent. The places of tourism are, in this sense, arbitrary cultural constructions.

Tourism is therefore a form of entertainment dependent upon exploitation – Urry has more recently conceptualised the mode of appropriation as 'the tourist gaze' (1990), a way of seeing that is both appropriative and non-involving. It could further be argued that this not only exploits the host culture but also demeans and trivialises the touristic culture. It seems inappropriate, however, to jump too quickly to aesthetic condemnations of the spectacular drama of tourism. Rojek (1993) argues that in touristic excursions the audience are actors in their own dramas, so that they are escaping not to alternative realities but rather to a more complex sense of the pleasures and constraints of the reality they are constructing.

The experience of mass tourism, in conjunction with all the ways in which consumer marketing makes every facet of cultural exoticism routinely available in your shopping centre, has led to the blurring of cultural boundaries. We can buy exotic fruit and vegetables at any time of the year, we can buy fabrics, furnishings and artefacts from any culture, and every town and shopping centre will have its array of international restaurants. This is not the place to explore theories of global culture (Featherstone 1990), but there has been a significant blurring of the specificity of locality in metropolitan society (Ritzer 1992). However much the tourist travels in a cultural capsule of their own society and sees other cultures through a prism of their own, tourism has been part of a enormous extension of the boundaries of many people's everyday world. For the same reason it has also encouraged a more widespread sense of the arbitrariness of any cultural order. Rather than being a prisoner of one's culture, there are important ways in which we need to conceptualise culture as a matter of style and choice.

The chain of argument I have been following has led to an emphasis on certain aspects of culture, an emphasis on fashion that immediately directs our attention to what is often called street culture (Collins 1989). Cultural studies has gained a lot of interest and notoriety through being willing to theorise the oppositional and innovation of youth culture in particular. One thinks immediately of those studies which have provided a commentary upon and interpretation of subcultural themes in mass society (Hebdige 1979; Willis 1978; Brake 1985). An important reason why this work has become well known is that it could be adopted and publicised within the endless reflexive consciousness of popular culture. The topics of youth and its exotic cultural efflorescence have been an infinitely productive staple of magazine and newspaper journalism and televisual commentary. Not all of this has taken the form of horror or moral panic at others' cultural excess; more generally it has served a role of explaining and publicising cultural diversity to its audience. One of the central themes of this cultural commentary is that style is a matter both of choice and of meaning. In the manner of your dress, the music you listen to, the books you read, the films you watch and so on, you tell yourself and others what sort of person you aspire to be.

I talked in the previous section of a recognition that the self is a form of representation, I am not just echoing that point when emphasising here that the theme of consumption and style is centrally concerned with the implications of the malleability of culture. We have come to appreciate the variety of ways in which we can see culture to be a political project, that is as a struggle to influence the dominant terrain of social consciousness. In the previous chapter I discussed some aspects of the subculture literature and I do not want to reiterate these here. The important point is that the early work on subcultures was pursued as a political innovation:

> The importance of spectacular subcultures here is not that they represent the whole of "youth" in some homogeneous "youth culture" but, in their practices of "winning space" within and against the hegemonic order, they constitute fragile, transient and minority forms, issuing symbolic challenges to the dominant culture and its definitions.
>
> (McGuigan 1992, p. 96)

It has often been pointed out that this politicised view of fashion necessarily involves a very selective use of examples and a judicious disattention to aspects of cultural forms that are inconsistent with an oppositional reading (an optimistic approach that has not disappeared from Hebdige's work – see his 'excavation' of alternative Britain: 1992). One of the most trenchant versions of this criticism came initially from within the Birmingham Centre itself and concerned the gendered biases of most subcultural writing (McRobbie 1991). Further work on the more privatised dimensions of different aspects of a culture of femininity, initially neglected by more overtly oppositional male posturing, has come to see even conventional consumer culture as offering opportunities for new forms of personal autonomy (McRobbie 1989; Nava 1992; Gammon and Marshment 1988).

The arguments here are beginning to consider the possibility that the indiscriminate egalitarianism of mass culture does not necessarily reproduce the structured oppressions of previous social order. Or rather, that these oppressions can more easily be subverted and deflected by the very diversity of life-style that consumerism encourages: 'One route into this project is the examination of teenage life-styles: of their asemblage on the production line of commodities for the teenage market, and their deconstruction, appropriation, subversion and reassemblage by teenage girls themselves' (Carter 1984, p. 198).

More generally, the popular music industry has been colonised by a number of cultural forms which have provided the most pervasive framework for stylistic heterogeneity in the later twentieth century. These are the most obvious examples of cultural themes with which audience members can identify, giving them the status of a particular cultural identity. A number of authors have seen popular music, more specifically rock'n'roll, as a form of cultural revolution that is in constant danger of being subverted by the crudities of commercialism (Marcus 1989). Less romantically, music has acted as a template or the basis for a cluster of life-style characteristics so that in everyday experience the most commonly used cultural items to frame personal biography are songs, records and performers. Writing on popular music has generated a lot of useful ideas and information on the development of a culture industry, although accounts have disappointingly tended to concentrate on narrative analysis rather than the social occasions of participation (see amongst others Frith 1983; Chambers 1985; Lull 1992; Negus 1993).

I have so far written about more positive reappraisals of patterns of audience behaviour as generally being sanctioned by theories in which it is denied that interest in mass-marketed products is equivalent to exploitation (see for example Fiske 1989a, 1989b; Willis 1990). In this respect interest in consumerism is obviously consistent with a broader theorisation of the 'active audience' discussed in the first chapter. One of the strongest features of this approach has been studies of the audiences for what might otherwise be seen as highly formulaic exploitative material (on for example soap operas see Geraghty 1991 and Nochimson 1992; see also Brown 1989). These studies have insisted that the meaning of mass cultural material cannot be predicted from textual analysis alone. To say this does, however, generate some ideological tension as, for many brought up within the Gramscian camp of over-arching hegemony, it opens the floodgates to populist relativism (a chaos of meaning).

Theoretical reconsideration of audiences for cultural products cannot be limited to forms of performance but extends to a broader conception of consumer culture. As Featherstone has pointed out this term 'refers to the culture of the consumer society. It is based on the assumption that the movement towards mass consumption was accompanied by a general reorganization of symbolic production, everyday experiences and practices' (1991, p. 113). He goes on to amplify the notion of a reorganisation of the frameworks for meaning by arguing that 'consumer culture through advertising, the media and techniques of display of goods, is able to destabilize the original notion of use or meaning of goods and attach to them new images and signs which can summon up a whole range of associated feelings and desires' (ibid., p. 114).

Once again we are picking up a theme of the destabilisation of meaning in contemporary culture, this time through the goods of fashion and leisure losing their moorings (see also Wernick 1991). Featherstone sees the theme of consumption and style taking us to the heart of the postmodern claim that there has been an aesthet-icisation of everyday life (Featherstone 1992). I am sure he would recognise, however, that this theme also opens up a broader perspective on a culture of mass entertainment. Work on the innovations in cultural form pioneered by the development of department stores (Chaney 1983b), allied with new forms of display in exhibitions, fairs and festivals (Williams 1982), has interacted with work on the social theory of the culture of modernity (Frisby 1985), to underline a history of euphoria in the ambiguities of urban experience. Archaeologists use a notion of style to detect a culture in fragmentary evidence, and I would like to suggest that, in the play of consumption and style, the practical actors of everyday life formul-ate their own versions of cultural diversity. In all sorts of ways the forms of the popular have, for over a century, been providing practical lessons on theorising culture.

CONCLUSION

I have emphasised repeatedly that what I have called the turn to culture can be seen to have been generated by a confused sense of the need to confront popular culture (Schudson 1987). This is especially true of intellectuals' understanding of their changing social position, but is more generally true of all the ways we talk about the rights deriving from membership of society (citizenship) in mass culture (Merelman 1984). The backdrop to a recognition for a need for change in theorising culture was the Romantic legacy of culture. This was based upon a number of claims for the privilege of Art (and artists). Although these privileges could be married to folk theories of natural culture, they decreed a civilised distaste at the mediocrity and vulgarity of the common culture of the urban crowd.

The growth of metropolitan culture and in particular the development of industries of mass communication and entertainment initially intensified this polarity; but, for a number of reasons, the ability of intellectuals to sustain the privileged claims of (and their authority for) a cultural sphere began to be dissipated. I have said at several points in this chapter that the histories of cultural forms and new cultural industries are essential components of any more general history of modernity. But in this conclusion (and Chapter 5) I will go further and argue that the culture of the new constituencies of mass society provides a vantage-point from which we can begin to trace the unravelling of modernity.

The popular has come to be seen as the political as well as social and cultural area (terrain) in which alternatives to an exhausted tradition of cultural discourse have become possible. The term 'alternatives' has been chosen as deliberately vague but sufficiently inclusive to cover some of the ideas discussed in this book. A paradox has, however, dogged the emergence of popular culture on centre stage in that the conceptual vocabulary of cultural discourse, as the form of address which has come to seem necessary and appropriate, has become increasingly abstruse and inaccessible to popular audiences. I do not want to glibly join the common criticism that social theory makes the everyday abstruse, but it is regrettable that a consequence has been that the positive results of the focus on culture that I have been trying to describe can seem to exist in their own world without consequences for popular experience.

Here I shall sketch in what I suggest are the outcrops in popular discourse of some aspects of the turn to culture at the level of theory. The points I shall mention are: (a) the contested character of cultural meaning; (b) an acceptance that cultural formations are constructed; (c) a paradoxical – given (b) – concern to assert and defend essential cultural difference; and (d) a widespread use and acceptance of interpretive methodology.

I mentioned in the section on cultural representation that a major force in politicising theories of representation was the publication of critiques pointing to forms of misrepresentation. So, it seems eminently contrary to natural justice, and likely to perpetuate injustice, if, for example, women, blacks and gays are consistently portrayed in pejorative ways. This sort of political concern has entered everyday experience, has been recognised by workers in media industries, and is taught in schools as a sort of counter-ideology training (which is not of course to say that there are now no sexist or racist stereotypes in media discourse).

It is a small but important step from what we could call defensive readings of popular culture (in that they seek to guard against prejudice), to more interventionist readings where members of special interest groups attempt to exercise influence over cultural content to further ends that they see as desirable. An example has been provided by Geraghty's discussion of soap operas and their representation of reality in contemporary Britain (1992). One instance she cites are those episodes in the serial *Brookside* which dealt with parents coping with their son coming out. The show:

> realistically represented the panicky and uncertain attitudes of many parents faced with a gay son. . . . But the representation was unlikely to satisfy those in its audience who were looking for . . . a hint that gay politics could challenge the ideology of the family rather than be incorporated within it.
>
> (p. 143)

This has the authentic hectoring note of someone seeking to use popular culture as a medium of social engineering. The politics of this, or any other example, is not what I want to explore here; it is rather the situation that all media content or mass entertainment becomes seen as endlessly contestable. In one way this immediately appears a development to be welcomed as it is an extension and politicisation of the active audience. Rather than being passive couch potatoes putting up with whatever is offered, a new form of public sphere is being constructed through the interventions of special interest groups. The other way of seeing these interventions is less positive in that it focuses on the censorship of the morally righteous.

Although I wrote earlier about a recognition of the need for change, I also noted that very often the growth of mass culture has been seen as a threat. A fear of the unpredictability of meaning amongst mass audiences has been inherent in the discourses of popular culture. The liberal norms of the public sphere traditionally presupposed elite constituecies, but faced with the prospect of unlimited access by the masses there have been a variety of programmes for positive intervention from religious fundamentalists through to women against pornography, and gay rights groups. The common theme in these activist interventions is that the mass audience needs to be protected against itself. My purpose here is only to point out that battles over 'right', 'fair', 'appropriate' media content are now an inescapable feature of the politics of mass society. Culture has been institutionalised as the battleground for a discourse of identities.

This leads neatly into the second point I want to make about the intrusion of culture into everyday experience. What I mean by the phrase 'discourse of identities' is that we can trace the development of a wide-ranging debate about the terms and forms within which group and cultural identity are to be phrased (a potent and hard-fought version of this debate can be found in the history of battles to prohibit racist categorisations). The essential premiss of any contest over identity is an acceptance of cultural relativism, that is that any behaviour, values, symbolism have to be understood within the context of a form of life, and as such cultural relativism is fundamental to the history of the human sciences.

The inflection of this theme that has come to be influential in the later twentieth century is, as noted earlier, signalled through a notion of construction. In all sorts of contexts and in all sorts of discourses it has become part of our taken-for-granted wisdom that social reality in general (formulated very influentially as a theory by Berger and Luckmann 1967), and the organisation of each particular social world are constructed entities. We therefore accept that the forms of social practice and interaction – custom and culture – are malleable and arbitrary (perhaps to the extreme that we take as a criterion of the modern world that everything solid seems to melt into air – see Berman 1983, 1992).

As we saw in the section on representation, the logic of emphasising the arbitrary character of the terms of culture is to accept images and representations as the basic matter, the stuff, of social experience. In turn it becomes possible to argue that constructing images has become the dominant mode of production. Lash, for example, has suggested that we can point to significant features differentiating the agrarian societies of the eighteenth century from the industrial societies of the nineteenth, and both from the semiotic societies of the later twentieth century: 'If social practices in agrarian society found their regulating principle in *agricultural goods*, and those in industrial society in *industrial goods*, then social practices in contemporary, semiotic (capitalist) societies find their regulating principle in signs, or *representational goods*' (1990b, p. 146). He goes on to argue that features of the production system of a semiotic system are that it is innovation-intensive with associated characteristics of being knowledge-intensive and design-intensive. What others have described as the predominance of the tertiary or service sector he sees in more complex ways as the growing significance of the production of discursive goods.

The relevance of this type of theorising to our present concerns is that it brings into focus what is often held to be a feature of the later twentieth century – an emphasis on the ways in which we apprehend reality rather than reality itself. One controversial aspect of this characteristic is that it has been blamed for the success of politicians who stress images of desired values rather than display any intellectual or practical competence. In general, however, constructionism has been seen as a radical input to public discourse. It has been accepted that to stress the arbitrary character of social categories is both liberating personally and should encourage greater tolerance in public life in general.

In introducing this section I noted that the third theme in some ways contradicts the second. Contradiction is not quite the right word – while constructionism has become pervasive and a principle of social attitudes it also underlies distinct modes of strain in contemporary culture. I will briefly mention two forms of strain to illustrate the third point of theoretical influence on everyday life. The first form is a recognition that for groups seeking to assert the distinctiveness and value of their identity it is somewhat undermining to have the basis of that identity questioned. Thus as

Henderson has pointed out there is a contradiction for gay and lesbian resistance between being constructionist in theory: 'though essentialists as we mobilize politically, demanding that the state comply because this, after all, is *who we are*, not who we are today or who we have become in recent history' (1993, p. 123; emphasis in original).

The problem here is clearly that some sense of essential difference is necessary in order to justify and sustain a threatened identity. This need not be restricted to those who are members of oppressed cultural minorities, but generates a second more general form of strain in contemporary culture. This can be summarised by saying that if all social categories, especially forms of identity, are arbitrary and relative then any individual's sense of self can be called into question. Thus there is what has been called an ontological insecurity in the meaning of personal experience in contemporary culture (a form of risk that has been extensively explored by Giddens 1991 and 1992; see also Lash and Friedman 1992). It seems likely that such a fundamental source of strain will generate for many members of society a perceived need for more transcendental reassurance. This has taken the form in some cases of the development of new religious sects, and in others has led to continual experimentation in the search for sources of meaning as amongst those caught up in new forms of mysticism and spiritual beliefs.

The fourth point concerns the influence of cultural theory on popular experience. This is that the theory has generated a space which is outside the domain of conventional science. I have put it in this somewhat awkward way because I do not want to say that the theory is based on or legitimises irrational beliefs. It is rather that, while not denying the general force of scientific rationality, it has become respectable to recognise areas that are outside the scope of that episteme.

This process can be detected on two levels. The first is within the human sciences and stems from an emphasis that cultural discourses are essentially concerned with understanding the meaning of representation. From a wide range of sources (one of the most influential theorists has been the cultural anthropologist Clifford Geertz – see 1973 and 1983) a distinctive position has been marked out which says that a form of analysis in which concepts should be able to be rendered in forms that can be measured is highly inappropriate. The alternative – although it can take many forms – is that analysis has to have an hermeneutic character, that is that we 'read' cultural phenomena in ways that continually discover new meanings.

It should be easy to see that such a methodological principle will be attractive to those trained in the humanities, so it has enabled a turn to culture across a much wider disciplinary framework than the limited horizons of scientism. More popularly, I believe that an acceptance of alternative dimensions of evaluation and interpretation can be seen in new social movements such as environmental and ecological activism, holistic medicine, widespread interest in new forms of therapeutic intervention, and spiritual development through personal and communal forms of life.

It is inherent in the challenge of these movements to hold that there are problems in the most technically advanced societies which need to be addressed in ways that are independent of the discourses of established knowledge (and this of course is why they are so frequently derided by representatives of institutionalised orthodoxy such as doctors, scientists and economists). This critique comes back to our starting-point that so many of the presuppositions of established knowledge have come to seem exhausted. As such the challenge of new forms of life is inseparable from all the ways in which we have made culture the dominant framework for collective experience; and exemplifies, in ways that parallel theoretical developments, a stress on the need for strategies of interpretation and evaluation.

Part II

Forms of culture

Chapter 3

Tolerance and intolerance in modern culture

TOLERANCE IN MODERN CULTURE

In this chapter I shall be concerned with some of the implications of what I have called the cultural turn. I have so far discussed aspects of that turn as theoretical issues in both how we think about culture, in particular popular culture, and in how we have come to use culture as various ways of explaining or understanding features of contemporary social order. I want now to look at the use of culture in popular discourse. In the concluding section of the previous chapter, I suggested points of contact between theoretical and popular accounts. Here I shall extend that approach, but look in more detail at what seem to me to be some unintended consequences in the implications of culture dominating everyday understandings of collective life.

I shall be especially concerned with the culture of modern societies that I shall call modernity. I shall discuss the various things modern and modernity have been taken to mean and focus on the significant implications of the dominance of industries of mass communication and mass entertainment for our understandings of modernity. To provide a theme for the chapter I will use pressures for, and counterbalancing qualifications of, the institutionalisation of tolerance in modern life. In the first part I shall argue that tolerance, itself deriving from increased awareness of culture, has become a dominant value in public culture. In order to simplify the presentation of my account I shall accept for the rest of this section that the value of tolerance is a dominant influence, and will set on one side all the disturbing evidence of persistent intolerance in modern culture. This artificial approach better enables me to make some points about the character of modern culture and to show the cultural contradictions at the heart of mass society.

A recurrent theme in the preceding chapters has been the significance for intellectual discourse of the development of industries of mass communication and entertainment. Another way of putting this is to say that issues of analysis and interpretation of popular culture have swamped cultural debates. The established privileges of intellectuals' authority in relation to cultural matters have been continuously called into question by new modes of production, innovation and appreciation that fall outside the canons of traditional cultural institutions. One style of response has been to enthrone tolerance of a diversity of tastes and means of expression as a basic cultural value. As Bauman has put it, writing of a broader vision of cultural matters: 'The overwhelming tendency today is to see culture as the ground of perpetual, irreducible (and, in most cases, desirable and worth conscious preservation) diversity of human kind' (1992, p. 18). Treating tolerance as a cultural value takes many forms and is significant because it is implicated in what I shall argue are the most intractable contradictions of the turn to culture.

The immediate basis of Bauman's generalisation is the vast corpus of knowledge of other cultures, and institutional practices in areas such as the family, religion, sexuality and property rights, that has been accumulated in the human sciences over at least a century. It has passed into the commonsense knowledge of everyday life that customs and traditions can make sense of different social practices that might initally seem strange or repugnant. Widespread patterns of migration, both limited and permanent, from richer to poorer societies and vice versa, have meant a much greater personal familiarity with cultural diversity. King (1991a, p. 6) has suggested that the First World has imported cultural diversity from the Third to the extent that 'Culture is increasingly deterritorialized'. There is also of course an enormous fund of secondary knowledge of global cultures through access to documentaries and news reports available through the mass media.

It has, then, become one of the staples of contemporary political discourse that we all have to confront the implications of living in multi-cultural social formations. The idea of communal diversity is frequently challenging because we are forced to confront the legitimacy of what we might otherwise take to be normal and natural. This, in its turn, has the implication that who 'we' are can also be called into question: 'These days questions of culture seem to touch a nerve because they quite quickly become anguished questions of identity'

(Rosaldo 1993, p. ix). The premiss of tolerance as a cultural value is that as members of social groups we should treat it as unremarkable that there are a variety of ways of arranging common social themes, and therefore that any form of social order is a pragmatic construction. The central prescriptions of tolerance are, then, that difference is to be respected, and that alternatives to what we consider normality should be accepted.

The values of tolerance presuppose moral relativism and, as I have argued in the previous chapter and at other points, a deep and pervasive awareness within popular experience of the arbitrary character of any form of social order is one of the most important consequences of modern cultural sophistication. This means that not only do we accept that there is no natural rightness to any set of social institutions, but also that the groups we naturally feel ourselves to be members of have at best only an uncertainly clear identity.

We tend, as I have said, to think of this as a feature of modern cultural sophistication, but such a confidence in our distinctiveness becomes more complicated if it is argued that the ideas of social relativism can be traced back to the point of transition from the feudal to early modern world. If this is so it means that we need to be able to accommodate the view that intellectual appreciation, of the degree of rupture in the basic frameworks of social knowledge caused by a realisation that society is a human creation, goes back to the inception of distinctively modern attitudes (and in fact can be taken to a prime criterion of the existence of a modern outlook).

The immediate consequence of introducing this new historical dimension is that everybody is completely confused by all this talk about how the notion of modern can be used in relation to society. The problem is inescapable because there are indeed a number of ways that modern has been used as a device in historical intepretation. But for the purposes of this chapter I shall distinguish two uses. The first is when we speak of our modern culture referring to the era that has been dominated by industries of mass communication and entertainment – roughly the past century. The second usage is to speak of a modern sensibility in relation to, amongst other things, notions of individuality, an historical consciousness, and the idea that there is civil society and that it is a human creation. It is in this second sense that we can trace the history of modern social concerns back to the decline of feudalism and the Renaissance in Western Europe. Although very different in that these two usages are part of separate discourses, I will argue that in important ways aspects of what we take for granted about the first use of modern have drawn heavily on characteristics of the second.

I shall very briefly set out what I mean by connections between the two meanings of modern and will suggest that there is a further deeper connection, picking up again the theme of the value attached to tolerance; in the next part of the chapter I shall discuss reasons for the principle of tolerance in a culture of mass media. In setting out these arguments I shall be saying something important about how we use a concept of culture. As a first step along this road I shall point to some aspects of the process of transition to a modern sensibility in the second sense as characteristic of civil society, that have, in turn, become more pronounced in the subsequent transition to mass culture.

The most important of these is reflexivity. This is a technical term that can be used to describe social consciousness of the instability of order: 'Reflexivity involves a profound and deep undermining of any assumptions that the order of things should be, indeed could be, taken for granted' (Tester 1992, p. 12). I do not want to slow the argument down by a digression on concepts but it should be noted that reflexivity can be used in at least two slightly different ways, and that a term that is a close synonym of this use of reflexivity but sets up an interestingly different set of connotations is irony. Tester takes the awful recognition of reflexive consciousness (awful because once the move has been made you can never go back to a naive trust in appearance), as the constitutive precondition of an imagination of civil society.

The intellectual history of theories of civil society is not my concern in this chapter, although we will be drawn back to aspects of that theme, such as citizenship in democratic society. I do, however, want to note three aspects of Tester's account of civil society that are also defining characteristics of our notions of culture in the modern world. The first is a contrast between the natural and the social. When it became possible to appreciate that any form of social order is humanly constructed, then the natural became both pre-social and anti-social (see also Tester 1991). As a place and a state, nature was increasingly, and is still largely, seen as the 'other' or negation of civilisation (a complementary account of changing discourses of human and natural is Thomas 1983). The second point is the development of an almost parallel distinction between public and private spheres, in which the former is both more formal and civilised (or at least more explicitly social) – and emphatically masculine. Later we will need to consider the notion of the public sphere in greater detail.

The third point is an argument that an essential trigger for reflexive consciousness is a normalisation of awareness of strangers. When in village society the everyday world is contained and highly predictable, the arrival of a stranger is possibly a divine intervention but more probably a threat as an intimation of disorder through difference. The essence of our modern consciousness is that strangers become routinised, so that it becomes harder to preserve a sense of the normal from which they differ: 'Quite the contrary, the fleeting appearances and relationships of the urban milieu indicated nothing other than the ceaseless possibility of different kinds of social relationships' (Tester 1993, p. 33; see also Frisby 1985). This has been a powerful theme in sociological accounts of modernity (see in particular Simmel's influential essay in Wolff 1950), and has been especially associated with a stress on the significance of the development of urban societies and metropolitan culture. Indeed the implications of urban anonymity can arguably be seen as the underlying theme of the sociological perspective.

The sociologist who has taken the issue of managing everyday life in a world of strangers most seriously is Erving Goffman, who begins, as Manning puts it well, by challenging us to recognise 'That the world is even in the slightest a predictable place is an extraordinary and largely invisible accomplishment' (Manning 1992, p. 10; see further references therein). Goffman's sociology can be read as an extended articulation of a fascinated horror at the fragility of our ways of managing this accomplishment. To the extent that social order is inherently and deeply artificial in Goffman, he emphasises for us that trust and tolerance (complemented of course by a pervasive wary distrust) are the prerequisites of reflexive social consciousness.

Goffman is notorious as someone who wrote without an historical frame of reference so that the deliberately contemporary character of his account brings us back to the culture of late modern societies. It seems to me that Goffman is saying that strangeness is so inherent and all pervasive in mass culture that we have no single culture as a clear, stable and practical universe of meanings. That is that the idea of cultural diversity is more than a recognition that there are no fixed or naturally right ways of organising social life. It is more generally that cultural diversity means 'our' culture is continually being reinvented and elaborated as we go along: 'people find out about their worlds by living with ambiguity, uncertainty, or simple lack of knowledge until the day, if and when it arrives, that their life experiences clarify matters. In other words, we often improvise, learn by doing, and make things up as we go along' (Rosaldo 1993, p. 92).

There are ways in which we structure and organise processes of interaction sufficiently to sustain the fictions of a common culture (and none better than Goffman at dissecting the rituals of reciprocity in that task), but as he makes clear it is akin to pulling ourselves up by our own bootlaces. Speaking of 'the dance of talk' Goffman says:

> Every conversation, it seems, can raise itself by its own bootstraps, can provide its participants with something to flail at, which process in its entirety can then be made the reference of an aside, this side remark then responsively provoking a joking refusal to disattend it. The box that conversation stuffs us into is Pandora's.
>
> (1981, pp. 73–4)

What I am arguing for can now be summarised as saying that the modern mass culture of urban-industrial societies, the culture brought into being by industries of mass communication and entertainment, has a number of features that derive from the modern sensibility. They are, first, that social experience is deeply reflexive, using it here in its ironic sense that any particular order or structure can be destabilised by being seen from a different perspective (what Giddens 1990 has characterised as the fundamental 'double hermeneutic' – the continuous interaction of practice and theory – of modernity). The second is that social life is artificial. This is not to say that it is false but that it is a human invention, or perhaps more accurately an imagination – something we conjure into being. Another way of putting this point is to say that we are constructed (made) through all the ways we perform relationships.

This leads to the third feature of ambivalent relations with what is seen as nature or natural. If culture is invented so must be nature, and thus nature as the reverse of culture is likely to bear both aspects of idealisation and fear and distrust. The ambivalence of our attitudes to nature will not just relate to spaces on the edge of society, and how we draw those boundaries; but also to how we might seek to enshrine differences between ourselves and other life forms, and at the same time understand the 'nature' within ourselves. The fourth and final feature is that it is a culture of anonymity – a culture of strangers. Impersonal, mass, public forms of communication will necessarily take on far greater significance in this setting in what I have called the performance of social relationships.

I suggested above that the two understandings of modern are not only linked because one is based on features of the other, but also by a deeper connection with the value attached to tolerance. The salience of tolerance to both discourses stems from the uncertainties that follow from the dominance of relativism. One reason for this dominance is that an ironic consciousness of the ways that difference is arbitrary finds it difficult to defend the 'obvious' authority of locally dominant cultural forms. A further reason is that in a culture of strangers there is a logic of egalitarianism. There are specialised markets and audiences and expertise within producers and audiences, but a more pragmatic populism has infiltrated traditional structures of privilege so that a multiplicity of different forms of subcultural prestige are indifferent to ascribed status.

Finally, another reason why a high value will be attached to tolerance are the very uncertainties in the dialectic between nature and culture. Where the boundaries can be asserted and sustained with conviction nature can confidently exist as a resource for exploitation. It is precisely our sentimentality about nature that makes our exploitation at once both savagely indifferent and pathetic through a variety of ways of searching for authenticity. In subsequent sections I will explore the illusions of tolerance but for now I want only to sketch in a positive case.

I have also promised that tracing the salience of tolerance in two uses of modern would lead to a reconsideration of the concept of culture itself. Put briefly, this is that marking off 'a' culture from another now seems considerably more difficult. And yet there clearly are marked differences in forms of life if we compare cultures in different settings, as there are if we explore cultural change through time. As an example of this duality I can point to the distinctive differences in the feel of the culture between European countries, and yet in important respects, such as the values attached to individuality, there are strong continuities. In order to broaden our grasp of modern culture, and to give a different slant on the significance of tolerance in modern culture, I shall turn to Norbert Elias' study of the civilising process (1978, 1982).

Elias is concerned with the behaviour of people in society, and with the emergence of standards of propriety and decorum during the development of what we have called civil society, standards that came to be treated as prerequisites of 'civilisation'. Elias is therefore providing a history of manners, that is a series of changes in conventions governing such areas of life as eating, bodily functions and interpersonal aggression. The civilising process is a series of developments in the self-conscious manipulation of cultural resources by social actors. It is one aspect of a notion of reflexivity, in that people came to pay a great deal of attention to how they could structure the organisation of social life in order to express specific values.

Elias' research process is to read a vast number of tracts and advice manuals published over centuries in several European countries on manners and forms of deportment appropriate to civilised people. The changing values he detects are consistent with features of modern culture we have already noted. There is, for example, the trend whereby 'people, in the course of the civilising process, seek to suppress in themselves every characteristic that they feel to be "animal". They likewise suppress such characteristics in their food' (1978, p. 120). Another value displayed through the elaboration of civilised conduct is the strength of individuality. Although codes of conduct are based on social judgements, individual failure to meet others' expectations is a source of shame. Manners are therefore a measure of the extent to which individuals can exercise control of their self: 'The increased tendency of people to observe themselves and others is one sign of how the whole question of behaviour is now taking on a different character: people mold themselves and others more deliberately than they did in the Middle Ages' (ibid., p. 79). And further, the changing balance between individual and community in determining conduct is itself a chart of the social forms which structure how actors stand in relationship to each other.

This, I think, helps to give us a better sense of the character of tolerance in modern culture. It may seem that an increasing stress upon the observation of an elaborate code of manners is a new form of intolerance. And yet, precisely because individuals have to take greater personal responsibility for their conduct, they are both more likely to innovate – believing it will secure status, attention etc. – and to be sensitive to the multitude of reasons why others might make mistakes or other lapses. In the exercise of what Goffman called civil disattention we both honour the existence of interpersonal codes and find ways of recognising that another's shame might so easily have been our own. The further possibility, that we will seek to copy others' infractions as worthwhile innovations, introduces the dimension of fashion as an inevitable feature of a form of community in which we are all spectators continually monitoring others' performance.

Elias' reading of the significance of manners in civil society is meant to illustrate his broader theory that changes in one institutional area are necessarily related to all aspects of discursive identities: 'The question why men's behaviour and emotions change is really the same as the question why their forms of life change' (Elias 1978, p. 205). Elias vehemently denies that the concepts of individual and society relate to two different types of object – they are rather two interdependent processes, and I think we could include the concept of culture as another. Elias offers a concept of figuration to illuminate these processes of dependence – it is through networks of relationship that cultural forms are given identity, and they signify through distinctive modes of representation. Reminding us of Goffman's dance of talk, Elias offers the example of the figuration of social dance as: 'relatively independent of the specific individuals forming it here and now, but not of individuals as such' (ibid., p. 262). It is how culture as a complex of figurations has come to be seen as the prerequisite of a basis for identity in the imaginary communities of mass culture that will be our concern in the rest of this chapter.

THE PUBLIC SPHERE

I have just described something of what we mean when we talk about the modernness of modern culture. I suggested some reasons why tolerance has come to be deemed a dominant value in accounts of modernity (accepting that this may be an idealisation that might have to be radically modified by experience). The trouble with the phrase 'dominant' value is that it conceals a number of different interpretations. I shall mention three different ways in which we could understand dominant value.

The first is prescriptive in that tolerance is seen as a value that all right-thinking people ought to agree is a good thing. In this approach it will be tacitly recognised that there may be many lapses from such a moral expectation, as with the injunction not to commit adultery, but it is still a way of ordering conduct to which we should aspire. A second more pragmatic way of understanding the dominant value of tolerance is as what could be called a functional necessity. Thus, it could be argued that tolerance is a rational response to the uncertainties of the modern world. Again, those holding this view could accept that there are and have been many infractions of the value of tolerance, but this would not impair a principled need for greater tolerance.

In the third version tolerance is in effect being seen as a structural principle rather than a normative expectation. What this means is that tolerance is argued to be a constitutive feature of modernity; and therefore lapses from tolerance, by individuals or as features of social policy, are unfortunate anachronisms that mar but do not deflect the course of modern evolution. It is in the spirit of this third sense that I have pointed to the intimate interdependence between the principle of tolerance and the erosion of cultural boundaries, and the nature of the modern culture that is based on industries of mass communication and entertainment. Another way of putting this is to assert that there is a logic to the modernisation of mass culture, which ordains that all types of society will be driven to adopt institutional values that will at least pay lip-service to the importance of tolerance.

If we hope to critically consider the proposition that there is a structural predisposition to tolerance in mass culture, we need to go back to what I have so far asserted: that a distinctively modern cultural world has been generated by the rise to dominance of industries of mass communication and entertainment. I will therefore begin by proposing three aspects of the ways in which the development of industries of mass communication and entertainment can be said to generate modern culture. In describing these different forms of the interdependence of communication forms and the character of modernity I will further describe my understanding of that term. This will lead to a discussion of what I will call the public discourses or public culture of mass society. This approach focuses on the nature of citizenship in mass culture, the significance of principled tolerance, and some reasons why the institutions of democracy are proving inadequate to their own goals.

The first aspect of the generative power of processes of mass communication begins from what we have called the anonymous culture of mass society. In a highly reflexive consciousness we are aware that our (whoever 'we' are) culture is both deeply felt and worryingly ambiguous. In these circumstances it is not surprising that new assertive forms of collective identity have developed: 'Beneath the decline of sacred communities, languages and lineages, a fundamental change was taking place in modes of apprehending the world, which, more than anything else, made it possible to "think" the nation' (Anderson 1983, p. 28; for more general accounts of nationalism see Hobsbawm 1990 and Smith 1991). Innovations in how we apprehend the world took the dual form, according to Anderson, of new forms of collective ceremony and a new language of time shared by the members of a community of strangers.

I can explain this argument a little more clearly. Nations, despite their aura of historical inevitability are sociopolitical inventions of the modern world, and central to the artifice of new social entities is held to be the imagination of community (see also Hobsbawm and Ranger 1983). The idea here is that as the boundaries of the known world even within a single city have expanded beyond the grasp of any single individual, the reassurance and control of continually being known to others have been supplanted by a more abstract imagination of a world shared in common. The anonymity of a world of strangers is masked and given structures of meaning by discourses of new forms of collective identity: 'My point of departure is that nationality, or, as one might prefer to put it in view of that word's multiple significations, nation-ness, as well as nationalism, are cultural artefacts of a particular kind' (Anderson 1983, p. 13).

Anderson's central theme is that the rhetorical power of nationalism is a distinctively modern imagination of community, which is articulated through the impersonal media of industries of mass communication, and, further, that this imagination will be equally shared within the relevant community. It is a basic principle of processes of mass communication that it is impossible to contain them within the privileges of hereditary elites – they are indiscriminately available (an idea provocatively formulated some years ago by Enzensberger 1970). And the history of nationalism in the European states of the nineteenth century shows that the equal participation of all became a precondition of the imaginations of community: 'it is imagined as a community, because, regardless of the actual inequality and exploitation that may prevail in each, the nation is always conceived as a deep, horizontal comradeship' (Anderson 1983, p. 16; emphasis is original).

The theme is that new media of mass communication not only make the content of the new cultural artefacts of nations available, they also provide the form through which the artefact is imagined. It is this idea of the form of imagination that will furnish the second aspect of the ways in which industries of mass entertainment can be said to generate a modern culture.

I mentioned earlier that the possibility of innovations in the language of time is crucial to new social forms. In the modern world time becomes expressed through abstract, impersonal and uniform units (see the discussion of time in modernity in Young 1988 and Adam 1990). Whether it is broken up into years, decades, reigns, presidencies or movements, the periodic framework advances through succeeding waves with, a vast number of heterogeneous happenings being collected under the impersonal heading of the era concerned. Anderson proposes the newspaper as the ultimate symbol and physical display of this process. Newspapers create a fiction of public discourse each and every day. The stuff newspapers print (and television broadcasts etc.) is therefore the content of national life, but in its indifference to any particular story – all news is grist to the mill – the newspaper is also a symbol of the logic of bureaucratic neutrality.

In the excited chatter of screaming headlines and dramatic happenings it may seem absurd to describe newspapers as indifferent. But their commitment is to the principle of drama rather than to any specific story. Their commitment is to the principle that there are always stories of interest, concern and relevance to all members of the reading public simultaneously. In this openness they symbolise the bureaucratic indifference of modern rationality. The principle of bureaucratic process is that the messy diversity of personal experience can be resolved into a number of procedural stages. I do not believe it is a distortion to see the relationships between daily news and daily life as sharing the same form. It is when news loses its indifference to what is being processed, when it becomes committed and partisan, that it becomes propaganda. The defect of the managed stories of state authorities is not that the stories they tell are 'wrong' but that in the manner of their imagining they deny the reflexivity of citizenship (and, I will go on to argue, thereby cannot transcend modernity).

The idea of an implicit bureaucratic neutrality, or indifference to the meaning of news, in mass communication industries, and this is of course another (possibly less positive) way of rendering the values of tolerance, can also be captured through the 'voice' of public address. I mean by this that there are conventional registers of speech in public life, especially in the forms of expression in news or discourse of actuality, that appropriate a privileged neutrality (see the fuller discussion of this notion in Chaney 1993, Chapter 4). Through the use of this voice a terrain of normality, with attendant ways of seeing, speaking and behaving, is given prescriptive force as that which can be taken for granted even within the diversity of a culture of strangers.

At least two aspects of the politics of culture follow from this practice. They are both too important to be left as brief references so I will take them up again in a subsequent section. The first is that the authority of the public voice will mean that those who have mastery of its cadences will have by that alone a powerful resource for colonising those with different voices. But it should also be recognised that those who are excluded from access to this mode of cultural capital may well emphasise their linguistic estrangement as a way of symbolically insisting upon their social refusal of normality. Exaggerated dialects amongst the young and ethnic minorities can in this way stand as deliberate forms of outrage.

A second aspect of the politics of cultural voices is that it seems to me to be consistent with an ideology of public voice that one of the major social consequences of mass communication has been the acceptance, within a polity, of a standard national language. Even without the existence of dominant communication industries there will be strong pressures within nationalist ideology to display an appropriate national language, if necessary by invention, or alternatively by reviving an archaic form. There are, however, distinctive further reasons why mass broadcasting facilities will initially be eagerly welcomed as an opportunity to stamp out the relics of linguistic particularism such as dialects and minority languages. In this way the history of national broadcasting can be seen to have been implicated in the project of inventing a national culture; a project which functioned at a number of levels, including the discovery of folk traditions, and the delineation of a national literature. (Almost paradoxically, the mechanisms of cultural imperialism, in particular the export of American entertainment to global audiences, has meant a further degree of cultural homogenisation that transcends the autonomy of national languages.)

The second aspect of modernity that is at least greatly stimulated by the development of processes of mass communication is therefore themes of standardisation. This leads well into the third aspect which focuses on the nature of citizenship. Citizens are those who enjoy, as of right, full access to participation in the political processes of a state. I have stressed that I believe there to be an interdependence between the imaginations of nationalism and an acceptance that all those who can legitimately claim a particular national identity can also, by so doing, claim the rights of citizenship. This lays the basis for the mass citizenship of democratic politics, and has become a constitutive principle of modernity with several further implications.

One of the most important has usually been understood to mean that in modern states there is a fundamental illegitimacy about denying any group of inhabitants citizenship rights on the grounds of some shared collective feature such as their religion, race or gender, or even economic status. To say there is a contradiction does not mean there are not instances of constitutions in which discrimination is formally inscribed, such as apartheid in South Africa, the position of Arabs in Israel and the attempted extirpation of Jews in Nazi Germany. But these cases have usually been seen as grounds for international boycott or other forms of exclusion. There are of course many other examples of unofficial, if systematic, discrimination but these are usually held, by spokespersons of the states concerned, to be illegitimate violations of the relevant constitution.

Two further corollaries of mass citizenship are that in order to be able to participate in the political process citizens must have access to adequate sources of information and commentary if they are to grasp salient features of issues; and that the presentation of all such information and commentary should be governed by norms of rational relevance and coherence. Not only do citizens depend upon media of mass communication in order to have a basic form of participation in public life, but those media also create a distinctively modern form of citizenship. Perhaps it will be helpful if I describe this modern form as consumer citizenship. Put very baldly, the idea is that there are formal parallels between the character of mass national markets and mass national political publics. The practice of citizenship involves the same form of relationship between the individual and collective opinions as that between the individual customer and patterns of taste and fashion. It is being able to create and sustain national markets that is an essential criterion of modernity and the basis of mass society.

I shall briefly amplify what I mean by the claim that there are parallels between markets and publics. Because markets have been given the character in contemporary economistic ideology of almost metaphysical abstract structures of determination, I should make it clear that by 'markets' I mean what could more aptly be called audiences for the myriad goods and services of consumer society. One of the most distinctive features of the development of the modern world has been the dissolution of local economies into national and subsequently, in important areas, international economies (clearly paralleling the development of national culture). Goods and services are not geographically or socially focused but are indiscriminately and simultaneously available to an anonymous crowd of potential customers.

The development of national markets has been dependent upon processes of mass communication in two ways. First there have to be transformations in systems of physical communication so that the constraints of time and space are effectively conquered. The rapid transport of goods and messages means that manufacturers can market on a mass scale and draw resources from a global reservoir. Second, the developments in national media of communication mean that potential customers can be made aware of and encouraged to desire the goods of a consumer culture. In short, mass advertising, drawing upon the media and the forms of mass communication, encapsulates in its practices many of the defining features of modern culture and thus provides one of the most representative cultural forms.

To argue that mass advertising is one of the most pervasive cultural forms of modernity and that it represents the essential form of mass communication would have seemed very depressing to many early commentators on the culture of modernity. This is because advertising seemed at best parasitic and probably deceitful, and because the logic of mass marketing was thought to be an inescapable search for ever larger audiences, with consequent vulgarisation in order to provide sensational appeals to the unsophisticated (the history of tabloid newspapers seems to confirm this gloomy analysis). In practice neither criticism has proved adequate to account for subsequent developments in mass culture, if only because the anonymity of mass audiences has not meant an uncritical homogenisation, but rather a more critically engaged variety of styles of negotiation in making local accommodations with mass cultural materials. Realisation of the opportunities this provides has led to more profitable narrow-casting, or more focused marketing, rather than the indiscriminate orthodoxies of crude mass appeals.

So consumerism shares a common form with industries of mass

communication and entertainment in the generation of markets or audiences. This is, however, to concentrate upon the later development of civil society. What I have called the mass publics of democratic citizenship are a relatively recent form of national government. To understand their distinctive character we need to look at their basis in an earlier phase of transition in Western Europe and North America. The later eighteenth century was characterised by the emergence of the public sphere or the discourse of public culture. An influential account of the characteristics of the public sphere by Habermas (1989; originally published 1962) further helps to clarify our understanding of the character of modernity associated with new forms of public discourse (for recent discussions of Habermas' contribution see Calhoun 1992).

The public sphere is held by Habermas to have been generated by: 'new commercial relationships: the traffic in commodities and news created by early capitalist long-distance trade' (1989, p. 15); each element in this pairing is as important as the other: 'For the traffic in news developed not only in connection with the needs of commerce; the news itself became a commodity' (p. 21). The significance of the innovation of the public sphere is more than new forms of economic relationships, however: 'The bourgeois public sphere may be conceived above all as the sphere of private people come together as a public' (p. 27). And it is this duality of values of rational discourse complemented by a concern to explore, develop and defend personal subjectivity that marks the citizenship of civil society (see also Gouldner 1976).

Of course this new mode of social being did not develop in a vacuum but was grounded in specific social settings which, although they varied in different national contexts, shared a number of institutional criteria. Those concerned disregarded ascribed status in principle; they disregarded boundaries between sacred and profane areas of discourse, and they recognised that the discussions of public life could not be confined to specific social groups but had an intrinsically universal relevance: 'Wherever the public established itself institutionally as a stable group of discussants, it did not equate itself with the public but at most claimed to act as its mouthpiece, in its name, perhaps even as its educator – the new form of bourgeois representation' (p. 37). Two consequences of this mode of institutionalisation are that everything is yielded up to the reflexivity of discourse, in which none can be excluded from the author-ity of participation, and that all privileges of status are inherently questionable.

The innovation of the public sphere is therefore radical and populist – it spawns that necessary fiction of democratic politics which it called public opinion. In the later eighteenth century public opinion was an essential fiction of liberal society in that it provided the forum within which 'the public competition of private arguments came into being as the consensus about what was practically necessary in the interest of all' (Habermas 1989, p. 83 italicised in the original). The idea of public opinion articulated a reflexive consciousness of bourgeois society: 'The self-interpretation of the function of the bourgeois public sphere crystallized in the idea of "public opinion"' (ibid., p. 89), but not in a way that challenged the 'natural' restriction of the public to educated male property-owners. Even within these narrow social confines it was recognised by contemporary writers that the effectiveness of public opinion depended upon publicity through the untrammelled operation of impersonal media of communication, namely the press (see also Burns 1977b).

We can see then that the self-understandings of mass democratic politics have been grounded in notions of citizenship which are inseparable from the constitutive power of impersonal media of mass communication (see the essays discussing the relationships in Dahlgren and Sparks 1991). The purpose of Habermas' study is, however, not only to lay bare the distinctiveness of a modern social formation, but also to criticise what he sees as the processes of transformation whereby the illusions of liberal society have been turned into the managed deceits of mass society (see also Sennett's (1977) development of this historical perspective). I would argue that there are many flaws in Habermas' account of the transformation of the public sphere; largely because I see it as part of a broader spectrum of mass culture critique, interestingly shown by his use of strands within the American mass culture debate of the 1940s and 1950s as authoritative sources. My theorisation of mass popular culture in the essays in this book runs counter to the terms of Habermas' approach, which I see as clinging to a sense of cultural practice that idealises certain norms of literary representation. There are, even so, two themes in his account of transformation which are particularly important as they have persisted as dominant themes in the discourse of modernity.

The first is that the interdependence of the private sphere of critical interpretation of personal experience with a public sphere of rational debate has been fractured: 'Inasmuch as the mass media today strip away the literary husks from that kind of bourgeois self-interpretation and utilize them as marketable forms for the public services provided in a culture of consumers, the original meaning is reversed' (Habermas, 1989, p. 171). And secondly, the role of the media in facilitatiing the rational discourse of the public sphere has been transformed by shift to a more directly mobilising role. The argument here is that by changing from first acting as dealers in public opinion to then generating publicity for the institutions of the modern state: 'Publicity loses its critical function in favor of a staged display; even arguments are transmuted into symbols to which again one can not respond by arguing but only by identifying with them' (ibid., p. 206). These themes together generate a powerful critique of the nature of public opinion and opinion formation in mass society. Rather than being the creative fiction of a new political order it is seen to have become a rhetorical fiction of institutionalised elites. Lacking any independent sites for development and expression it becomes something conjured into being by interested groups to rationalise and legitimise the play of institutionalised politics.

The theme of the public sphere takes us to the heart of any judgement about the validity of democratic institutions. Implicit in the idea is a belief that the mode of imagination, which we saw Anderson arguing has been made possible by impersonal, mass media of communication, can be given vitality in the flow and shift of endlessly forming and changing patterns of public opinion. In this way the anonymous mass of citizens can be given a means of participating in and constituting the government of their state. If, however, it is believed that those citizens are little more than consumers, seduced by advertising into failing to see that the language of politics is only a spectacular show lacking any substance, then the promise of the public sphere for mass democracy has been made into a sham. Fears that this radical critique may be justified cluster around two distinct themes which I shall briefly discuss: the nature of public opinion in mass society; and the organisation, ownership and financing of media organisations.

Sociologically inspired critiques of mass democracy have often observed that an appropriate symbol of the trivialisation of the public sphere in contemporary society is the concept of public opinion. They argue that it has slipped from being the collective imaginative fiction we have been describing, to the collection of individual attitudes and opinions on every possible issue by polling organisations (in brief, that a form of collective life has been made meaningless by psychologisation – a more general critique of consumer relationships). While I have a great deal of sympathy for an argument that social concepts cannot be atomised, it is still possible to derive relevant ideas from the literature on opinion measurement and formation. Zaller (1992) has recently addressed this issue of the relationship between elite formulations of political issues and the data of multitudinous opinion studies by proposing a model of opinion formation that is predicated on the weaknesses of opinion polling.

Zaller clearly demonstrates that there are a number of 'noise' variables which have been found to greatly affect people's responses to opinion studies. By noise variables I mean factors such as the ways in which questions are phrased, the order in which elements in questions are presented, the instability of response patterns over time, and the significance of context in framing responses. Variability due to collection variables such as these is conventionally dismissed as a problem to be overcome. Zaller, however, argues that this is to mistake their significance and that a model faithful to this evidence

> abandons the notion that individuals typically possess preformed attitudes that they simply reveal when asked by a pollster to do so. It instead adopts the view that people possess numerous, frequently inconsistent 'considerations' relating to each issue, and that they base their survey responses on whichever of them are at the top of the head at the moment of response.
>
> (1992, p. 54)

His approach is based on the centrality of ambivalence, with the further implication that the rhetorical fictions of public opinion, even when they are based on 'data', are an attempt to corral heterogeneous uncertainty into ideological blocks.

This does not necessarily mean that there is even less substance to public opinion than we had previously supposed: 'If by public opinion one means the hopes, fears, feelings, and reactions to events by ordinary citizens as they go about their private lives, then certainly there is public opinion whether or not there is a pollster to measure it' (ibid., p. 265). What Zaller seeks to deny is that survey responses constitute public opinion. In this his account of public opinion is much closer to the version of culture that I have been advancing in these essays. I therefore find this approach congenial, particularly as Zaller does not deny the powerful effect of elite consensus in generating blocks of opinion on certain ideological themes. It is, however, true that the weight of Zaller's analysis runs counter to Habermas' expectations for the public sphere, especially when the theme of uncertainty is combined with data on very low rates of information on factors relevant to social issues and high rates of reported apathy and lack of interest amongst citizens.

The second theme. of the organisation, ownership and financing of media organisations, has been more extensively discussed in relation to the nature of the public sphere and the possibilities of effective citizenship in mass society (Curran and Gurevitch 1991). Critics have argued that it has proved all too easy in drawing up an ideology of democratic freedoms to accept that there is an equation between a free press (standing for media in general) and the absence of state controls on news content, in which the latter guarantees the former. While this equation is obviously important, it may be dissipated if media organisations are controlled by small groups who use their power to impose their own agenda on public discourse. A concern with this possibility does not just have to depend upon a belief that a class or social elite has been able to use its economic power to retain ownership of media organisations; it can be argued that processes of professional socialisation and organisational practices will also work to create orthodoxies of representation of public life (cf. Tuchman 1978; Fishman 1980). It is because the media create the possibility of public opinion that their operation shapes and determines that opinion (Thompson 1990; and see for example the analyses of the organisation of the news published by the Glasgow University Media Group 1976, 1982; and Eldridge 1993).

Garnham has developed this point by arguing that: 'changes in media structure and policy . . . are properly political questions' (1986, p. 37), and are of as much significance as any other feature of political organisation. The issue of the relationships between state power, means of financing and media organisation has been distinctively inflected in Britain by a history of what has been called public service broadcasting (see the comparative media histories in Curran and Seaton 1992). Recent technological developments, in particular satellite and improved cable broadcasting facilities, allied with government policies favouring the provision of public utilities by commercial agencies governed solely by market criteria, have meant the virtual collapse of traditional values governing broadcasting policies (Murdock 1993). If this British experience is put in the context of analogous policy developments in Western Europe and North America (see also the essays in Ferguson 1990), it is easily understood why there are widespread fears that it will be increasingly difficult to believe that the classic functions of the public sphere are being sustained by the organisation of the media of mass communication and entertainment.

A recent paper by Scannell (1992) has tried to reconcile a recognition of the seriousness of concern about the structural organisation of public communication, with a more positive account of the role of broadcasting in the democratisation of everyday life. Put very briefly, in this revisionary view of the public sphere Scannell stresses the ways broadcasting has reshaped the codes of the public voice – changing the calendar of national events, broadening the range of styles of address and facilitating a whole new repertoire of topics and styles of performance: 'The world, in broadcasting, appears as ordinary, mundane, accessible, knowable, familiar, recognizable, intelligible, shareable and communicable for whole populations. It is talkable about by everyone' (1992, p. 334).

The implication of Scannell's account is that broadcasting does not sustain a public sphere through mediating or reflecting an independent realm of discourse. It is rather that new forms of public discourse are being generated, forms which are indigenous to their setting. It is therefore inappropriate to look for Habermas' rational discourse, based as that is on a particular model of literary appreciation and articulation: 'I prefer to characterize the impact of broadcasting as enhancing the reasonable, as distinct from the rational, character of daily life in public and private contexts' (Scannell, 1992, p. 342).

There are interesting parallels between Zaller's account of public opinion and Scannell's version of the modern public sphere. Both stress pragmatic meaningfulness rather than the more theatrical vision of manipulation and deceit fostered by the ideology-critique of the hegemonic tradition. It is, however, still true that the citizens and their politics are at best ill-informed, deal in stereotypes and clichés, and tend to judge policy programmes by the personalities of their proponents and opponents. Thus we come back to the criticism that 'political communication which is forced to channel itself via commercial media . . . becomes the politics of consumerism' (Garnham

1986, pp. 47–8). In the political discourse of marketing, intellectuals fear that issues are simplifed by being massaged into life-style choices. Thirty years ago Habermas pointed out the dangers for political life of news management by a then new industry of public relations. Since then, state and commercial organisational investment in the development of public relations expertise, and news organisations' active compliance in publication of such news management (see Ericson *et al.*, 1991), have meant the active propagation of ideological illusions as the framework for public discourse.

I referred above to the indifference of news, using this term as a way of making a distinction between news and propaganda. It seems now that in the public sphere of mass culture this distinction has become inadequate. It has to be amplified by a recognition of the implications of the introduction of ideological engineering through public relations. These implications can be described as working to stratify the possibility of effective political participation by those with access to influencing media policy and those lacking that access (except for exceptional circumstances). The power of access can be understood as a particularly significant form of cultural capital (using Bourdieu's fruitful concept) that is not only markedly unequally distributed, but has also proved to be easily appropriated by dominant organisations. The meaning of the public sphere in different social formations must be continually inspected, unless its failures are persistently to rob the concept of citizenship of effective meaning.

CENSORSHIP

In the first part of this chapter I indicated some of the ways in which tolerance can be seen as a central value of modern culture. In the second part I addressed the argument that tolerance is more than just a desirable or appropriate feature of modernity, but is rather a prerequisite of, or constitutive of modernity. I did this by looking more closely at the nature of relationships between institutions of mass communication and entertainment and the character of modern culture. I mentioned new forms of collective imagination, new ways of ordering and regulating public discourse, and new forms of citizenship in the political discourse of mass society. Discussion of these led to a closer look at the theory of the public sphere and some important reasons why the 'classical' model of the public sphere has been seen to have been transformed by later developments in the mechanisms of public discourse in mass society.

It may seem that the theme of tolerance has been lost in the progress of this account. But rather than being lost it has been put on hold while other aspects have been pursued so that the significance of tolerance in modern culture and some of the paradoxes of observing these values can be seen more clearly. At the heart of the classical model of the public sphere lies a privileged sense of tolerance. This is a principle that all citizens have the right and capacity to participate as political actors and none should contradict that right. Any system of mutual respect for others' rights entails the prerequisite of tolerance. If, however, there are good reasons for believing that the joint factors of ownership and operation of media organisations, allied with the ways in which public opinion is staged and articulated, have subverted the rights and capacities of citizens, then tolerance can be argued to have been hollowed out, to have become a principle without substance.

I will now develop the theme of constraints on tolerance by discussing the principles that have generated controls on the content of public discourse. So far I have only considered constraints on the principle of tolerance which can be seen as implicit as they do not stem from intolerant or elitist policies (or not policies that are likely to be publicised). There has been, however, a mode of constraint since the development of mass media of communication which has been more or less explicit and has been legitimised by being seen as necessary to the public good. This is the system of controls on publication, performance and presentation which has acted as a framework of censorship. (The difference between implicit and explicit constraints can also be described by saying that censorship is articulated in ideology as necessary, whereas other modes of constraint are hidden in ideology which denies their operation.)

Although it can be argued that an essential feature of the exercise of political power in any form of government has been a strategic use of secrecy in manipulating the flow of information, the idea of censorship is closer to the cultural form of advertising than diplomacy. By this I mean that the essence of censorship is a series of systematic controls or constraints on what can be broadcast/ published to anonymous audiences (diplomacy seeks to mislead known others). The principle of censorship is made possible by processes of serial reproduction of communication in which the projected audience is largely impersonal, in the sense of being a public. Censorship is the frequently unacknowledged child of the public sphere, an uncomfortable recognition that the promise of modernity can be as threatening as it is liberating.

The rationale of censorship is that some 'things' should not be said, heard, seen, read about or acknowledged. The necessity for control may be phrased on either or both of the grounds of what the 'thing' is or who it is that might be in the audience. It has been widely reported, for example, that in Maoist China, in addition to a number of newspapers and other publications sponsored by various agencies of the state, a restricted circulation newspaper was published which gave a résumé of news that had not been deemed appropriate to be reported in the official record of public life. It is consistent with the bureaucratic management of knowledge that this hidden source of news was made available only to senior party cadres and other important functionaries.

In this example we see a combination of two common elements – the exercise of state power and the stratification of the potential audience into two or more layers of knowledgeable and ignorant. It is unusual for those who can exercise the power of censorship to hope to completely suppress or forbid that which is forbidden (it is instructive to compare and contrast heresy and censorship). Rather, censors seek to protect the putatively innocent from too much worldly wisdom.

The ways in which the practice of censorship hedges the principled tolerance of the public sphere is therefore by asserting that all members of the relevant or possible public cannot be presumed to be equally rational or responsible. I have noted that classically the public sphere was limited to those who possessed social attributes such as education, wealth and masculinity. It will come as no surprise to see that those who are most frequently pointed to as being in need of protection through censorship are those who lack these attributes – the young, women and the working class (famously in the trial of the book *Lady Chatterley's Lover*, the serving classes). More recently especially in relation to television, the elderly have been introduced as another group who need to be protected from what they could be expected to find disturbing. The warrant for intervening to constrain the free flow of information and ideas is a claim either that what is proposed will eventually lead to anarchy, or that it will be repugnant to public opinion, or both. Both grounds have been advanced by the British government to defend their ban on direct interviews with members of the IRA on broadcast networks.

The counterpoint to intellectual fears of the drive to banality in mass culture has been a series of moral panics spread over at least a century concerning the dangers inherent in commercial exploitation of the weaknesses of the mass psyche. In fact, fears of dangers, such as moral corruption, incitement to criminality and sloth and dissipation, which have been held to be likely to stem from un-controlled access to yellow journalism, comics, the popular cinema, cheap literature, television and videos, can easily be seen as part of a much broader current of concern with the modern crowd. It is also consistent with the ways in which a mechanistic marketing view of public life has translated public opinion into the data of polling agencies, that the discourse of concern with mass culture has been addressed by an enormous industry of the measurement of effects (Cumberbatch and Howitt 1989).

Despite the vigorous commitment of those eager to sustain their belief that there must be specifiable effects which can be seen to stem from the pernicious influence of cultural corruption, it has in practice proved impossible to identify causal associations. The reason is that becoming a deviant (or criminal/sexist/immoral/drug user or a member of any other illegitimate category) is not a process like choosing between two pairs of virtually identical jeans. Becom-ing deviant is a negotiation of identity, a process of staging and enacting a variety of elements from interpersonal and cultural resources (a view strongly influenced by Matza 1969). It is pre-cisely because the forms of popular culture have become the main discourse for identity that we monitor its roles and images so carefully; but that does not mean that we are mirrored refractions unable to play with the variety of ways of dressing up that they make possible.

Any system of censorship will depend upon rhetorical fictions concerning the form and character of public discourse. Censorship is a form of imagination which is riddled with contradictions. This is brought out more clearly if we broaden the range of 'things' repressed to include representations of human behaviour, princi-pally sexual behaviour, most commonly generalised under a heading of pornography. The history of pornography, largely in its modern sense an invention of the nineteenth century, also supports my argument that censorship hinges on the mode of publication rather than on what is depicted. It is the possibility of unregulated mass consumption that censorship is created to control.

The problems with regulating representations of sexuality are:

that any attempt to define scope in detail instantly becomes ridiculous; that the process of repression generates the publicity that repression seeks to deny; and that attempts to stratify the audience involve unsustainable and frequently contradictory criteria: '"porn-ography" as a field of discourse was mined from the start with impossibilities, not the least of which was that it turned writers and readers alike into amateur psychologists, who never asked what an object was, only what was meant by it' (Kendrick 1987, p. 31). As Kendrick goes on to say, pornography 'names an argument, not a thing'. The regulation of pornography is therefore caught in the detailed mapping of minutiae of publication and performance. Factors such as place, price, manner of presentation and medium will all be used to evaluate the extent to which pornography (or other genres of representation such as human aggression and demonic possession) can be held to violate public taste.

I have so far been concentrating on the use of some notion of public opinion as a legitimising warrant for the exercise of state power, but earlier I mentioned a parallel use of a fear of anarchy as an equivalent reason for censorship. The reasoning here goes back to the idea that censorship is a form of imagination. That which is denied is denied because it conjures into being what has not previously been said or indeed sayable. Hence the classic status of the Marquis de Sade writing at the birth of the hubris of modernity – that is the later eighteenth century at the beginning of the French Revolution; here the imagination of revolution is turned into ever more baroque forms of physical transgression. In this view censor-ship is a bulwark against the possibilities of chaos inherent in the constructions of civil society.

I described censorship as the unacknowledged child of the public sphere, but although its presence may create discomfort it is not illegitimate. Censorship takes us back to the creative reflexivity of modernity, except that in the pornographic imagination the boun-daries of normality are visualised. Censorship is a form of collective consciousness in public discourse; it displays the perniciousness of culture (an idea I shall take up again later in this section).

It is consistent with this account of censorship patrolling the boundaries of the possible for any discursive milieu, that those who transgress these boundaries are often denied human status (cf. Segal's (1970) innovative discussion of this theme). It seems to me significant that pornographic behaviour, and violent and terroristic behaviour, are so often characterised in popular reports as animal-like or the actions of 'beasts'. Public sexual display always trembles at the edges of what is civilised, using that term as in the first part of the chapter, to mean a code of manners. To stage such actions in the expectation of audiences may be creative, transgressive, innovative or sordid, according to the framing conventions of a particular context, but it is always threatening because it invokes the imagination of disorder. It goes back to the points noted earlier about the salience of the ways we talk about nature and the natural in civil society. In this sense pornography is literally on the edge of culture.

I think it becomes easier in this context to see certain forms of intervention through censorship as attempts to constitute a version of culture as a set of normative expectations rather than lived experience. One of the earliest and most frequent ways of 'prettify-ing' culture was by expurgating texts. Kendrick has pointed out that the practice grew up in the eighteenth century and was a method: 'well suited to anthologies, another eighteenth-century invention, designed for newer members of the reading public – the middle class, and particularly women' (1987, p. 50). The most famous exponents were Dr Bowdler and his family, which led to the neologism, 'bowdlerization', meaning a sanitised version of a cultural classic for unsophisticated audiences. Although the practice has become less common in relation to literature, the practice of re-editing films for television broadcast can be seen as a more contemporary version of making performances culturally innocuous.

Another nineteenth-century form of cultural intervention is provided by the collectors of folk-songs and tales and other aspects of popular customs (Burke 1978; Shiach 1989). Inspired by a belief that socio-industrial change was destroying the cultural base upon which this material had grown up, as well as a strongly national-istic sense that the distinctiveness of national cultural traditions lay in these authentic folk roots, collectors in Britain and other European countries embarked upon extensive projects of docu-mentary record. What is interesting is that the ribaldry and vulgarity of material collected was usually thought to be inappro-priate. (For an account that locates the tensions of appropriateness in emergent class consciousness see Colls 1977.) Popular culture was often thought to be both too coarse to be genuine and in any case unsuitable for a wider audience. Here the censorship is clearly working in terms of idealising a version of culture as it should be. An analogous more recent practice is the unease with which liberal commentators greet homophobia in rap lyrics for example. This again often leads to calls for censorship on the grounds of more appropriate cultural tastes.

I have depicted the turn to culture, in particular the discourses of popular culture, as a response by the intelligentsia to the institutional transformations of mass society. Throughout this turn to culture there has clearly been a pervasive feeling that the novelties of mass society have required new languages of aesthetics and interpretation. In this chapter I have approached the same theme through an exploration of citizenship in the cultural forms of modernity. Although the term 'citizenship' harks back to earlier forms of urban society and government, in its contemporary use in mass democracy it describes new modes of social association. These modes of association, which we can call the publics of mass society, are cultural in that they are forms of imagination. It is precisely because they have to be continually imagined that the anxieties betrayed in censorship are so pervasively present. I think it now reasonable to argue that the intolerance of censorship is not an anomaly of the public sphere but part of a broader search for ways of expressing aesthetic judgements and values in mass culture (which is also what I earlier called collective consciousness).

I have also argued that those involved in this search have consistently sought to justify their interpretations through some form of sociologism. It is therefore appropriate to invert the critical strategy and to try to understand censorship through the sociology of knowledge and power, in part because the practice of censorship so clearly dramatises the uncertainties of authority. Those who draw up the codes of what is permissible have to intervene on behalf of culture, or more precisely those who could not be expected to cope with the complexity of cultural diversity. The sociology of knowledge directs us to ask who could see themselves as competent to fill this role, a legislative task that the intelligentsia would eagerly accept in mass society. (As indeed it was in countries whose governments were inspired by self-conscious ideology so that the state had taken for itself greater and more explicit powers to regulate the public sphere. The past tense relates to countries of the Soviet empire; there is no reason to believe that this form of government will not recur.) The problem is that the intelligentsia are split into numerous fractions by cultural diversity.

Rather than refer to the intelligentsia as if it constituted a coherent category, it is more appropriate to use the metaphor of cultural capital briefly mentioned at the end of the previous section.

Holders of cultural capital have the resources to be able to invest in and thus influence the cultural agenda. As Bourdieu has so clearly demonstrated (1984; see also the essays in Featherstone 1991), these resources are used according to a number of patterns. Some will see themselves within the romantic ideology of creativity so that they will welcome work which transgresses current norms of representational propriety; for others certain sorts of performance such as displays of violence and aggression are objectionable because they will be seen to cater to the dominant expectations of fractions of the audience such as males.

It is also consistent with a theory of cultural capital that a number of studies have found that 'moral entrepreneurs' of campaigns for increased censorship have largely been based in social groups who are likely to feel they have been marginalised and that their 'assets' have been devalued. That is, groups who, by reason of their age, social status, occupation or who, by reference to other more privileged groups feel disadvantaged by what have been presented as the accelerating changes of modernity (see for example Tracey and Morrison 1979; Zurcher and Kirkpatrick 1976). For those impoverished by cultural inflation the campaign to outlaw deviant forms of representation can easily be assimilated to broader concerns with threats of disorderly permissiveness, particularly as these are seen to have been encouraged by minorities who are typically associated with urban sophistication.

For certain groups, then, the moral authoritarianism of censorship functions as a way of denying the tolerance of diversity in favour of some utopian sense of traditional normality (a very distinctive imagination of community). It is then appropriate that an idealised sense of cultural identity, used as an ideological contrast to the ambiguities of diversity, should seek to project itself as grounded in implicit consensus. Hence the frequent and of course unjustifiable claims of proponents of reactionary intolerance to be speaking on behalf of the 'silent majority'.

Campaigns on censorship share certain ideological themes with other types of moral authoritarianism such as political movements against the provision of abortion facilities, or for the teaching of a single religious orthodoxy in public schools. As I have indicated, sociological accounts which have studied the social background of those who become involved as committed partisans in these campaigns have illuminated the social structural location of moral entrepreneurship. There is, however, a further dimension to these movements in that they represent an exemplary elaboration of the more general turn to culture. I believe that it is useful to study the discourses of control as ways of talking about culture as well as power, for censorship offers a distinctive slant on the progress of cultural triumphalism that we have come to call postmodernity (this is more fully taken up in Chapter 5).

Censorship is a reflexive discourse on culture for two reasons. First, I have argued in this section that censorship conjures the possibility of the edge of culture, and, second, that censorship implicitly uses culture as a mirror for different modes of collective identity. Forced to confront the arbitrariness of cultural conventions, order can no longer seem natural. (Censorship is both a response to and a confused recognition of what I earlier called the awful realisation that nothing is natural and that we live in a world without nature.) The premiss of the perceived need for censorship is that who we and others are are fictive enterprises. To put this another way, censorship hinges on the realisation that cultural discourse is representation.

I mean by this more than an argument that modern culture has been swamped by an anarchy of images. It is rather that images have been destabilised. Meaning is governed by context and therefore any way of picturing or representing can be radically shifted in meaning by being seen from a different perspective. In the reflexivity of modern culture we have invested the dramaturgy of representation with constitutive powers, and therefore to misrepresent (or be misrepresented) in this universe of discourse is disabling because it blocks off certain possibilites for who the subject might be. As Kappeler (1986) has forcefully argued, to try to measure the 'harm' of pornography through effects on individuals is to sociologise in a way that mistakes the character of the offence: 'women . . . experience pornography not only as a nuisance, but as direct assault upon their image, their dignity and their self-perception' (p. 21; see also the collection of papers on representations of women in Bonner et al., 1992).

I hope I can now begin to explain the paradox of later modernity that has hung over the discussion in this chapter so far – that in important ways we have not become more tolerant as we have become more aware of cultural diversity. Or, to put it more accurately, the paradox is that we have both a more widespread and well grounded appreciation of the significance of tolerance in cultural diversity, and a more tenacious sense that 'our' culture, whichever that might happen to be, is both an essential protection and needs protecting. The reason for saying this is that the privilege of censorship is no longer reserved for moral conservatives who would seek to deny any dilution of cultural authority. There are in addition many cultural perspectives associated with particular groups whose members seek to forbid collective cultural slurs. Thus cultural minorities, or those who feel disadvantaged by the hegemony of white, educated, males whether they are numerical minorities or not, feel authorised to campaign against discriminatory characterisation in public discourse.

It is initially reasonable to think of censorship as a form of propaganda – those who would censor are clearly not indifferent to the character of news. Censorship has, however, precisely because it is arbitrary, become a means of engagement with contemporary culture. Far from censorship withering away as our culture matures in greater mutual trust, it seems more likely that there will be an ever-increasing clamour to intervene in the dramatic languages of mass culture. It has proved a small step from the conviction that members of the mass audience need to be protected from representation in public discourse, to the realisation that public discourse needs to be protected from itself.

To say that the number of interested parties who would like to be involved in some form of censoring how they are represented in different cultural forms is constantly increasing does not mean they are all or equally successful. It is rather that there is a more widespread sensitivity to the implications of representation. We can describe as cultural activists those who are actively involved in campaigns to prevent women being regularly seen as victims of sexual violence, or to prevent smoking and drinking being seen as glamorous activities, or to prevent those with a disability such as autism being depicted as victims who lack any autonomy in their life-circumstances. They are articulate proponents of specific agendas who react with outrage when they feel their cultural identity has been insulted (again). But their vociferousness does not mean that their concerns are not shared by 'ordinary' members of that group; indeed their concerns have become ubiquitous.

It has become one of the clichés of late twentieth-century culture that media of mass communication and entertainment provide a convenient whipping-boy with which to explain or to be blamed for anything undesirable. Political failure, cultural disadvantage, eating disorders, urban riots can all be viewed as, possibly unintended, consequences of dominant media discourses. (Paralleling this style of cultural explanation, there is an enormous number of advice agencies, counsellors, therapists and professional consultants who can offer accounts of personal failure – or insufficient success – in terms of image, deportment, presentation etc.) The ease of explanation that the media offer allows an easy slippage into believing that media discourse is sufficient. The means of representation come to supplant the intrinsic merits and faults of what is being represented, so that correcting the image, that is making it conform more to what seem to be favourable or attention-getting expectations, comes to be the dominant goal of politicians, organisations and all forms of public institution.

A sensitivity to the need for control through censorship and an acceptance of the infinite regress of representation are both grounded in cultural pluralism. As dominant characteristics of modern culture they are not arbitrary hiccups but are inherent in contemporary cultural forms. It is only to be expected that this particular conjunction of authoritarianism and relativism would come to be particularly focused in language. As a dominant medium of discourse language can be expected to collect tensions and contradictions in the relationships of individual and community. Fifty years ago George Orwell writing in England saw the crucial significance of language in shoring up a system of political repression once it became an arbitrary medium of prescription as well as representation (a persistent concern of Orwell's: I am thinking in particular of his novel *Nineteen Eighty-Four* (Penguin 1954)). More recently the phenomenon of political correctness provides another dystopian orthodoxy of sanctioned discourse.

In Orwell's version of authoritarianism a single political figure acts as the focus for mythologising culture. In order to systematically pull language away from experience towards ways of talking that constituted an idealised reality, Orwell saw a political class using a charismatic icon to author-ise shifts in representation. It is actually more consistent with the politics of mass democracy that we have usually not proved dependent on such a figure, but have instead created informal practices of monitoring and controlling each other's speech, writing and performance. In the authoritarianism of political correctness all are entitled to act as censors of their neighbours' speech. As any form of reference can be examined to see whether it is slighting, disparaging or encouraging 'unhealthy' or 'inappropriate' attitudes; there is an infinite regress of correction because language is not being shifted towards some more accurate forms of representation but rather is being remodelled towards continually changing expectations.

As a form of censorship political correctness is a rhetorical fiction much as any other, but it is a fiction in which a diversity of culture is continually being reimagined as a form of politics. At its most extreme, political correctness moves from being sanctimonious to more insidious forms of authoritarianism. I said above when discussing collective consciousness that censorship displays the perniciousness of culture. What I mean by this phrase is that the turn to culture can generate a concentration on the infinite distinctiveness of cultures. To recognise the dramaturgy of others' forms of life is respectful and enlightening, but to assume that difference commands an autonomy in description and imagination that must be protected by sanctions, whether informal or enforced by the state, is to create a barrier to intercourse that is the antithesis of tolerance. The reflexivity of culture demands that we are continually open to the play of other perceptions not isolated by self-serving fictions.

CULTURAL INTOLERANCE

In the previous section I discussed censorship as a form of constraint upon our expectations of the classical model of the public sphere. I argued that censorship expresses distrust of the public in that it discriminates amongst audiences and because it discriminates within topics and their representation. I further argued that censorship is not an anomaly that we can hope to transcend in a more enlightened democracy. The roots of the institution of censorship are buried deep inside the notions of culture with which we have tried to enact new forms of collective identity. This has generated a fundamental ambivalence within and about the value of tolerance as a general name for our consciousness of cultural diversity and relativism; an ambivalence that has had the almost paradoxical consequence that the moral authoritarianism that censorship articulates has become more pervasive and virulent. It seems that for censorship to become generally seen to be superfluous will require new ways of staging and performing fictions of collective life.

I referred to the development of new agendas for censorship as paradoxical, and a good illustration of this point is provided by the lack of consistency within objectives for censorship. The problem is that many of those who would see sexual displays, for example, as exploitative and degrading are also in principle libertarian, particularly in respect to the exercise of state powers. This has led to fierce debates within feminism between anti-porn and anti-anti-porn over the extent to which individuals can control the meaning of representations (Bonner *et al.*, 1992). It is important to appreciate that these debates are not locked in futile squabbles over degrees of explicitness, but are expressions of politicised concern with cultural practice: 'What is at stake, then, in recent feminist discussions about whether it is possible to distinguish between pornography and erotica, or in disagreements about the role and relevance of censorship, are not only different understandings of pornography, but also implicit models of culture' (Franklin *et al.* 1992, p. 101).

This sort of debate helps us to understand that having some stake in setting the agendas for public discourse has become one of the crucial areas for political struggle in contemporary culture. (By public discourse I mean all the ways in which the politics of social life are staged and enacted – not just talked about – in the media of mass communication and entertainment.) It is precisely because for many their political commitments are focused on cultural topics that it has become a means of emancipation to attempt to rewrite the scripts for different modes of identity. To be imprisoned within the terms of a subjectivity that is composed of elements emphasising irrationality, animality, perversion or disability is as much a form of victimisation as a denial of legal or other human rights.

There has been an interesting interaction between grass-roots struggles and contemporary social theory in this respect. The turn to culture has generated more widespread innovation in life-styles than previous forms of social radicalism, as well as a much greater interest in, and a willingness to see the relevance of, theoretical work in mundane experience. The commitment to theory has moved in two waves over the past thirty years. At one stage sociology was very influential and there was a consequent emphasis on the arbitrary construction of social reality, in particular the processes of construction of roles, identities, norms and deviance. These ideas made concrete the principle of reflexivity in civil society. At a later stage theoretical work associated with postmodernism and deconstructionism became expecially important in helping to articulate a politics of representation.

There is no history of strong intellectual influence on English-speaking political life, so the innovations just mentioned reinforce a feeling that politics has been transformed into culture; or, one should say more accurately, there is a growing divide between the institutionalised politics and an alternative politics. The former has been characterised by political parties competing for control of government machinery, and it is a politics that is increasingly irrelevant to an alternative life-politics of struggles over the autonomy and dramaturgy of identity. It is therefore not surprising that so much of the rhetoric of alternative politics has focused on slogans concerned with raising consciousness, or pride in identity, on campaigns to assert rights and a refusal to accept others' characterisations. It is the latter politics, in its reflexive concern with the symbolic vocabularies of social forms, that is cultural and that increasingly engages the passions of citizenship.

The consequence of emphasising distinctive cultural identity, however, has been on the one hand to intensify feelings of cultural diversity, while, on the other, to exacerbate certain forms of an intransigent intolerance of difference. It is as though the form of imagination through which we conjure our communal identities has become more intense, less able to accommodate ideas which stress the indeterminacy of culture. It seems as if the turn to culture has created monsters which now threaten to destroy the promise of modernity. I shall briefly discuss several forms of cultural identity, beginning with nationalism, in order to get a fuller reckoning of the costs and benefits as we confront the unravelling of modernity (and thereby begin to chart the outlines of postmodern social forms).

The imagination of national identity is an institution of modern culture that has, as I have said, been particularly associated with processes of mass communication (while also being dependent upon infrastructural features such as transport networks, bureaucratic initiatives and a state education system). Indeed, an unquestioned and 'natural' goal of nationalist movements has been, as Smith says, to act: 'as an ideological movement for attaining and maintaining autonomy, unity and identity on behalf of a population deemed by some of its members to constitute an actual or potential "nation"' (Smith 1991, p. 73; emphasis in original. Although I have quoted Smith in this context I should point out that in this publication and his papers, 1988 and 1989, he contests the cultural accounts of nations of purely modern inventions and draws a distinction between civic and ethnic understandings of national identity.)

What an ideological account of nation-ness means is that a nation is being constructed to be equivalent in all important respects to a culture: a culture that has an identity through being distinctively different and thereby creates an identity for its members. Here identity should be understood in two senses: as creating a community of common purpose; and as a shared or distinctive way of being (who 'we'/'I' are). In part this dual sense of identity is sustained through public dramas of processions, rituals, places and occasions that map a symbolic history; and in part by a public discourse that reiteratively points to forms of entertainment, in particular sporting heroes and occasions. In addition there are, as Scannell (1992), has argued ways of structuring news and public events, as well as representations of the repetitions of everyday life (especially in advertisements) that function as features of a world 'we' share in common.

It has, however, seemed reasonable to argue that the urgency of national affiliations should gradually become less intense as commercial and technological pressures within media organisations have led to transnational media mega-corporations, and thus that there will be complementary trends towards a globalisation of culture (King 1991b; Featherstone 1990; Albrow and King 1990). There has been for many thinkers a drift towards a global culture in which national idiosyncrasies should become relatively unimportant, a process also held both to stimulate and to have been stimulated by parallel trends in the production and marketing of consumer goods and agricultural marketing. As Giddens has put it: 'Modernity is inherently globalising' (1990, p. 63). Further pressures towards globalisation have been detected in post-industrial moves towards an information economy in which 'capital' is necessarily rootless and the production of goods and services is independent of specific places set in space and time. There has also been evidence of a diminution in national sovereignty apparent in the development of supra-national economic and political unions such as the European Community.

It is all the more paradoxical then that in so many ways in the last years of the century the intensity of national affiliation has increased rather than diminished, and that the number of nations continues to increase. Although it could be said that the profusion of national sentiments unleashed by the break-up of the Soviet empire is merely a case of a history that had been artificially repressed for fifty years suddenly breaking free, I think the extraordinary intensity of some of the hatreds that have been revealed has surprised and dismayed everyone. Above all, in the former Yugoslavia people who had lived in what had seemed harmony for generations have turned upon their neighbours, seeking not just to turn them away but to deface and exterminate their culture through mass rape and attempted genocide. The frenzy of national consciousness seems to have been fuelled as much by hatred, and fear, of others as by passion for new communities.

In Western Europe and North America intercommunal antagonisms have not in general been enacted through military conflict. This does not mean that nationalist movements in Scotland, Wales, Catalonia, Northern Italy, the Basque country, between Flemings and Walloons in Belgium, and the Quebec liberation movement, to name some examples, are not powerfully evocative struggles which frequently transcend the conventional parties of class politics and occasionally lead to terrorist bombings or assassinations. The breadth and vitality of these movements, and the constant possibility of new struggles, makes it clear that nationalism is not an exhausted dynamic. It is, however, when a nationalist revolt is intertwined with ethnic conflict, with religion providing the traditional basis for communal identification, as in Northern Ireland, that sectarian bigotry is displayed in full, vicious intensity.

The example of Northern Ireland in particular, but also many of these nationalist movements, illustrates that the anomaly of nationalism in the context of an increasingly global culture is in part explained by strong feelings of ethnicide. That is, members of a self-identified cultural minority feel threatened to the point of extinction by a combination of local circumstances and an encroaching amorphous mass culture. Thus in Ireland a Protestant minority seeks desperately to cling to their hegemony in a small part of the country. To do so they enact their sense of living in a cultural laager through a symbolic repertoire that looks back several hundred years, and a cultural outlook that combines a fierce anti-Catholicism with a deep suspicion of the tolerance of modernity. One can also see that some members of the Muslim community in Britain have sought to resist incorporation through emphasising traditions of distinctiveness and cultural autonomy. Thus in some cases local groups have resisted educational practices which might subvert the intolerance of gendered discrimination, for example, and, most famously, local groups have supported the extreme censorship of prescribing execution for an author of (what seemed to them) a famous heresy.

Communities that feel threatened often throw up leaders who can and do use culture as a ground for stressing the intransigence of difference. Rather than seeing our knowledge of other cultures as a way of appreciating the arbitrariness of difference, new forms of fundamentalism claim the impossibility of mutual comprehension and use the necessity of defence as a reason for the development of a multiplicity of nations within a state. Of course it cannot be emphasised too strongly that the threats ethnic minorities face in the post-industrial economies of late modern culture are not just of the loss of identity in global assimilation. The informal hidden iceberg of vibrant nationalism in majority cultures has created a climate of terror and hatred for ethnic minorities that soils and sickens any hopes one might harbour for cultural tolerance. The violence inflicted upon victims ranges from that sponsored by organisations of neo-Fascist racism, to the occasional physical violence and persistent insulting hatred of local antagonism (an antagonistic climate that, it must be admitted, has been made worse by institutionalised racism in the media – Van Dijk 1991).

The very ubiquitousness of the menace of racial attacks means that it escapes the dramaturgy of news and sinks into the 'normality' of routine social order. It is against this background that what is often the defensiveness of cultural identifications seems so clearly comprehensible. It is clearly important that a pride in the distinctive traditions, festivals and heroes, cuisine, language or dialect – what we can call the cultural places of a group – can be sustained and expressed, particularly when often so many of these markers of identity become flashpoints of antagonism between the subordinate and the hegemonic ambitions of majority culture. It is also true, however, that a cultural politics in seeking to exploit the dynamics of embattled identity can insist upon the necessity of difference (and these remarks are not specific to ethnic minorities). Culture in this usage is being torn from the imaginative fictions of social theory and reshaped as particular ways of being closed to outsiders.

Most controversially this can lead to forms of cultural essentialism in which attempts at intimate cohabitation are spurned. Thus it has been argued that it is likely to be damaging to black children to be brought up in white households. This is principally because it is claimed that they will lack role-models to faciliate pride in their identity, and a community of experience with which to cope with degrading insults from outsiders. I do not belittle the hurt and pain inflicted by cultural insults, but neither do I believe that cultures are unique discourses that act as forms of life-worlds or buildings that you have to live inside in order to be able to understand the experience. The point of the turn to culture is precisely to teach us the irony of cultural shibboleths; that we can use our fictive imagination to combine elements from different discourses. Those who would use social theory to deny the creativity of new forms of intimacy are guilty of bad faith.

We have also, however, to confront the extremes of cultural intransigence and remember that genocide is the darkest invention of the modern imagination. There have of course been many tyrants in history who have massacred huge numbers including whole city populations, but the systematic attempt to exterminate a culture is peculiarly modern (Bauman 1990). For native North Americans and Aborigines in Australia, specific classes in Stalinist Russia, the Cambodian intelligentsia under the Khmer Rouge, and above all the Jews in Nazi Germany it seems to have been a denial of their culture that made their physical extermination both thinkable as well as practicable.

It is against this background that other forms of modern intolerance and violent abuse such as the physical assaults and particularly sexual assaults on women, violent attacks on gay men and particularly the violent stigmatisation of AIDS sufferers, and increasing rates of child abuse and sexual assault begin to coalesce into a picture of demonic violence. Far from the liberal civilisation that is the theoretical fruit of modernity we seem to have created a form of social order where violence is suppressed into (and explodes through) the jagged edges of cultural interaction. If an earth-poisoning pollution is the pernicious consequence of the spectacular life-styles of consumer culture, then it seems analogous to suggest that for some an intensifying rage against difference is the pernicious consequence of the reflexive arbitrariness of postmodern culture.

It seems then that the processes through which in the late modern world we have come to emphasise the creative significance of representation in social order, processes that I generally summarise as the cultural turn, have had at best, a confused relationship with the structural principle of tolerance. The more we have sought to ground or root a language of identity in imaginative affiliations, the more we seem to create tensions in sustaining the distinctiveness of others' claim to recognition. I would like to say authority rather than recognition here because being someone/something gives us the right to speak for (as well as the security of being recognised as one of) that group. This is a creative power which is a form of authority for those who are largely otherwise anonymous. To be challenged in this claim to recognition or authority is, as I have said in relation to censorship, to put another's social existence into question.

I have suggested that the intensely cultural representation of identity in later modernity generates both freedoms and new tensions of insecurity. An equivalent duality can be seen in other grounds for a secure sense of self, such as a comfortable pleasure in one's body. Here a feeling that this physical form exemplifies the self has to some extent been whittled away by moves towards the civilisation of manners I described earlier (on contemporary re-thinking of social theories of the body see Featherstone et al., 1991). Elias' account of the increasing controls upon the body associated with the historical development of individual self-consciousness stresses, as we noted, how these controls are deemed necessary as the body is seen through others' eyes. Another way of putting this is to say that for each individual in modern civilisation their body becomes a thing to be evaluated or judged in terms of aesthetic criteria. Rather than just being the medium of sensuous engagement it acquires a further level as an image and thereby as an object of moral discourse.

Of course it can be objected that such generalisations are inevitably over-stretched. The variety of the ways in which we experience embodiment are too diverse to yield to a neat sentence-long summary (Synott 1993). And yet it is clear that the civilisation of the body has meant the development of new forms of insecurity, particularly in relation to the ways in which our identities are embodied. One only has to note the plethora of clubs and centres where bodies can be trained and shaped, the insistent moral discourse on the appropriateness of exercise and fitness, and the parallel discourses of anxiety about food and the amounts and types we should eat as responsible citizens. In all late modern cultures the streets of cities and lanes of the countryside are filled with sweating and grunting men and women running and riding as dedicated aesthetes because, in a triumph of ideology over experience, they feel convinced that they feel better.

So I would argue that in important ways, the body has become a cultural form and that the experience of embodiment (how the self experiences its physical form) is intertwined with other images of (or ways of image-ing) identity. Although the culture of the body is an important topic that deserves much fuller consideration, for the present in relation to a theme of intolerance I want to explore the implications of the physical degradation of the body by agencies of the state. In the discussion so far of how nationalist sentiment and other forms of collective identity have been used to justify or make sense of aggression against those who are different, I have drifted between various forms of more or less spontaneous violence. To turn now to assaults on bodies, including both physical and mental torture, is to address more systematic or bureaucratised violence. My reason for including a reference to the prevalence of torture by modern states is that it seems another form of institutionalised degradation of cultural difference (I draw heavily here on Peters 1985).

We have become used, following Foucault (1977), to conceiving the history of punishment as falling into two phases. The first consisted of a series of spectacular degradations of the body, followed by a second phase where the body is secreted from society and becomes the vehicle for a number of disciplinary regimes. To the extent that physical violence is minimised in the second then torture should, in an evolutionary perspective, have become anachronistic; and indeed it was the great hope of Victorian enlightenment that torture like slavery would become impossible in civilised societies. Recent evidence from the later twentieth century that torture in a variety of forms is routinely practised by all governments, not just totalitarian regimes, seems to be more than a failure of enlightened optimism. The institution of modern torture draws upon themes of the cultural representation of identity rather than just displaying a casual brutality of the mindless.

Torture attacks the image of the body as it grounds the various dimensions of identity for the self. Through pain and fear and disgust the body is degraded so that as a representation of the self it is literally fractured before the victim's eyes. Thus, although it may seem an eminently physical assault, in its practice modern torture is an assault upon culture. All the ways in which culture sustains a meaningful world are attacked and eventually broken, not, however, as by a demonic fury but as a routine practice of occupational expertise. Those who have been trained as torturers in places such as Greece and Chile have spoken of learning to 'de-culture' victims. They did not have to be hated or feared but rather made into the 'other' of a stranger – someone outside the cultural embrace of recognition and reciprocity.

While it is infinitely distressing that torture can be so widely practised, it is possibly an even greater cause for despair that it is so easy for agencies of the state to be able to recruit those willing to act as torturers (we are reminded of psychological experiments in which well-educated, secure undergraduates were easily 'persuaded' into inflicting physical violence upon their peers). All that seems necessary is for sufficient institutional authority to be exercised to persuade actors that those they are dealing with are outsiders, pariahs, strangers (in itself a mocking commentary on the community of strangers that is a principle of modernity). The process is facilitated, of course, if the victims can be labelled communists, or fascists, or blacks, or gays or atheists or abortionists or any one of the other communal identities that threaten normality, but the stigma is easily arrived at. In a culture of appearances where everyone is potentially a stranger, difference is easily found and can usually be inscribed into social order as a reason for victimisation.

The character of solidarity between different cultural identities is of central concern for any hopes we might harbour for the culture that succeeds modernity. Discussing the issue I raised above of whether the pressures towards a global culture are likely to lead to diminution of the significance of the nation as the dominant form of collective identity, Smith combines a negative answer with a critique of constructivist accounts of nations as phenomena of modern culture (1991, especially Chapter 7). He seems to feel that there is a theoretical continuity between those who would treat the nation and its traditions, symbols etc. as inventions of a collective imagination, and those who would attempt to impose the artificiality of postmodern eclecticism on contemporary culture. The failing both strands of thought share is to miss the positive functions of nationalism in generating an historical context for individual experience: 'the *longue durée* of ethno-histories have furnished the very languages and cultures in which collective and individual selves and their discourses have been formed and continue to bind and divide human beings' (Smith 1991, p. 160).

As an argument for an organic basis to national culture and identity this seems to me to be remarkably circular, but it does suggest that the power of national fictions is in response to the ironic ambivalencies of pervasive reflexivity. As the normality of everyday life becomes increasingly hard to sustain so the threats of abnormality are both fragmented and intensified. It may be, as Smith seems to suggest, that the power of the nationalist imagination is its metaphoric association with the family. In so many ways nations use a language of familial relationships to characterise the emotional bonds of identification, and perhaps these appeals become all the more persuasive because for so many their personal experience of family life fails to conform to stereotypical expectations. Similarly, other forms of community, whether they be spiritual, political, ethnic, sexual or national, as voluntary overlapping commitments can be seen to be consistent with the more common sense of ourselves as a multi-faceted identity in late modern culture (Schlesinger 1991).

The dynamics of affiliation, or what we could call the appeal of imaginative fictions, is not my primary concern at this time. I am instead trying to see whether our multi-cultural societies can offer the hope of a liberal tolerance or if we must look forward to increasing fundamentalism and intolerant denial of others' rights. If the latter nightmare is to be avoided and there is to be any hope it surely must be not through a denial of difference but through a celebration of interdependence. The history of modernity shows too clearly that to identify with others necessarily creates others' difference: a community of affiliation, whether it is race or gender or generation, creates a divide between those who are members and those who are not. Kristeva (1993) has argued that in a search for certainties we must not create a cult of origins out of these differences, or treat them as displays of some cultural essence

As an alternative Kristeva looks back to Montesquieu and a classical theorisation of the public sphere. She argues that this tradition invites us to take pride in the particularity of each community, while recognising that any affiliation is necessarily embedded in further overarching communities, and thus we should 'think of the social body as a guaranteed hierarchy of *private rights*' (1993, p. 31). My family, my region, my gender, my race etc., are overlapping rights and responsibilities: 'Understood in such manner . . . [a nation] . . . is at the same time affirmed as a space for freedom and dissolved in its own identity, eventually appearing as a texture of many singularities' (p. 32). The same idea is taken up in another essay in the same collection where she talks of the multiplicity of identities in a modern nation as: 'a polyphonic community' (p. 63).

THE NEW PUBLIC SPHERE

I concluded the discussion of the strains of intolerance in modern culture with a brief account of Julia Kristeva's plea for nations without nationalism, which I could adapt for this chapter to read cultures without culturalism. As well as being a passionate argument for fictions of community that are not mutually destructive, this approach also helps us to reconcile the persistence of nationalism, and other modes of cultural identity, with international mass culture.

It is unlikely that a major process of cultural change such as late modernity will collapse neatly into one side or the other of a contrast-pair such as nationalism or globalisation. It is far more likely that there will be contradictory trends in different spheres. For example, while the power of America as the foremost global economy will probably come under increasing threat, pressures intensified by pretensions to global military hegemony, at the same time the power of America as global mythologist through acting as technical and imaginative centre for the production of alternative realities is likely to increase (a theme I take up again in Chapter 5).

Against this backdrop the urgency of local experience will create a multiplicity of (for example) gay or black or ageing cultures. Experience shows that they will be able to emphasise their particularity within a mass popular culture that is increasingly able to accommodate a variety of modes of innovation and replay them to curious but rootless audiences. The dominant organisations controlling industries concerned with this endless process of harvesting innovation and repackaging it for mass audiences will continue to be American (with significant exceptions).

There will therefore be a continual interplay of local cultural identities which are focused on specific concerns – frequently oppositional to what they take to be conventional culture – but at the same time unconcerned about their adaptations from and use of a global leisure/media culture. In this way local cultural identities, however urgently felt, will be increasingly imaginative fictions. They will need to be continually invented and reinvented using vocabularies of style and historical imaginations to sustain their distinctness for members and to mark off outsiders.

Balancing the eclecticism of local cultural use will be what I called earlier the bureaucratic indifference of media organisations. I was writing then primarily about news, but the point holds for entertainment as well. For the culture industries products are as arbitrary as they are as signifiers for audiences. It is in their indifference to how they are used that global cultural coroporations facilitate consumer citizenship. Programmes of social engineeering through communication and entertainment are locked into the revolutionary hubris of modernity, and it was in their failure to facilitate a playful dramaturgy of representation that state propaganda organisations remained caught in the coils of anachronistic aesthetics.

I have so far written of a contrast between mass and local cultures, suggesting that they can live in a curious interdependence. To develop the idea further it will soon become necessary to distinguish between several levels or types of local culture. For example, there will be nations such as Ireland, Scotland or Britain, and then cross-cutting communities of religion and class such as Protestant and Catholic, or working and middle class, and then further affiliations between white and black, street-wise and straight etc., etc. (on some of the ambivalencies of contemporary Britishness see Chambers 1990, Chapter 2). These local cultures will differ in their ability to set agendas for different media of mass communication and entertainment, and in the sorts of ways they use collective ceremonies to dramatise particular forms of identity (Morley and Robbins have begun to address very interestingly what they have called the politics of identity – 1989; 1990; 1992; see also the work of Dayan and Katz on mass dramatisations of collective ceremonies, for example 1987 and 1988).

A number of writers have begun to focus our understanding of these developments in late modern culture by arguing that in negotiating new political commitments and identities we are also redrawing the contours of the public and private spheres. I have argued that the classical model of the public sphere was destroyed by a simultaneous movement of being absorbed into international mass culture, largely through the power of media mega-corporations, on the one hand and on the other by a privatisation of public discourse. This I described as being the result of a related concern with the development of public relations and an incorporation of public opinion into the rhetoric of consensus politics. Both aspects are moves towards privatisation in that they generate what I called consumer citizenship – individuals shopping in the market-place of politics for something they feel comfortable with. To this account we should now add the ways in which new strategies of mass communication are transforming the structures of lived experience for mass audiences.

Morley has begun this process by arguing that for research to focus on the domestic context of reception is not to trivialise or privatise the public sphere, but rather to recognise that: 'the sitting-room is exactly where we need to start from, if we finally want to understand the constitutive dynamics of abstractions such as "the community" or "the nation"' (1992, p. 283). Amongst these constitutive dynamics Morley mentions two structuring processes; first, the ways in which all pervasive media of mass communication frame and allow for the infinite reframing of forms of space and time, in particular new technological developments that give audiences much greater control over the time and place of reception; and secondly, the constitutive power of what we could call leisure resources in sustaining domestic rituals. Households, families and living units and their idiosyncratic patterns of appropriating entertainment forms are all instances of what I called above the use by local cultures of mass entertainment.

The significance of these processes is that they call into question the possibility of defining a firm boundary between public and private spheres. It is rather that there are a multitude of levels of appearance. The figures of public life, the stars, heroes and celebrities, are given a public identity but they are also of course private figures watching their own and others' show. What we mean by the public sphere is a series of ways of talking about, dramatising and responding to the dramatisations of identity. Accepting the inescapable role of audience, we are ambivalent about anonymity. It is both a profound security against the dangers of exploitation (see the development of this theme in the next chapter), and an arbitrary state. Recognising that identity is infinitely malleable, and buttressed by innumerable tales of unpredictable fate which selects figures at random for a form of public identity or fame before oblivion, there is no reason not to believe that we do not all contain the seeds of our own greatness.

Habermas, in his essay on the public sphere, at one point quotes Burke, who wrote at the end of the eighteenth century that: 'In a free country every man thinks he has a concern in all public matters; that he has a right to form and a right to deliver an opinion on them' (1989, p. 94). The fruit of these separate deliberations subsequently came to be called public opinion. It seems to me an appropriate analogy that as public opinion has been transformed into the polling exercises of marketing consultants and public relations experts, so our understanding of citizens' rights has shifted to a common ability to judge the character and authenticity of public figures – whether it is a pope, or a terrorist, or an alleged homosexual politician, or the victim of a kidnap. In these absurd little judgements on trustworthiness and good faith we seem to be enacting a politics while remaining firmly within the secure space of conformity.

It is possible then to see the emergence of new more active publics – a diversity of identities and styles we can call a multiplicity of cultures. And perhaps it is in this profusion of choice that we avoid the contradiction of both institutionalising tolerance as a dominant value, while at the same time feeling the persistent insidious tug towards new forms of moral authoritarianism and intolerant particularism. The generative paradox of mass democracy is that while becoming ever more skilled in the play of cultural vocabularies, we simultaneously appease the gods of intolerance with an acquiescence to the conventions of conformity.

I am led to this idea not just by the moral authoritarianism of political correctness, but also by a growing social politics in which it is increasingly accepted as appropriate to punish the victims. Those who are seen to be so irresponsible as to continue smoking can legitimately be denied further hospital care because they have not observed the prescriptions of healthy citizenship. At the same time that there seems a dominant climate of tolerance of moral diversity, so that domestic living arrangements have never been so heterogeneous, there is an intolerance of those who cannot or will not be active citizens. The island of normality is felt to be precariously balanced – at risk not just from a collapse of culture but also from environmental catastrophes that are more or less adequately guarded against by social structural arrangements (Beck 1992). In a culture of appearances or representation we are most concerned to avoid the risk of exclusion, and thus a loss of social identity, by transgressing the conventions of our local cultures.

I have started a number of 'hares' in the course of this chapter. I have not had the space or the ability at this time to pursue many of these issues, such as whether the contradictions in the practice of tolerance that I have described can be explained within the broad terms of Elias' theory of the civilising process (relevant aspects are explored in Dunning and Rojek 1992, particularly the essays by the editors); or, more seriously, how, in the light of this discussion, we should understand the status of the stranger in modern and postmodern culture (a line of thought that has been stimulated by Lash 1993). I have instead tried to confine myself to aspects of the ways in which the use of culture has become a central theme in modern public discourse, in particular how culture is used as both a descriptive framework and a source of social policy. My intention has been to show that these aspects of the turn to culture have generated consequences and contradictions that I find pernicious. It seems to me that the tasks and promise of modernity have still to be adequately addressed.

Chapter 4

Spaces and places: consumer culture and suburban life-style

INTRODUCTION

One of the most commonly reiterated themes in social theories of culture is that the culture of a community structures and orders everyday life. Culture imbues personal experience with meaning and significance: in part through the provision of a repertoire of local sayings, frequently repeated values, and the use of categories of admiration or mockery in relation to local figures and so on; and, in part, through the provision of a ritual calendar that provides a structure of festivals and symbolically important transitions for individual lives as well as communal festivals marking seasonal change, the accession of new rulers and occasions and sites of licensed transgression etc. Culture therefore works on a number of levels and through a number of forms to give a structure of predictability and continuity to the practice of community life.

I hope that most of us reading this passage would agree that this is a reasonable summary of the function of culture in a simpler society. People may query particular terms and certain elements that should be included or given greater stress but that would not invalidate the general perspective. There may, however, be considerably more argument over whether such an integrative view of culture has any validity in relation to the complex social orders of the post-industrial world (Archer 1988). In the countries of that world there is a generally felt sense of history and cultural change such that it seems reasonable to characterise the differences of our greater social complexity as the modern world; and to many it is increasingly appropriate to call upon an idea of transcending modernity to late modern or postmodern culture. It has been the premiss of the preceding chapter that in modern experience culture is no longer coherent, definable and authoritative in the ways it might once have seemed to function.

In this chapter I want to look at the organisation of personal and collective experience more closely. I shall do this by confronting one aspect of modern culture directly. Part of the force of our sense of culture in pre-modern society is that it seems reasonable to presume that a form of life is tied to a territory in a precise and specifiable way (although reasonable, this generalisation is obviously inadequate to encompass the diaspora of the Jewish people for example). In this sense culture traditionally defines a lived environment as well as a world of acquaintance and familiarity. Central to the dislocations of modernity has been an uprooting of culture. For an increasing proportion of society culture creates a social space but co-exists in physical space with other cultural forms, summarised by King as: 'Culture is increasingly deterritorialized' (1991a, p. 6). Obviously important in this process has been the development of metropolitan-based mass communication and entertainment networks that provide a level of cultural homogeneity overlaying the diversity of spaces and places.

I shall therefore use the social organisation of space as a theme upon which I can introduce, and I hope illuminate by discussing in this way, accounts of distinctive features of our concern with culture. Amongst these harmonic variants on the theme of space, I will discuss the meaning of acting professionally, some characteristics of suburban living environments, tourism, shopping centres and the aesthetics of life-style in consumer culture. Such a long list means that each cannot be dealt with in great detail, but, accepting a degree of generalisation, I hope that something coherent can emerge about the cultural organisation of lived experience.

PROFESSIONALS AND SPACES

I shall begin by making some notes on the authority of professionals. I do this because I believe professionals can be characterised by their ability to control social space in important ways. I will justify this statement in the course of the discussion. One of the distinguishing features of the professionalisation of an occupation or a trade is that the members see themselves as bound by a different code of conduct to that which would conventionally be expected of tradespeople. It may be that this code merely regulates those matters that are of immediate economic interest to members of the profession, or that the code is generalised as a set of expectations for every aspect of their social behaviour (thus doctors and barristers have professional tribunals which can examine a colleague's behaviour, and if found wanting the colleague can be barred from further practice). In either case the distinctiveness of the code is what assures members of the privilege of membership; it gives them an identity which marks them off from the world at large. This identity is commonly reinforced through a number of social processes such as ceremonies, a particular calendar, feast days, traditions, costumes, and distinctive language, which are peculiar to the profession.

The recognition of an occupation as a profession has usually served as the basis of a higher social status and the granting of a certain authority and intrinsic 'character' to members. (Thus in Britain applicants for a passport can have their photograph confirmed as a true likeness by the members of a number of professions.) Professions have traditionally sought to defend and sustain their privileges by, as I have said, codes governing members' professional conduct, controls upon training and entry to the profession and a high degree of autonomy in regulating working practices.

In post-industrial societies the traditional professions (including the law, medicine, education and the priesthood) are losing the structural basis of their authority. The trend of deprofessionalisation has been inflected by local considerations in relation to specific trades, but it can be summarised by saying that the function of independent expertise filled by professionals in an era of entrepreneurial capitalism is no longer appropriate in the disciplines of corporate bureaucracy. Professionals claim obligations which derive from an independent code – attitudes which generate suspicion in the corridors of government and commercial bureaucracies – and their status has implied a career-long expertise which may be unsuited to a rapidly changing technologically based occupation.

Although traditional forms of professional organisation are losing their substantive power there is an ever-increasing number of occupations and trades that seek to claim the rhetoric of professionalism. Given the distinctive rewards enjoyed by traditional professionals it is easy to see why a number of different occupations will seek to enhance their own status and encourage a we-feeling amongst co-workers by setting up some show of professional organisation even if it lacks disciplinary powers. Thus, for example, builders, hairdressers, journalists, even policemen, now claim to foster professional values amongst new recruits. The extension of a rhetoric of professionalism has meant that the sense of distinctive expectations discriminating between insiders and outsiders which I took to be a function of professional codes of conduct has become routine in discourses of identity. I intend to develop this idea and its implications, particularly for our understanding of cultural forms, initially through a discussion of the film *Reservoir Dogs*.

The film concerns the aftermath of a robbery that has gone wrong. The film takes place in two main settings – a diner where the robbers spend some time before going off to the robbery, and a warehouse where they had arranged to meet after the robbery and where those who are still alive gradually reassemble. There are a number of flashbacks to other locales anticipating the robbery but these are not essential to the main narrative theme. The robbery failed, in part, because the gang had been infiltrated by a member of the police posing as a gangster. The police are thus able to be present at the robbery; when an alarm is sounded there ensues some confusion during which time a number of people are shot. In the discussions that take place at the warehouse two themes emerge that are relevant to my discussion of the rhetoric of professions.

The first is shown in their conversations when the gangsters invoke the idea of acting like professionals i.e. behaving calmly and coolly and considering their options rationally. (It seems that this theme is reinforced by racist remarks throughout the film in which the supposed inability of blacks to act in these ways is invoked in order to emphasise difference.) A second theme is closely related: one of the robbers is held to have behaved badly (unprofessionally) by losing control in the robbery and firing indiscriminately. His behaviour is seen as reprehensible on two counts: because he endangered his colleagues; and because he failed to observe a distinction concerning appropriate involvement. The second professional value is that in any situation there are two types of performer present: those who happen to be there but are only 'noise'; and other professionals. It is necessary to frighten the first group and discourage them from heroism, but they are essentially civilians whose neutrality should be respected. The police on the other hand are professional players and are legitimate targets in all circumstances.

The robber who engages non-players wantonly is held to be a moral failure; he is classified as sick and therefore dangerous. (I am not suggesting that these robbers observe the dominant moral code of the wider society, but one of the strong emphases of the film is that armed robbery is a trade like any other with its own working practices in which violence is inherent but used discriminately.) A professional, then – and this refers to the class rather than just to bank-robbers – is somebody whose experience leads them to rationally assess how a scene is likely to 'play', and to ensure that they accomplish their (or their client's if they have one) ends as effectively as possible. The idea is that there is a fundamental distinction between those who know what is going on and are able to manipulate the dramatic resources of the setting, and those innocents who are in some sense victims or imprisoned by the setting.

The distinction between players and civilians formally echoes the tradition of that between professionals and their clients, and is one that has been taken up in many unlikely trades where the rhetoric of professionalism has taken hold. Within these trades there is an extensive argot to label innocents – tricks, johns, punters, civilians, straights etc. Except of course that we are all sociologists now. We have all seen films, watched television and read books in which processes of exploitation and manipulation are displayed and/or admired. We are all therefore suspicious to some degree; our consent to play the role of punter, however involuntary, is hedged around with a reflexive sophistication that makes us ironically aware of the frames that others seek to impose.

As I have said, one reason why we are suspicious of exploitation is that as audiences for popular culture we are aware of how in different settings we are cast as innocents, but, perhaps more fundamentally, the great majority of us perform or work on a number of stages. On some we are cast as innocents but on others we change footing and take command of the setting. So pervasive is the rhetoric of professionalism that we are all in at least one of our roles professionals who seek to manage our business as economically as possible and at other times customers who are only too aware of how the service being provided trades upon our good-humoured complicity.

My point is that as part of normal social competence we monitor the ways in which we are used, positioned, set up by others' working practices. As long as these practices observe certain minimal moral expectations we comply with the presumption of innocence upon which they are based. I imagine we might all try to humanise our involvement, by for example getting on first-name terms with the garage mechanic who services the car. In this we believe that we are picked out from the mass of punters and our needs are treated with greater respect. We may even try to signal our shift in alignment by trying out some humour at our joint cynical recognition that the gullibility of other punters is a sad necessity of professional organisation.

I want to link this approach with a discussion of another cultural source that initially will seem to have very little in common (certainly with *Reservoir Dogs*). In one of the *Just William* stories two Americans, an older man and a young attractive woman, visit William's village. The William stories, written in the 1930s, feature a group of boys who live in a mythical English village and who endlessly get into scrapes with various forms of adult authority. The visitors are tourists who are looking for Stratford-upon-Avon. Despite William's usual misogyny he is smitten by the woman's charms and, in order to please, he pretends that the village they are in is indeed Stratford. This leads to a number of farcical episodes in which features of the village have to be presented as Shakespearean sites. There is a considerable strain of sly humour in all this at: (a) Americans' enthusiasm for culture; and (b) their innocence of history. In this case then it seems, to use the framework that I have established, that Englishness is a form of professional expertise in stage-managing history for transatlantic punters. This idea of an inherent national sophistication in culture and its history is deeply ingrained in British national mythology; arguably it has been a considerable impediment to finding an appropriate post-imperial national identity.

The more substantial point that I want to take from the story concerns the conventional character of places. Where somewhere is depends upon a number of expectations (or we could say the conventions of that sort of place) being met. We would recognise I expect that we can be in a giant metropolis such as London or New York and not have seen the 'real' London or New York. A place is formulated in terms of a number of markers that make it distinctive and recognisable. We also have to recognise that what I call markers can be of several different types. For example, some places are constituted, at least in important respects, through physical signs – so early discoverers of slums looked for certain traces of poverty such as dirty children (Warner 1983). (In my personal experience visitors to an area of extreme social deprivation in a large English city can express disappointment that it does not look luridly poor.) Other places such as a bohemia are constituted through the people one might meet, although there might also be associated physical symbols such as cafés, clubs or galleries. Then again, a third type of place is constituted through the involvement of participants, as in the case of a church or a theatre. A meeting for worship or a performance can transform the meaning of any site by the use of a small number of symbolic markers. When we are in the presence of those markers then we are where we set out to be – a space has become a place.

Although these two stories are couched in very different genres they share a common theme in the management of social space. Both touch on negotiating an environment, if this term is understood as not just a physical setting but also a social setting with appropriate norms of conduct etc. – that is as a form of stage. I have described professionals as those who claim a certain expertise in the management of a specific setting – they command a technology of both machines and habitual responses. Those who are managed are therefore treated as naive but more or less willing collaborators. William's female visitor was such a collaborator, but she was also a tourist, suggesting the idea that tourists are particularly good examples of naive social participation. There is no evidence in the story that William's visitor was aware that as a performer she was conforming to another's script, but even if she was so aware her complicity led to a satisfactory outcome.

This I believe to be the heart of the reason why the tourist is a revealing social type: tourists are visitors to places who accept that others in this respect are professionals: 'Essentially tourism is about an experience of place' (Ryan 1991, p. 2). They might resent an ever-present suspicion of exploitation but as long as the place delivers the sorts of occasion that could be expected the tourist is unlikely to be unruly or disrespectful (unless of course that is the sort of visit they had in mind, as when some followers of English football teams visit the home towns of other European clubs).

The idea that tourists have always been sensitive to the management of the place they're visiting means that I am not persuaded by Urry's argument that there has been a recent development of what he calls post-tourists cynically tolerant of stage-management (Urry 1988). It seems to me that the reason MacCannell's use of a distinction between front and back stages in relation to tourism has been persuasive (1977, Chapter 8) is precisely because we are aware that as naive non-professionals we are embarked upon an infinite regress in searching for the authenticity of reality.

What I have called the sophistication of social competence has involved a more or less explicit acceptance of a practical distinction between professionals and punters in types and places of social activity. Armed with this possibly rueful knowledge, there is an ironic pleasure in sometimes successfully guarding against the exploitative perils to which the truly innocent can be seen to succumb. A lot of the humour in everyday life turns on stories about friends, colleagues and acquaintances who, either through naivety or due to factors beyond their control, find themselves betrayed by a setting turning out to be completely other than it appears. This principle has also been exploited by a number of television shows in which the victim is secretly filmed while trying to cope with some disaster or a tear in the fabric of reality. I assume that much of our laughter at all these happenings is a form of relief that this ever-present anxiety has come true for someone else this time.

There is, however, another dimension to this play of social consciousness. If the performed dramas of our industries of entertainment as well as personal experience constantly tell us that we are prey to the subterfuges of the cynically knowing then we may seek to retreat to the securities of private spheres where ties of love and blood might seem to offer some minimal bulwarks against exploitative intrusions. Another way of putting this is that the recognition of the fragmentation of professionalism can be used as an explanation for a widespread flight from public life. The private home is an enclave within which others' professionalism can be excluded except when it is needed, and thus a collection of private homes lacking any productive focus, such as a suburb, can be seen as a place where the civilians and the punters can gather for mutual reassurance. A place for the celebration of innocence.

In this chapter, as the title makes clear, I intend to explore the utility of concepts of space and place. One reason is that there are always currents in theoretical interests. The metaphors of space and place in relation to social action have become more prominent as part of the turn to culture that is the central theme of these essays. In one sense a minor by-product of interest in these physical metaphors has been the opening up of (dare I say?) a space for greater contributions from geographers to central themes in the human sciences (see for example Agnew and Duncan 1989). Although these contributions have been stimulating, a more important aspect of the use of physical metaphors has been a recognition of the centrality of formalist themes in accounts of culture as ways of life. I shall explain what I mean here by talking more directly about the culture of suburbanism.

This leads me to a further reason for this chapter. A central institution of the suburban life-style has become the shopping mall: a somewhere that is clearly both space and place for playing with and playing out the imagery of cultural artefacts. In a previous paper (1990) I discussed one instance of the cultural form of the out-of-town shopping centre as a poverty of utopian imagination. Here I shall go back to the idealisation of place that the centre articulates and try to develop the theme of a distinctive culture of consumerism as somewhere that tourism and life-style overlap.

meaningful spaces

SPACES AND PLACES

I have tried to suggest some unusual aspects of how we build in an implicit sense of being grounded in space as a dimension of normal social experience. To the extent that these ways of experiencing space, which I could also describe as formulating space or manipulating it, are integral to how we make everyday life meaningful, then the organisation of space is fundamental to the distinctiveness of a culture: 'Places encapsulate and communicate identity' (Mills 1993, p. 150).

I do not want to become bogged down in theoretical niceties, but there has been such a marked increase in interest in the cultural meanings of the physical environment that it has become one of the defining features of the turn to culture; authors who have specifically addressed the significance of culture for geographical theory include Jackson (1992) and Johnston (1991); more recent collections focusing on the culture of place are Duncan and Ley (1993) and Keith and Pile (1993). Following an exploration of the meaning of place I shall propose a way of discriminating between space and place. We will then be better equipped to tackle an account of suburban places.

Until recently it would be true to say that the majority of work published in sociology has at best been uneasy with the initiatives of Simmel and other theorists of modernity in their concern with space and time as the parameters of human society. (I go on to consider space in greater detail. For an example of new thinking in relation to institutionalised time see Frankenberg (1992); more theoretical concerns are expressed by Adam (1990) and Young (1988). In commonsense terms they are physical givens of the material world upon which the infinite creativity of human society can devise innumerable ways of periodising, marking out, framing significant intervals, etc. The extent to which optimistic assumptions of scientific imperialism, that is that fundamental criteria for measurement were definable, now seem mistaken need not concern us; both Kern 1983 and Finlay 1990 have discussed the interaction of relativism in physical theory and new forms of representation in the arts as central to modernism.

What is relevant is the widespread acceptance now that the organisation of the physical environment is actively used in the constitution of social order: 'The term "place" cannot be used in social theory simply to designate "point in space", any more than we can speak of points in time as a succession of "nows"' (Giddens 1984, p. 118). In contrast, Giddens argues that the parameters of location should be seen as the context within which action is to be understood. Giddens' privileging of space and time in his theory of structuration has been centrally important in stimulating new theoretical concern; see the critical discussion by Gregory 1989; Clark et al., 1990 Part 6; Urry 1991; see also Agnew 1993 on the neglect of place in social theory.

Space in abstract is infinite, it needs to be broken up or structured in some way to become meaningful. Space is therefore defined by the form of its organisation – the categories of organisation are necessarily human interventions that underlie formal distinctions. It could be argued that nature provides different types of terrain 'naturally' which we then label, but the point is that it takes human culture to make differences in the physical world meaningful. (As a social theorist committed to studies of the constitution of lived experience I am immediately attracted to Werlen's action-oriented theoretical critique of traditions in social geography which begins from his insistence that 'space is neither an object nor an a priori, but a frame of reference for actions' (1993, p. 3).)

We should expect then that the ways in which members of a community organise different types of space – such as living, commercial, agricultural, religious and public – will symbolically display important values and structures of relationships for that community (and indeed that our metaphors of landscape and place will have a determining significance for common sense as well as intellectually self-conscious theories of the lived world). Although all communities organise space as part of the practical business of social experience, in some cultures there are specialists in the organisation and production of space: it will be a skill that has practical and ritual significance.

In post-industrial societies such specialists tend to be architects and planners, although there is input from other professionals such as engineers and communications experts. Although we might think of architecture as the professional mastery of surface and structure of built forms, these are, one could say, the content of architectural statements. The form or grammar of such statements is the organisation of space, within and between and around built forms. In this perspective no space is 'innocent' or devoid of meaning, so one would expect the culture of landscapes (including townscapes of course) to become an object of social inquiry (see for example Pugh 1990; Daniels 1993; as Urry has pointed out: 'landscapes are not only visible in space but are also narratively visible in time': 1992, p. 21). It is unsurprising that the idea of the landscape, as a way of structuring a lived environment, can become a metaphor for other types of 'terrain' such as the organisation of financial institutions or media organisations (Appadurai 1990).

The analogy of linguistic grammar is also useful in directing our attention to lines of analysis that address the contextual ground of interpretations of taken-for-granted features of social forms (Button 1991). Put briefly, the 'indexical' or contextualised theory of social meaning holds that signs, symbols, events, actions etc. are not meaningful in themselves but only as they are used. Thus an utterance not only has to be placed within a sequence or conversational strip and thereby be seen to be following the rules of conversation analysis, but it can also be seen to be a performance engaging parts of the identities of speakers, overhearers and setting (Goffman 1981). While the grounding in context of meaningful phenomena is inherent in all forms of social reproduction, there are specific features to institutional change in modern societies which have meant that the lived worlds of everyday experience have become self-consciously artificial: 'Together with the transformation of time, the commodification of space establishes a "created environment" of a very distinctive character, expressing new forms of institutional articulation' (Giddens 1984, p. 144).

My purpose in these notes is to recommend that we conceptualise the space for social action as a malleable sphere rather than as a fixed terrain. One way of describing this approach is to contrast the 'space' of the cinematic image with that of the theatrical stage. The latter is conventionally a flat space with clear boundaries and for any one member of the audience a constant mode of synopsis through the perspective of their line of sight. In contrast, a cinematic image which constitutes a framed space can become more intense or distant, it can become focused or discursive, it can even become agitatedly involved or serenely dispassionate. The spaces we occupy in the course of the daily round expand and contract in terms of both size and intensity as we are differentially engaged with other participants and projects.

What is to count as significant spaces for each individual, whether it is our domestic space, or place of work, or characteristic leisure haunts, will be a distinctive inflection on how that space could be mapped by different instrumental notations. As mapping in published texts is a process of charting social uses and inscribing structures of power and ownership in symbolic form, so our habitual routines of progress through space are pragmatic maps of mundane experience (this in turn raises the possibility of politicising space through what Jameson 1991 has called cognitive mapping).

I hope that it is now possible to see a clearer connection between the distinctiveness of professional status and the conceptualisation of space being developed. When describing the difference between a professional and an amateur as a metaphor used in a variety of unexpected occupational settings, I argued that professionals are marked out by their confidence in manipulative use of features of the interactional stage that is comprised by the exercise of their expertise. Thus when a trick stops his car beside a street-walker, the car, the street and wherever else they go becomes her stage. It is a space that is framed by their interaction. The variety of locales are in a sense a place and are set in a sequence of conventionally known places, but the specific trajectory of their transaction is not really *a* place, as conventionally understood (although the regularity of a specific mode of transactions may institutionalise a place), so much as a social space.

I mentioned in the first part of this chapter that, while all of us as citizens of modern worlds are innocents for much of the time, for some if not the majority of us there are occasions on which we become professionally responsible: occasions on which we gain and accept a moral responsibility through our command of the situation. This responsibility is often expressed and experienced as forms of power, and the reality of power is often quite constrained. For example, the prostitute is always at risk from unpredictable violence from her customers, and a restaurant worker, however cleverly they stage-manage customers' patronage of their place, is always at the mercy of irrational and malicious complaints which transcend their professional space. In general though, the use of what I have called the rhetoric of professionalism is a bid to talk out an effective ability to frame social space in such ways that those naively caught up in the space are at a practical disadvantage.

In the terminology I am proposing here, then, spaces are necessarily transitional projects. They exist for the duration of some interactional business but can evaporate when those who motivate them move on to other concerns: 'Location is only relevant – and this is crucial – when filtered through the frames of reference that orient individuals' conduct' (Giddens 1993, p. xv). In practice, such is the habitude of social order that spaces persist as grounds for reliable expectations and will in all probability become closely entwined with places. Thus, for example, the professional authority of the teacher is likely to be embedded in the architectural distribution of the place of the school, but not exclusively so (as will be appreciated by those who have led school trips overseas).

Another usage which is interestingly ambiguous is that of cultural workers, as we might call professional artists or performers, who commonly refer to their working area as 'a space' or 'my space'. These spaces are commonly set in institutional places but more generally are used as a tool for the practice of a craft. While the boundaries to these spaces need not be demarcated by anything as manifest as walls, they tend to be clearly understood or insisted upon by co-workers. This idea, which I believe is called 'Chinese walls' within financial organisations, to describe a form of professional autonomy, has been taken up as a metaphor within the dialect of New Age so that it is common to hear of individuals complaining of others intruding upon their space, or more positively agreeing to respect others' need to maintain a space.

Although the New Age language of self emphasises process and change so that identity is not fixed, and indeed in part becomes a matter of personal choice, in the use of a metaphor of space it harks back to the entrepreneurial individualism of emergent modernity. Stuart Hall has characterised this confident tradition of individuality as an old logic of identity that offers a certain guarantee: 'that logic or discourse of identity . . . gives us a sense of depth, out there, and in here. It is spatially organized' (1991, p. 43; it would be distracting, although tempting, to pursue here the idea of interiority as a spatial metaphor for the self).

Although Hall remains enough of a prisoner of the residues of structuralist Marxism to – in another use of the metaphor of space – still write of subjects being positioned, he does propose the emergence of a new identity generating a: 'politics of recognizing that all of us are composed of multiple social identities' (1991, p. 57). It is a constitutive feature of the cultural incoherence implicated in multiple identities that space becomes a form of play because it is a process of engagement, a strip of interaction, rather than a stable context for social action. Another way of describing this notion of play is by describing social space in theatrical terms as different types of stage. Daniels and Cosgrove have suggested that such a shift in metaphors is central to new social theory: 'The present cultural turn in human geography has introduced metaphors and analogies more in keeping with an emphasis on meaning than function . . . System and organism give way as metaphors to spectacle, theatre and text' (1993, p. 57).

Space is therefore inseparable from social forms, or what we should more accurately call institutional forms. These are normatively inscribed patterns of bahaviour, and forms of communication and structures of relationship that coalesce around themes of concern such as family meals, a group of friends at a fitness centre or an adulterous relationship. Although the effective space of any one occasion of these institutional forms is malleable, it will through processes of habituation tend to become sedimented in routinised forms. In these ways characteristic structures of social space will symbolise institutional form and will function as cultural resource displaying and prescribing identities for participants within and between generations. This is most clearly seen when the institutional form has become ritualised.

Rituals are particular forms of performance in which a symbolic repertoire is deployed in ways that call upon and constitute some sense of obligation to collective affinity or solidarity. This is why the organisation of space becomes highly charged in areas marked out for religious significance, but more prosaically the boundaries to spaces, rules governing access and characteristic expectations for deportment within a space will pragmatically reproduce social order. The structures of power and hierarchy implicit in social order can be made clear through the example of how ways of using specific spaces are always highly gendered (an early collection of papers taking up this theme is that edited by Ardener 1981; see also Katz and Monk 1993; on a broader range of aspects of the politicisation of place see the papers in Keith and Pile 1993).

I have noted that a number of authors have recently stressed the importance of cultural theory in rethinking the project of human geography. Soja (1989) has argued that theorists who have been inflential in the turn to culture have enabled critical theory to throw off the shackles of historicist traditions and productively engage with the significance of space in critical social theory. Rather than the imperialist mapping of traditional geographers content to see the many dimensions of the world as of a passive object to be bent to the authorial will, social space is to be theorised as a multiplicity of projects so that it is continually being staged and restaged in human practice.

In Soja's view spatiality, as the embodiment of human projects on a terrain, is 'never primordially given or permanently fixed' (1989, p. 122), but in its indeterminacy is also 'the site' for struggles over the meaning of space. He summarises his account in six propositions of which I shall quote two:

> 2. As a social product, spatiality is simultaneously the medium and outcome, presupposition and embodiment of social action and relationship; 6. Concrete spatiality – actual human geography – is thus a competitive arena for struggles over social production and reproduction, for social practices aimed either at the maintenance and reinforcement of existing spatiality or at significant restructuring and/or radical transformation.
>
> (pp.129–130)

In terms of the account being developed in this chapter we can say that the physical form of these struggles tends to be inscribed in the symbolism of places.

Organised spaces can thus be more economically thought of as places, with the implication that disorganised space – chaos (the wilderness?) – is without place. Places are culturally formulated ways of imbuing environments with meaning, but rather than just being a form of engagement, as social space is, a place also constrains interpretation by pre-existing as representation. Although every place will exist simultaneously on the level of each individual and group modes of using as innumerable projects, it will function as a form of inscription by having certain focused collective identities. It is clear then that in these facets of the organisation of social life there is another dimension of the turn to culture through the imaginative force of a distinct mode of representation. To illustrate this we can turn to Short (1991), who introduces his study of the social construction of the environment by citing Raymond Williams' *The Country and the City* (1973) as one of the two seminal texts that has inspired his approach.

Short is concerned with very large-scale, collective places – national environments – and uses three conceptual frameworks to illuminate their construction. These are: myths as representations of archetypal attitudes to three types of environment – wilderness, countryside and the city; ideologies as the inflections of such general myths in the creation of a specific national identity; and texts as a term for a cultural form in which for each national instance the myth has been articulated as ideology. The examples he uses are Britain, the United States and Australia. His approach allows him to make some insightful comparisons, as when contrasting the cultural function of the countryside as national heritage in Britain which has been used to symbolise an invented tradition of organic community, with the frontier in the USA. In the latter case the confusion of images of masculinity with community and independence has para-doxically helped to focus different discourses of social policies for the cities.

A more complex theorising of place as a mode of representation has been developed by Rob Shields (1991). Shields' ambitious attempt to sketch alternative geographies of modernity begins from an insistence that here images of places are to be understood as more than the multiplicity of impressions of personal experience, and rather as: 'the culturally mediated reception of *representations* of environments, places, or regions which are "afloat in society" as "ideas in currency"' (1991, p. 14). Shields' approach is consistent with my emphasis on the interdependency significant context and institutional form.

There is, however, in his book the desire, characteristic of converts to culturalism, to identify a transcendent level of cultural determination which grounds the haphazard character of experi-ence, thus:

A set of core images forms a widely disseminated and commonly held set of images of a place or space . . . To these, a range of more subtle or modifying connotations can be added. These peri-pheral images are more ephemeral or transitory. They result from idiosyncratic associations and individual experiences. Generally these find expression in descriptions only where they are set into the terms of more conventional and widely understood core images. Collectively a set of place-images forms a place-myth.

(ibid., pp. 60–1)

In a series of case-studies Shields' examines distinctive place-myths, identifying characteristic inflections of the thematic myth through images which can be associated with different social fractions.

This enterprise appears similar to other modes of hegemonic analysis whereby a system-need (or hegemonic impulse or place-myth) is identified so that it can then be used to explain different empirical forms. In practice, Shields is more concerned with places 'on the margins' of social order, or the histories of different mythologies of order. For this reason 'civilised' becomes a paradigmatic term around which a number of related terms cluster so that imageries of place are seen to be ways of talking about continually negotiated tensions between the normal and the extra-ordinary (Zukin (1992) is another author who insists on the significance of the liminal – Victor Turner's term for the transitional boundaries between cultural 'spaces' – in mobilising urban social configurations). In giving a notion of civilisation a privileged status in this way, he is consistent with the point made earlier that recognising a place is accepting a framework of meanings; the disorder of transgression is always a counterpoint to the normality of inscribed order.

In his conclusion Shields suggests that these myths and images can also be seen as yarns exemplified in particular narratives which both give place identity and all those social actors identity through their unremarkable familiarity with yarns of local and exotic places. In this 'dramatistic' conceptualisation of the staging and restaging of places Shields is close to my use of a notion of cultural form. In previous publications (principally 1993) I have argued that we can express the differences between systems of representation more accurately by using a concept of cultural form. Briefly, each cultural form is characterised by an interdependence of three types of material: (a) the social organisation of the relations of production and distribution; (b) characteristic narrative structures and themes; and (c) forms of social participation and appreciation.

As the concept of cultural form has been developed in order to provide a framework for distinctive differences between systems of representation, as well as changes within a single system through time, it should also be relevant to forms of representation which are not forms of performance as that term is conventionally used. I will therefore suggest that in the light of the distinctions between space and place that I have developed in this part of the chapter that places are cultural forms. I have already embarked upon this approach in two papers (1983b, 1990) on department stores and shopping centres respectively as places that are distinctive cultural forms. In the fifth part of this chapter I reprise the latter paper in the light of the following discussion of suburban places. Expanding the concept of cultural form in this way also hints at how it can be used to facilitate a broader account of the cultural economy of postmodernism.

In this brief account of the cultural character of places I have tried to marry together the three elements of: (a) a physical location acquiring a distinctive identity in social discourse; (b) an emphasis that identity is couched in cultural forms that embody distinctive projects of use; and (c) that the facticity of the ways in which forms of representations and images are inscribed in a physical terrain should not blind us to the processes of staging and restaging social order in the contours of places. If the transition from modernism has involved a loss of faith in the grand narratives of progress, as has often been held, then that process can be more positively phrased as an acceptance of the arbitrary character of the terms of experience allied with a pragmatic sense that our use of these terms is based on local and provisional knowledge.

In the terminology I am proposing here, then, spaces are distinguished from places by an element of authority that clings to individuals' commitment to sustaining that space. Places are an essential feature of the cultural repertoire of social order. They (places) provide itineraries for biographical journeys and maps of life-styles; they are therefore representations of possibility for cultures both local and global. I should also emphasise that a place, as I have conceptualised it here, can exist at a number of points on a scale of precision. We might think of a place as a particular spot, such as the street corner where Doc and his heirs hang out, or it might be a looser conglomeration of buildings such as a shopping centre, or again a large number of places such as the place of the city. The place tourists visit can vary enormously in degree of specificity.

It will be apparent to those with any familiarity with this field that I have so far avoided any reference to Bourdieu's concept of habitus and whether it duplicates either term or is a third dimension (Bourdieu 1977, 1984). I have done so because Bourdieu seems to combine elements of how I use both space and place and to keep the lived environment as a form of socio-structural category essential for its role in his accounts of social reproduction (see also Werlen's discussion (1993, pp. 152–8) of Bourdieu in the context of his analytic emphasis on the necessity of a theory of action). To trace an adequate exegesis of Bourdieu's thought is a separate project which, if attempted here, would unnecessarily confuse this project.

So there are at least two dimensions to any concern with the ecology of culture. I have briefly indicated in the course of this part of the chapter why I believe there is a necessary ecological impulse in a turn to culture. This is in part reclaiming an original dimension to the meaning of culture, as Williams insisted from the beginning (1958 and later): that of cultivation or productive engagement with a terrain. To insist that forms of collective life are grounded in representations which are a productive engagement with a terrain is therefore an appropriate recognition that turning to culture necessitates ecological consciousness. To see this as sociology climbing on the 'green' bandwagon is to miss the ways in which the bandwagon is itself a popular form of the turn to culture. We will now look to places that have frequently seemed far from ecologically sensitive.

SUBURBAN PLACES

In his entertaining dissection of the modernist intelligentsia and their fears of the impact of mass citizenship on culture, John Carey (1992) identifies the suburbs as one of the central themes and motifs of intellectual contempt: 'They [the suburbs] exacerbated the intellectual's feeling of isolation from what he conceived of as philistine hordes . . . The supposed low quality of life encouraged by suburban conditions became a favourite theme for intellectual ridicule or censure' (pp. 50–1). The suburbs were held to be impoverished because of their uniformity – intrinsically mediocre people were being given a ridiculous claim to dignity and status by their absurd little houses, the appropriate anonymity of their crematoria, and the ersatz quality of their taste for tinned food.

Carey continues that the lack of intellectual muscle in suburban culture was seen by the intelligentsia to be inevitable given what they felt to be the intrinsic femininity of the place – the suburb was a country ruled by women. At the same time there was another strand in the same discourse that feared that the very blandness of suburban landscape bred a penchant for secret vice. The wide range of suspicions went from anonymous sexual licence to a taste for socialism via yoga, vegetarianism and the Cyclists' Touring Club (were we updating today we would have to add the aesthetic vulgarity of grunting clumps of joggers pounding their twilit suburban streets).

In many ways it is easy to see that aspects of these themes survived the high modernist reaction to mass culture and have persisted in more populist cultural celebrations. It is for example not difficult to see that elements in culturalist identification with outsiders, such as Hebdige's postmodern Black stylists (1988, 1992) and Willis' celebration of lumpen proletarian values (in particular 1977), involve stepping over the mass of suburban culture. The popular can be made into an instrument of history when it is framed as counter-cultural, unselfconsciously bohemian and proto-revolutionary. Hall's frequently cited commitment to the study of popular culture as an instrument of class struggle (1981), is usually reported as a defiant identification with revolutionary optimism but it can also be read as a more traditional elitist disdain for the popular as merely successful.

If we assume, as seems reasonable, that the heartlands of mass audiences for popular (as in widespread rather than oppositional) entertainment are to be found in the suburbs, and bearing Carey's point about the perceived feminine qualities of suburbs in mind, it is relevant that the most sympathetic writing about mass cultural genres from within cultural studies has tended to come from women. I am thinking here of studies of audiences for romance literature, soap operas, women's magazines and adolescent comics (*inter alia* Radway 1987; Nava 1992; Hobson 1982; Winship 1987; Geraghty 1991; Ferguson 1982; Modleski 1984). Seeking to locate unfashionable genres within meaningful contexts, feminist writers have confronted the suburbs (sometimes ambivalently), and have attempted to deflect the workerist contempt of their more hairy-chested colleagues (I have cited before Stilgoe's surprise that when he began his social history of American suburbs he was frequently faced with dismissive remarks by colleagues that this was only a woman's topic: Stilgoe 1988, p. 16; Chaney 1993, p. 64).

In general, however, the new intelligentsia of the post-war consensus – in the main children of the suburbs themselves – have not thrown off the prejudices of earlier intellectual elites. In seeking some form of romantic redemption through culture, they have echoed their elders in their attempts to detect an uneasy coalition of decadence and the industrial proletariat against an uncritical acquiescence in domestic life of suburban places.

It is easy to see why the practice of suburbia has so persistently inflamed the sensitivities of the cultural intelligentsia. The suburbs are the architectural manifestation of the new citizenship of democratic politics. The serried ranks of mass housing are a cultural innovation that exemplify all the fears of herd-like mass publics. I have proposed the view that the new national polities of mass society were founded on a political citizenship dependent upon media of mass communication, combined with a populist egalitarianism of mass entertainment, and in the context of those developments the privatised families of new housing estates were an appropriate analogue. Faced as they increasingly were with the pragmatic platitudes of mass citizenship, it is perhaps not so surprising that the intellectuals of nationalism so often sought cultural legitimation for the collective fictions of mass society in the archaic traces of folk traditions and arcadian imagery (see for example Porter 1992; Daniels 1993).

While there is no necessary reason for suburban housing to be built as uniform or semi-uniform estates – indeed estates for wealthy customers such as that described by Stilgoe (1988) did often consist of a cluster of houses each unique – there are, however, major economies of scale in building from templates. This holds whether one is building apartment blocks, terraced rows of housing or single-household detached or semi-detached houses. It follows then that mass housing will almost inevitably be cast in terms of a local uniformity. This will mean that small variations of detail will take on an unlikely significance both in displaying differences in status level between housing types and as claims for individuality within a housing type.

The impression of uniformity is intensified because the premiss of a suburb is that it is a residential enclave. There are shopping clusters, maybe a street or a precinct, amid residential streets but otherwise no intrusions from productive enterprises. This is of course why the initial flight to the suburb (and the metaphor of flight is often used to evoke the negative urban qualities of crime, dirt, disease and confusion) is inextricably linked to the articulation of a distinction between public and private spheres (see Davidoff and Hall 1987 on the initial constitution of suburban places). The idea that social life can be divided into types based on public and private places must, in turn, lead to a concern with the cultural forms of private lives.

I have talked of the imagery of fleeing the city as a place associated with the social problems of modernity (although it is not the problems that are new or modern but rather the perception that suburban places are utopian constructions that should be free of such problems – a theme I shall return to later in this section), but the other side of the negative push was the positive pull of creating life-styles in the suburbs. Rather than work being the focus of community and the medium of practical creativity for ordinary experience, the suburb enshrines the idea that it is in the practice of familial relationships that life is given meaning. As families create their life-worlds through the design of possessions and activities, their suburban sites inevitably become the engine of consumer culture. This is because the suburban home becomes a privileged site for the display of life-style and other aspects of cultural status.

Consumer culture is not so much the feeling that there is a cultural imperative to continually spend and acquire new possessions, as that a hedonistic pleasure in conspicuous display should not be experienced as a cause of guilt. One could go further and say that the sorts of things which the consumer takes pleasure in acquiring, and the taste with which their acquisitions are displayed, become bound in with their identity (and in this way become a form of design). The residential place cannot be a neutral terrain, it cannot be just somewhere that you temporarily are – despite some, usually masculine, protestations. It is a set of choices about how the creative author (of these choices) is to be seen. A series of television programmes filming people in their homes and asking about their choices showed the sorts of investment that are made in the construction of these places. This type of commitment does not of course have to take place in a suburb but it is likely to be encouraged in a residential enclave where the appearance of one's self is grounded in the presentation of the home.

Complementing the symbolic significance of the home as a site for cultural meaning is the development of industries servicing the discourses of life-style. It has often been pointed out that the development of metropolitan department stores was an innovation directed at both the suburbs and, in particular, at female shoppers (Miller 1981; Bowlby 1985; Chaney 1983b). Department stores transcended the intimate, local transactions of pre-metropolitan cities. They provided a stage upon which images, fashions and styles could be piled indiscriminately, and from which the anonymous public could pick, choose and adapt to the particular circumstances of each suburb and household. The stores did not work alone but were intermeshed with what has increasingly been called intertextuality in cultural studies. This means other cultural forms which replay common themes such as, in this case, the development of mass advertising, consumer journalism especially in women's magazines, and books on life-styles, cookery manuals and domestic issues.

Other aspects of new leisure industries parasitic on the suburbs were the growth of gardening as a cultural activity with aspirations to aesthetic creativity supported by industries supplying tools, such as the new lawnmower, and advice manuals. More recently, the development of suburban leisure centres, offering a mix of sports facilities and training and other body-maintenance activities (again with appropriate instructors), provide new social centres as well as opportunities for a wide range of new acquisitions including costumes, the instruments of the activity (racquets, shoes, clubs etc.), and associated health and beauty products. To describe the place of suburbia as a cultural form involves a concern with the production of the practice of suburban life. The significance of activities such as new leisure industries is in broadening our understanding of the notion of production here.

A further aspect of production can be found in the transport networks between suburbs and city centres. Access to efficient transport facilities has been essential for the development of suburban places. This is because a suburb as a residential, non-productive enclave regularly has to export and import workers. A suburb will also have to bring in supplies and services from outside. From the beginning, then, suburbs have been associated with the introduction of rapid-transit networks. In different cities these networks have used several modes of transport such as horse-drawn trams and buses followed by other forms of mechanical power, both overground and underground (and elevated) rail networks, exceptionally riverboats, and private transport, infrequently bicycles but predominantly automobile, facilities. The automobile, as a privately owned usually 'family-sized' vehicle, perfectly complements the usual housing unit of a suburb and has of course become the defining symbol of suburban life-style. (Another level of association is that the car is a conspicuous piece of symbolic display. For most households, after the house, it is the second most expensive possession in their consumer repertoire. Like the house its style, decoration and maintenance are given semiotic and social significance.)

The symbolic dominance of the private car has been institutionalised to the extent that public transport networks to many suburbs have been allowed to atrophy (or in more exclusive developments were never made available). In a city of suburbs, such as Los Angeles, public transport is notoriously non-existent, so that the place of the city engulfs all constitutive social spaces and defies any form of synopsis in personal experience: 'its [Los Angeles] spatiality challenges orthodox analysis and intepretation for it seems limitless and constantly in motion, never still enough to encompass, too filled with "other spaces" to be informatively described' (Soja 1989, p. 222). Suburbs are therefore built on road networks with garaging facilities becoming an important feature of domestic architecture. It, further, seems appropriate that the roads of suburban housing should lead into super-highways or motorways, which are roads built without habitation.

Based on an idea developed in the 1920s and 1930s the superhighway takes as a model for road transport the railway line rather than existing roads or streets. The latter are thoroughfares primarily dedicated to human interaction. This might take the form of travellers meeting *en route*, or in villages, towns and cities the street was the focus of commercial activity. Frequently a site of production, particularly in the provision of services, the street was a type of stage upon which performers paraded, others admired and entertainers sought audiences for drinks, songs or tricks. (This idea of street-life has of course not disappeared but it is more likely to be preserved now in traffic-free enclaves, in pedestrian-only zones, where social life is in a sense thematised as an entertainment object as in a theme park.)

Even intra-urban highways strip away the random access of street life: they are dedicated to personal exploitation. Super-highways reduce danger and facilitate speed by regulating flow and interaction. The highway becomes a terrain for privatised transit as it is populated by nuclear modules. In the freedom of each individual journey they conform to an all-embracing disciplinary apparatus. Policed by road patrols, the social codes of the super-highway work through a multitude of private individuals conforming to a fear of the randomness of others. The paradox of claiming a complementarity between the super-highway, as a continuous place that overrides habitation in favour of a specific form of use, and the suburb, as a place dedicated to habitation, is then resolved through the interdependent themes of privatised experience and a rigorous social order. Zukin, writing of what she calls newer modern cities such as Los Angeles, says: 'Both landscape and vernacular were represented in freeways, shopping malls, and single-family houses, the whole a low-rise ensemble of auto-mobility' (1992, p. 226).

I have argued in the previous section that places can be separated from spaces by the inclusion of an element of constraint. Places are characterised by a social as well as a physical architecture that prescribes the meanings of relevant roles and forms of activity. In so many ways the place of the suburb is constituted through an implicit social discipline. I can illustrate the character of this discipline, what we could call the narratives of suburban places, by the form of participation that defines tourism. I said earlier that tourists recognise places through a semiotic vocabulary which gives each place a distinctive identity. To this we will have to add now that the vocabulary includes expectations of others as well as physical features of the landscape. In their expectations suburban residents are tourists in their 'own' places.

It may seem surprising to think of suburbs as tourist sites. Apart from connoisseurs of civic amenities and parties of architectural historians it is hard to imagine cultural visitors to the great majority of suburbs. Like Sunderland, suburbs are places that are rarely visited for their own sake. They are, however, more fundamentally places visited by their inhabitants. As tourist sites offer the construction of a place so a suburb offers the appearance of a community. In the artefacts, traditions, festivals and symbolism that could act as a semiotic vocabulary of communal life, the inhabitants are able to spell out a way of giving places an identity. In his study of a northern British suburb, for example, Young (1986) found that: 'In Woodlands [the suburb], local social organisation was characterised by the explicit declaration and celebration of communal identity' (p. 123). The inhabitants used this identity to organise and politicise issues of change and to assert and reiterate difference and distinction: 'Consistently referring to the idea of "Woodlands Village", developing and expressing idealised versions of local history, asserting the existence and superiority of local tradition, local rustic qualities, residential interests invested Woodlands with a distinct communal reputation' (p. 124).

In the mix of entrepreneurial provision and rhetorical construction that constitutes suburban places, MacCannell argues, appearance has come to be central: 'The archetypal postmodern community is composed of the physical and mental spoils of the tourist crusades: "nouvelle cuisine" and ethnic restaurants ... nostalgic elements including reconstructions of old homes, districts, and offices, and fairs featuring traditional handicrafts' (1992, p. 94). The reiteration of retrospective themes in all these accounts of suburban imagery might suggest that the past has acquired a sacred quality, but, as MacCannell goes on to argue: 'it is still more accurate to read these forms *not* as bearing traditional values, but as specifically designed to *appear to bear traditional values*, which is a different matter' (ibid., p. 96; emphasis in original).

It is in the emphasis on appearance that the common ground between the suburbanite and the tourist becomes apparent: 'Modern mass tourism is based on two seemingly contradictory tendencies: the international homogenization of the culture of the tourists and the artificial preservation of local ethnic groups and attractions so that they can be consumed as tourist experiences' (ibid., p. 176). Suburban inhabitants collude in the appearance of community in order to provide experiences that can be consumed. As social theory becomes routinised and adopted into everyday speech so they are able to borrow a concept of culture to provide a way of melding together form of life and place to give it an apparent identity.

I have argued that the very anonymity of the suburb further requires the imposition of a code of discipline which provides for regularity, continuity and respect while facilitating individual biographical journeys. It seems that in the appearance of social homogeneity the unpredictability and chaos of metropolitan life can be denied. MacCannell does give an extreme example when quoting from an information bulletin extolling the virtues of the planned community of Irvine, California: '"Neighbourhood committees make sure that dwellings are painted in bland colors and that lawns are trimmed. Even the citizenry is fairly homogeneous: ... 73 per cent own their own homes and most household heads are college graduates ... Urban fears are no part of life in Irvine"' (quoted in MacCannell 1992, p. 81).

Similarly, Soja quotes a resident of Mission Viejo, a suburb of Los Angeles, as reporting that: 'You must be happy, you must be well-rounded and you must have children who do lots of things. If you don't jog or walk or bike, people wonder if you have diabetes or some other disabling disease' (1989, p. 231). This may to the anarchic seem undesirable, and certainly unrepresentative of the more limited rules of everyday suburban life, although consistent with a climate of increasing moral authoritarianism discussed in the previous chapter. Certainly it seems that for many a homogeneity of culture as life-style is utopian, for as MacCannell goes on to point out: 'The official bumper sticker of the city of Irvine reads, "Another Day in Paradise"' (1992, p. 94).

In my previous book (1993, Chapter 5), I made the suggestion that tourism should not only be seen as a highly disciplined activity but also as an exemplar of shifts in collective life from being a crowd to an audience. Both aspects turn on the idea that, although the tourist as a holiday-maker is a hedonist usually concerned to suspend conventional constraints for the period of the holiday, tourism is a sophisticated mode of consumerism. The tourist, whether in a party or family group or by him/herself, collaborates with resource managers in traversing the place they are visiting. They are bound into certain routes, activities and modes of appreciation; deviant attempts to do something different will in all likelihood have been catered for and built into the repertoire of ways of visiting that place.

It will I hope be apparent that we have come back to one of the concluding themes of the first part of this chapter, and to the idea of fleeing the city. The first theme is one of the dominant myths of contemporary public culture, that is that public life is dominated by a multitude of forms of professional expertise that will exploit and corrupt unwary innocence, so that those who feel themselves to be predominantly others' punters will retreat to privatised spheres. It is very easy to read so many emphases in suburban imagery as precisely conforming to this idea of a turn away from public insecurities. One of the most important rhetorical vehicles here is surely the unquestioned positive stress put on notions of tradition, nostalgia, how things used to be, ideas of family, domesticity and above all quiet and stability. And yet, as it said very briefly above, it is not that the problems of city life are new. It is rather that in the realisation that places are arbitrary configurations, it becomes a normal expectation of consumer life-style to be able to choose to create a symbolic boundary between personal life-world and poverty, crime, and cultural alienation, etc.

It is against the backdrop of the suburban place as an arbitrary, invented culture that so many of the narratives of the suburbs are concerned with traditions and continuity. Stilgoe interestingly points out that the marketing of tools, manuals and kits for home do-it-yourself has never been primarily motivated by economic necessity. It has been rather that DIY has been seen to offer males an opportunity for a creative hobby, literally modifying and creating their domestic castle, and for passing on family values of craft and responsibility through (typically) the male line from fathers to sons (1988, Part 5). Above all, of course, suburban domestic architecture has been from the beginning and remains stubbornly rooted in images of the past. In British suburbs the most notorious example has been the popularity of 'Tudorbethan' as an amalgam of vague historical references on endless semi-detacheds; but more generally it is the ubiquity of mock Georgian doorways that is the most pervasive symbol of ritualised nostalgia. It seems likely that the conformity of appearance in the suburban landscape is not evidence of a lack of imagination so much as a source of reassurance through the security of predictability.

Although I have stressed the positive choices in suburban places, in order to explain how the representations of this cultural form function, we also have to recognise that many are dissatisfied with the options for identity on offer. For some it will be the implied cultural homogeneity of suburbia that is intolerable. Rather than flee the city they will actively embrace the cultural diversity of central urban life, and flaunt the tolerance of oppositional lifestyles. In Mills' study of gentrification in an inner-city district of Vancouver she notes how developers use a rhetoric of the self-consciousness of city life in contrast to the anonymity of the suburbs: 'residents are invited to become players in the urban theatre . . . Fairview Slopes is presented as not merely a place to "live" – that is, to reside – but also the stage upon which one may practise the art of living' (1993, p. 161).

Others will reject the arbitrariness of suburban places and seek to discover some greater authenticity by leaving the city and its environs altogether and retreating deep into nature (and quite often changing countries and thus emphasising cultural flight). In this they are looking to transcend the constraints of tourism by changing sides and hoping to disappear into some natural place, often only made possible if they become part of the tourist industry catering for urban visitors travelling from where they once were.

The ability to become natives to others' tourists is not of course unique to cultural émigrés; for most if not all 'natives' it is a prescribed feature of their lives imposed by patterns of cultural imperialism. And yet it is important to recognise that they are not just victims but also professional in their management of visitors' experience. Conforming to a script they have helped to write they are able to help the naive and worried visitor through the problems of managing an unfamiliar setting. I shall conclude this section with the suggestion that in their (the natives') ability to manage being the subject of others' visits lies a clue to the cultural fictions of suburban places.

I began looking at suburbs by suggesting that they are a form of refuge from the exploitative skills of professionals in public life, but now in conclusion it is necessary to recognise that in the management of the refuge lies a form of professionalism. Inhabitants of suburbia are both tourists seeking the appearance of community and professionals colluding in the construction and management of appearance. Reflexively aware of the frailty of community they are able to accept the necessity for conformity to others' expectations for the management of children, gardens, hedges, car, paintwork and life-style in general. In interpreting the manner of conformity each life is given distinction while remaining grounded in the form of place. There is in this view of the suburbs an intriguing interdependence of space and place. Spaces framed for personal authority in patterns of use, whether it is the household, the neighbourhood leisure centre, the local pub or the shopping trip, in adapting aspects of social institutions are also places in which forms of life are inscribed in an ecology. In the concluding part of this chapter I shall try to illustrate the relevance of all these terms and ideas for our understanding of the cultural form of the shopping centre.

SHOPPING CENTRES

I have advanced the idea that one of the ways in which social life is structured is by the ability of those playing specific roles to control their social environment (as it were a stage) on certain sorts of occasion. I claimed that this ability lies at the heart of what I called the rhetoric or persuasive power of professionalism. When I say control it should be clear that this is a loose power, not like the controls of agencies of the state, a power therefore which is subject always to a process of interaction.

The idea of controlling space led on to the more general idea of the social organisation of space, and thus the ways we can distinguish between spaces as exploitative projects and places as forms of inscribed representation. I suggested then that this some-what technical vocabulary can be simplified by seeing places as cultural forms, a perspective I have illustrated through a very generalised account of the cultural form of suburban places.

No doubt valid objections can be raised to the level of general-isation involved, but it can be defended by saying that the point of the exercise is to bring out the significance of representation in the forms of social life. Another way of putting this defence is to offer the method I have followed as an instance of a sociology of culture that is not confined to conventionally 'cultural' objects. I shall continue by going on to talk about the cultural form of place, and the associated theme of tourists as consumers of a distinctive leisure, a more specific discussion of a suburban shopping centre.

In the previous section I detected what I called a utopian strain in the cultural form of suburbia. This is based on an appreciation of the arbitrary character of a suburb, an arbitrariness that stems from the suburb being not a focus of productive activity but generated by social concerns with domesticity and leisure. And precisely because a suburb is a wilful, human intervention it represents, however implicitly, a moral version of appropriate community. It does not have to accept the frailties of 'human nature' as inevitable; the inspiration of a suburb is of a place where an idealised version of social experience can be a valid point of reference. This will seem grandiose as a description of the myriad individual decisions on buying houses in particular suburbs, and one would probably need to look at explicitly utopian communities as instances of self-conscious moral inspiration. I will still argue though that a suburb is a form of settlement generated by moral concerns, and in this way is a very modern place.

The implied utopianism can be found in the discourses of sub-urban associations, festivals and celebrations, the collective memory of the locality and inscribed in the imagery of place – in particular architectural forms. It has frequently been remarked since Raymond Williams first noted it in writing about the countryside (1973, Chapter 1), that community, in its most *Gemeinschaft* sense, is always something that has recently disappeared. There is a built-in nostalgia to places that aspire to be communities. They are con-stantly seeking to model themselves on a world they have lost.

This can help us to understand the development of what we can call nostalgia tourism. By this I mean the growth of heritage sites (parks based upon a now vanished form of life in the locality such as the Beamish open-air industrial museum in north-east England), and what Rojek has called literary landscapes (1993). These are areas that encourage tourism through reminders of how a locality has been colonised by a famous author as the basis of several novels. Examples would include Hardy country in south-west England and Brontë country in Yorkshire; we would also think here of more traditional guided visits to stately homes and historic places (for a critique of inauthenticity in much of this marketing see Hewison 1987). Nostalgia tourism offers an idealised version of the past for people who seek representations of community grounded in places. This form of tourism is clearly a commitment (an all-embracing turn) to culture.

There is then a paradoxical incompatibility between the modernity of suburban places and the retrospective discourses through which they understand themselves. I will argue that this paradox is displayed very clearly in the innovation of the suburban shopping centre; an innovation which constitutes a new cultural form. (A further level of analysis which I cannot pursue at this point is provided by the suggestion that myths of place have become more intense, as they are told against the backdrop of a global mass culture in which the particularity of local identity becomes increasingly meaningless. (These ideas are more fully developed in Meyrowitz 1985.)

The suburban mall or shopping centre is typically a purpose-built enterprise that is a single building large enough to contain a large number of different types of shops; opportunities for refreshment such as bars, cafés, restaurants and fast-food outlets; usually more specialist types of leisure provision such as cinemas, sports centres, and entertainment areas of rides and games; often tourist attractions such as simulated exotic locations; and parasitic functional agencies such as banks, a religious centre or doctor and dentist. The shopping centre therefore mimics the wider world – within its ambit it encapsulates the attractions and facilities of a town centre. This point is strengthened if it is borne in mind that surrounding the centre 'proper' there are usually a number of ancillary retail and wholesale outlets, such as furniture stores and home-improvement warehouses too big to go in the main centre, and associated facilities such as garages, drive-in burger joints and even hotels.

The shopping centre is, then, clearly an economic innovation with major implications for traditional social policy. For example, local taxation policies are conventionally based upon a sliding scale with city-centre sites at the pinnacle and rates diminishing therefrom. If a new shopping centre undercuts the viability of a proportion of city-centre trading, then areas change their social and economic character and go 'downhill'. There are now widespread fears amongst contemporary British urban planners that the success of out-of-town shopping centres will fatally endanger the viability of urban centres.

It this proves to be the case central areas are more likely to take on the negative social qualities that have come to be associated with city life. Other zoning policies are thrown into disarray and it becomes harder for local civic administrations to manage resources to maintain the urban infrastructure and the city as a cultural centre. This is one reason why it is impossible to maintain a simple distinction between economic and cultural change.

But although there is a shift in location from city centre to sub-urban location, the shopping centre does not constitute a significant advance on previous retail settings. For example, the opening of the Palais Royal in Paris in 1784 with its combination of shops, a multiplicity of entertainments and fashionable social venues such as the newly invented restaurant, all within a continuous covered arcade (where it is alleged that the Revolution was hatched five years later), could be seen as sufficient precursor (Girouard 1985, especi-ally Chapters 9 and 14). Further, the subsequent development in London and Paris of bazaars or arcades as fashionable shopping centres and social venues, so notably discussed by Benjamin (1973), are another instance of enclosed social worlds in which the purchase of goods is the ground upon which an elaborate social edifice is being created (on the 'Arcades' project and its theoretical signifi-cance see Buck-Morss 1989).

Continuities in form between these havens of mannered display do not, however, necessarily denote significant continuities in mode of participation. The shopping centres of suburban society differ not just in catering for a different social fraction or constituency; more importantly they articulate different relationships between public space and urban life. I shall attempt to show that the changes in relationships are best understood as cultural, and stem from the cultural form of the shopping centre.

I have previously (1990, 1993) tried to bring some consistency in the ways to which a concept of cultural form is used in culturalist writing. A cultural form is a distinct means of representation which is characterised by a combination of three elements or types of material: the social organisation of the ways in which content is produced, which can also be phrased as how things are made; the element that would most commonly be thought of first – the types of performance (or narrative) that are characteristic of this means of representation; and a distinctive mode of participation or form of social occasion for the performances of each means of representa-tion – so that there is a distinctive way of consuming the show. This model of a cultural form provides a sufficient framework for us to compare significant changes in a means of representation through time, for example the theatre, and between different representa-tional traditions – as between the Hollywood cinema and main-stream television.

I shall combine elements from my previous discussion of the MetroCentre in South Tyneside with further material in order to develop the thematic concern of this chapter with spaces and places in suburban culture. I have argued that the lack of monumental (or historical) features means that the suburban place becomes defined through social expectations – it is the appearance or the rhetorical imagery of community that grounds identity. More prosaically, we could say that it is the presumption of consistency, the lack of jarring differences, that gives suburbs the comfort of reassurance, that implies the community of commonality. The shopping centre in so many ways echoes and exemplifes these values. The fear of modernity, which can be seen to be the potent heart of the mythology of neighbourhood, is in this development rendered through a more general twee-ness in which the logic of scale and grandeur is undermined and trivialised even as it is being brought into being.

This mode of insincerity is consistent with recent developments in town planning where the functional purity of Mies-ian offices or large housing estates has been recognised as both an eyesore and impractical. (Interestingly planners, or their political masters, have not yet lost a suburban belief in the necessity of intra-urban highways to criss-cross and bound neighbourhoods.) Within town-scapes there has been a revaluation of intimate walkways, jumbled perspectives and 'quaintness' in aesthetic texture. Urban design now consciously seeks to display vernacular disorder, and even to overlay the rigid sequencing of a grid or radial design of a shopping centre. (Again it is worth noting that the implicit discipline of the planned environment is rhetorically denied even as it is being most forcibly enacted. To call all these traits of the shopping centre postmodern is not in itself enlightening; we have to explicate all the traits in order to explain the general concept.)

The rigid grid of the built form of the MetroCentre cannot, any more than the conventional suburban street, accommodate the heterogeneity of streetscapes and we therefore find a number of gestures to the intimacy of community. At frequent intervals along the walkways there are imported trees and other bits of living greenery (itself a semiotic paradox in that plants denote nature but here gloss an inescapable culture). Also interspersed amongst these gestures to the real are benches and other types of seating area. These are meant to be places where the weary can rest and the informal networks of community life be reaffirmed.

The MetroCentre lacks any of the distinctiveness necessary to become an exhilarating place; the crowds who rest here have much of the vitality of those who wait in railway station waiting rooms. Numerous carts parked in the walkways serve to break up the rigidity of the vista. These carts tend to sell the sort of ephemera that are sold at down-market beach resorts. Trembling on the edge of being souvenirs they heighten the impression that somewhere is being visited. Although the enterprise is modern in materials and scale (horizontal scale) the challenge of technology is subverted through the reassurance of brick finishes, greenery and touches such as incongruously aged clocks (that seem to mimic some prior example but end up as autonomous hybrid) functioning as 'street' furniture.

One form of attraction in the MetroCentre which directly borrows from the marketing of tourism and yet simultaneously honours the mythologies of neighbourhood in some ways, is the nodal points in some galleries which have been 'themed'. What this means is that the order of shop-fronts is broken up by the introduction of areas which are named and styled in ways to exemplify that name: 'The Antiques Village', 'The Mediterranean Village' and 'The Forum'. The process of styling involves the introduction of rather cheap, visual gestures towards clichés of the theme concerned. Thus in the 'Antiques Village', presumably to underline an equation that antique equals age, this section is tricked out with a laboriously turning waterwheel and several house frontages that cobble together vernacular styles from a number of centuries and regions in very unpersuasive chipboard and fibreglass.

Similarly, in 'The Forum', which is presumably an echo of Roman colonisation of this region, a number of shops have been literally framed with weak classical imagery of imitation marble and porticoes. The effect is rather undercut, as at the time of writing the bulk of the space here is occupied by 'Pam's Pantry' a café/ restaurant that has no discernible grounding in either classicism or colonisation. The interpretation of these themes is therefore eclectic, but it is not an eclecticism which is designed to reveal an implicit theme – itself a perceived quality of modernist thought – so much as a taking for granted that that which is recognisable is reassuring.

There is a broader argument here that there is a consistency between the casual appropriation of inconsistent cultural vocabularies and the eclecticism of tourism. Once a site has been established, associated attractions can be tagged on to the original 'hook'. They will offer something remarkable – a topic for visitors – and can therefore be framed as extraordinary. This consistency holds in the discursive presentation of the MetroCentre to the extent that the most mundane activities can be given a touristic gloss: 'Mouthwatering displays of fresh food – fruit, vegetables and flowers. Breathtaking butchery displays, delicious confectionery and sweetmeats from handmade chocolates to home baked bread' (MetroCentre n.d.; Readers should note the emphasis on craft in the handling of raw materials here, which is conspicuously absent in reality).

Tourist brochures, whether for ferries, shopping centres or campsites, work with similar oppositions and conventional expectations to naturalise the artificial: 'And when your meal is over relax in MetroCentre's newest attraction the beautiful, Tranquil Garden Court, an idyllic retreat away from the hustle and bustle of everyday shopping' (MetroCentre n.d.; it is a suburban truism that city centre shopping is difficult and tiring. Here, where much of the uncertainty has been designed to be removed, it is symbolically reinserted to give the appearance of vitality.) The tourist as social voyeur savours the interplay of life-styles and the consumer tourist is able to indulge in a confirmation of the banality of difference.

So insistent is the rhetoric of appearance in the presentation of the MetroCentre as tourist attraction (and it must be remembered that the imagery of tourism that I am exploring is not just metaphor – a large proportion of the visitors to the Centre come from outside the locality, sometimes very considerable distances) that the theme could be characterised as a myth. We do not have to treat a myth as simple deception but can see it as a more complex recuperation of contradiction in an autonomous level of symbolisation. In this case the myth is an imagery of neighbourhood as market sustained through networks of gossip and informal association. Although writing more generally of the ex-urban postmodern landscape, Zukin captures well three elements concentrated in the Metro-Centre: 'it is a stage set, a shared private fantasy, and a liminal space that mediates between nature and artifice, market and place' (1992, p. 232).

But for the visitors the imagery of neighbourhood and the communalism of staff, such as the presence in the Centre of a full-time priest and dentist, cannot overcome the logic of what makes the Centre possible. Not only is it hedged about with life-giving motorways that preclude casual association and informal gatherings but national identity means that more than any city centre it is a place of metropolitan anonymity. The mythology of neighbour-hood elides the impersonality of anomic society.

The autonomous level of symbolisation through which these contradictions are resolved is articulated by an abrogation of any firm distinction between public and private spheres. The practical organisation of an environment is suppressed in favour of idealised social arrangements which are independent of that environment. It is not so much that the values of one domain are arbitrarily or inappropriately purloined for another as that there is a mutually constitutive interdependence of our languages of the 'good life'.

The rhetorical trick of this mythology (see Chaney 1986 for further discussion of the 'trick' of myths and rituals) is that spec-tacular features previously associated with a metropolitan centre are now used in a closed environment from which the terrors of urban life have been excluded. In the publicity for the Centre the nature of these features is only seen positively; it stresses cinemas, restaurants and bars, etc. and the safety of the setting, in that there are no threats from traffic: 'The new Disney stores springing up across North America may point towards a new phase of enter-taining consumption: instead of hiring store clerks, Disney has hired "cast members" trained to treat customers cheerfully as "guests". Stores are meant to offer the "magic" of theme-park experience' (Warren 1993, p. 174).

But implicitly and more importantly, there are no threats from the anonymity of urban life. Even in the quietest moments it is hard to imagine anyone being raped or mugged in one of the walkways. Here, there are none of the anonymous spaces and dead vistas of urban landscapes as quaintness has been suppressed in favour of incorrigible visibility. An all-pervading sense of social visibility is also doubtless responsible for the self-conscious manners of customers. People walk here, if not quite with the decorous timidity of the museum visitor, then as if their conduct might be called into question at any moment. There is little to disrupt the sobriety of this type of leisure.

It is not just the design that is responsible for a fabrication of virtue (a phrase borrowed from Evans 1982), there is also a marked absence of the extremes of the social spectrum. Across the range of retail and entertainment outlets and generalising across the mass of customers the predominant tone is of the lower middle class. There is very little exclusive or expensive marketing and at the same time there is a tremendous consistency of social register. (Although it is interesting that through time the Centre is gradually becoming zoned as in any urban centre, with the quarter immediately adjacent to the public transport facilities, and therefore inevitably having a higher proportion of a poorer clientele, taking on a recognisably seedier feel.)

It is unclear whether the unobtrusive security guards actively discourage their visits, or whether they find the ambience unappealing or inaccessible, but there are very few instances of social dereliction or marginality strolling these walkways. In his quest to discover popular insurgency Fiske (1989a) has argued that shopping centres are prone to appropriation by the dumb insolence of the feckless young who recolonise malls into public space. To an extent that is true of the entertainment quarter of the MetroCentre but for a variety of reasons the suburban shopping centre has not pulled those who are publicly aimless into its ambit.

The predominant atmosphere of quiet suburban restraint is, then, rarely disrupted by those whose life-style could be seen to be too disorderly. A symbolic facet of this implicit order, which may or may not be a deliberate echo of a theme-park motif, is the efforts devoted to keeping the walkways free of litter and the general ambience clean and tidy. Litter has come to stand as a powerful physical symbol of urban decay and its absence speaks to a revived sense of social propriety. And yet as another utopian feature the order is sustained with very few explicit markers of the organisation and use of power. The management may be proud of the low rates of crime within the environment but, as we know, that may also be seen as a display of a more insidious authority.

The social ambience of the MetroCentre might therefore be

described as one of limited aspirations. There is nothing extravagant here, or hard-edged; the dominant aesthetic is a combination of whimsy with a use of spectacular vocabulary in very unspectacular ways. Two examples are glass-sided lifts which smoothly climb in the courts where galleries meet, and fountains which provide another focus for these courts. (In another instance of how tourist vocabulary can be borrowed indiscriminately, visitors have started throwing coins into the fountains here in an echo of other more famous superstitions. The fact that there can be no possible rationale for the practice other than memorialising the transient emphasises that it is the appearance rather than the specificity of places that is significant.) In both cases the imagery is drawn from public display, one trenchantly modern the other traditional, but as the Centre is only two storeys high the scale is absurdly fore-shortened. The dinkiness is appropriately suburban, there are no threats here to the paucity of visitors' ambitions.

I mentioned that the suburb has been conventionally marked as a gendered space. One reason for this association is that in its translation of public place to private concerns, the suburb has been held to exemplify thematic values of continuity, reassurance and the stability of family life. (The fact that these are myths in the sense of not corresponding to empirical reality has not been of determining importance; a contradiction that may help to illuminate the political sociology of conservative voting.) The ways in which these values are stressed in the imagery and rhetoric of the shopping centre may, in combination with the various aspects of safety already discussed, help to explain the attraction of the Centre to female shoppers (see also Morris 1988).

One way of indicating this attraction is by comparison with the neighbouring city centre where the absence of small boutiques and specialist clothes shops for women is remarkable (and made the more remarkable by the comparatively large number of specialist shops selling expensive leisure-wear for young men). In the Metro-Centre there are all the usual national chain stores, pitched at a variety of levels of sophistication and style, but in addition there is a large number of 'one-off' shops specialising in marketing to women. This does not mean, however, that the variety of shops provides opportunities for innovation and creativity. Both within the ranges carried by national chains and in more specialised shops there is a complete absence of 'high' fashion – either as expensive or as different. And in fact throughout the whole spectrum of the

MetroCentre, whether in clothes, furnishings, food or leisure goods, there is very little that deviates from a very mundane consensualist middle-of-the-road orthodoxy. It still seems very marked that the city is for the unorthodox when compared to the suburban shopping centre.

The MetroCentre is then a place in which the narratives of suburban places are picked up and told in clearer and more concentrated ways. It is also a place in which the contradictions inherent in suburban community are dramatised. Rather than the intimate interdependence of village society (leaving on one side how mythical that ideal-type is), the public space here is populated by anonymous crowds integrated by their ordered mingling. The suburban shopping centre therefore constitutes a new form of public space but in order to see how that works we have to see the shopping centre as a system of representations on a number of levels.

The first mode of representation is of consumer culture. Here shopping is elided with leisure, it becomes a hobby, it becomes a way of enacting an identity. One goes for its own sake rather than necessarily to achieve a particular purpose (to the extent that some commentators have queried the financial viability of the Centre although it is regularly packed with visitors – they look but buy insufficiently). The process of revelling in commodities as entertainment is of course heightened by presentations in the centre which emphasise the touristic features of a visit.

The second mode of representation is of community. As I have stressed throughout my account, the Centre, as something marvellous and extraordinary, presents itself as spectacular innovation, but the detail of the spectacle is expressed through denying difference. In all the ways the signifiers of exoticism are naturalised and neutralised the unquestioned ordinariness of implicit community is underlined. Visitors may and will come from any one of a hundred suburbs, they will differ in socioeconomic level, in the trajectory of their visit, and how much they find the insistent sociality of the Centre wearing, but it requires definite and persistent estrangement to metaphorically stand outside what has been called in earlier section the myths of place, in this case the security of ordinariness.

This leads on to a third mode of representation, which is of authority. Both types of representational theme I have described so far work to authorise the customer. This is a distinctive type of citizenship in which there is privatisation of public authority. And this is where we come most clearly back to the opening discussion of professionalism in post-professional society. I argued then that the rhetoric of professionalism has been appropriated to serve in a more or less cynical management of social spaces. There will of course be many varieties and levels of this form of professionalism operating within the suburban shopping centre, but it will be represented in ways that do not insist on the innocence of the 'tricks' and 'johns' that throng the walkways.

Visiting tourists need not fear that their everyday claims to authority and a little dignity will be discredited by the professionals who surround them. There is of course the ultimate threat that professional robbers can burst in and use violence shrewdly to transform a place into their space for the duration of their business. That nightmare is an ever-present spectre in suburban consciousness – and is the theme of innumerable horror and crime films and plays – but to the extent that it can be suspended, suburban places guarantee the innocent a certain latitude in their claims to competent sophistication.

Part III

Immersed in culture

Chapter 5

Postmodernism and popular culture

CULTURE AT CENTRE STAGE

The essays in this book are about how culture has come to dominate intellectual work in the human sciences in the latter years of this century, and the significance of this development. In the first two chapters I described the main themes that have formed the substance of the turn to culture. I indicated the socio-intellectual context within which these themes have been generated and suggested what seem to me to have been the greatest strengths of this paradigm shift, as well as why the same developments have sometimes ended in intellectual blind alleys. These chapters are not, then, a straightforward intellectual history but also offer a critical engagement with some of the central ideas and values that have been built into a theme of the study of culture.

In the next two chapters the style changes away from a review of the field to an approach in which a key theme in contemporary culture is explored in some detail. My reason for doing this has been that by taking themes such as citizenship and the meaning of places, both of which might not be immediately seen as cultural in conventional terms, and showing how they have been colonised under the remit of the culturalist theorising, I have been able to tackle more directly a cluster of associated ideas and themes that are implicit in that paradigm. I have been undertaking the tricky job of talking about the culture of post-industrial societies, and principally British culture (or cultures within Britain), in order to find ways of talking about theorising culture.

In all these chapters the theme of modernity has been dominant. The reason is that rather than just having intellectual history as our subject, it has also been necessary to consider social and cultural history. Another way of putting this is to say that theories have been trying to catch up with changes in the 'real world' as well as being driven by internal theoretical developments.

I have put the phrase real world in quote marks because one way of describing the changes in forms of culture is to emphasise that it is no longer possible to mark meaningful distinctions between culture and society: the real world no longer exists in its own terms but only as it is staged, performed, enacted, imagined in cultural forms. So drastic is this suggestion, and the nature of the changes that are implied in even beginning to think it, that to many (both theorists and inhabitants of the real world) it has seemed that we must have transcended the modern and become postmodern. I have therefore thought it appropriate to include a final chapter on triumphant culturalism – the postmodern world as the apogee of the turn to culture. The purpose of this chapter is to both unpack some of the ideas so briefly summarised and to consider our options in a world when culture does not just provide the meaning of experience but is also the terms of that experience.

The first step is briefly to review some of the theoretical concerns that have been collected under the heading of postmodernism. Although this is not, as such schools never are, a consistent intellectually homogeneous grouping there are sufficient traits commonly held to generate a paradigmatic unease about the adequacy of 'traditional' accounts of culture (although some theorists still cling on to the possibility of theorising: see Best and Kellner 1991). I will then describe some features of contemporary culture that might be seen to exemplify these theoretical concerns. It might seem easier to reverse the order and theorise from the evidence (although this would not be consistent with the history of postmodernism), but in fact the significance of specific cultural changes could be said to need a theoretical context. I will then attempt a conclusion through some notes on the concept of culture in the light of all this attention, and in particular on our understanding, at the end of the century, of the concept of popular culture.

Having just said that I will begin with a theoretical discussion I should, even so, describe a little more what I meant when I said that in the paradigm of postmodernism forms of culture refer to or represent other cultural practices rather than traditional forms of experience. (I have taken the term paradigm from Scott Lash,

1990a, to refer to the shared features of cultural practices, and thus a dominant style. The term is attractive because it reminds us of Kuhn's use of paradigms as generic frameworks for scientific inquiry: Kuhn 1970. It is of course true that in the history of culture traditions and genres have provided formal resources and characteristic themes that are continually drawn upon. What seems to distinguish postmodern cultural practice is that the universe of cultural imagery can be pillaged indiscriminately.

Primarily in pictorial imagery (even in non-pictorial media), a great deal of technical sophistication is employed in order to provide an impression of verisimilitude that is not allied to complex content. Indeed, meaning is often subverted, ironicised and made ambiguous to the extent that representations are displayed as spectacular shows with no further significance. Sophisticatedly knowing postmodern cultural practices seem consigned to a form of decadent irrelevance in which ethical or aesthetic significance is assumed to be impossible.

I can begin by reiterating the point that there has been a tradition, in those countries with a mass citizenship and a culture based on industries of mass communication and entertainment, of intellectual dismay at what were perceived to be the consequences of cultural production largely dominated by catering to mass tastes. It is not inappropriate to read a lot of postmodern theorising as a continuation of that tradition (Featherstone, 1991, makes the same point in his essays on postmodernism) – although in its most recent forms there is a considerable unease about the appropriateness or the character of that dismay. Lash, for example, has suggested that amongst the sociological factors explaining the development of postmodernism are pressures to restabilise bourgeois identity and the fragmentation of traditional cultural forms of the working class (1990a, esp. Chapter 1; and although I have referenced them before it would be absurd in this context not to cite Bauman's essays: 1990; 1992).

The significance of the point about intellectual crisis is that while there is widespread agreement in the literature that postmodernism is a shift in cultural paradigms, it is associated (to put it no more strongly) with changes in dominant modes of production usually summarised as post-industrialisation. Calhoun has described the import of these changes as follows: 'A new centrality is posited for media, information technology and the production of signification (for example culture industry) as an end in itself' (1993, p. 78). Not only do these forms of production throw up new fractions of the intelligentsia, but they are also bound up with a crisis in confidence in the authority of established intellectual formations and programmes. The turn to culture both expands the scope of intellectuals' domain while dissolving the basis of hierarchies of privilege within that domain.

I shall take from Lash (1990a) the concept of de-differentiation to describe the crumbling of the foundations of the edifice of culture. Lash has also been influential through his related conceptualisation of a distinction between discursive and figural regimes of signification to illustrate the differences between modernism and postmodernism (1988, reprinted in 1990a); although the essential idea has been well described by Featherstone: 'If we examine definitions of postmodernism we find an emphasis upon the effacement of the boundary between art and everyday life, the collapse of the distinction between high art and mass/popular culture, a general stylistic promiscuity and playful mixing of codes' (1991, p. 65). The idea of de-differentiation obviously depends upon a prior use of institutional differentiation which Lash takes from the classical sociological accounts of modernisation (I used the idea of the differentiation of the cultural sphere as a criterion of modernisation in Chapter 1). Cultural differentiation in this tradition turns on the development of clear distinctions between the spiritual and the social, the process of secularisation. The development of the cultural sphere centres in this account on the delineation of a repertoire of representation.

The idea here is that in the early-modern world there was institutionalised a set of values and practices concerned with the pragmatic re-creation (representation) of forms of experience. The purpose of these representations varied (amongst others) from being the exploration of phenomenal reality in the sphere of science, to an educational resource for imparting both ethical values and practical skills, and a means of inspiration and recreation that was exploited in the Renaissance innovation of trading in culture. (In due course, with the development of the fully-fledged modern world, the handicraft trades of culture developed in distinctive ways into the culture industries that are the recurrent theme of these essays). In delineating the character of differentiation I do not agree with Lash that we should make a distinction in type between symbolism and representation, as it seems to me that symbolism is a mode of representation that survives in modern cultural forms. What is significant though, and it is a point which I shall take up again in greater detail shortly, is that the language of realism became increasingly dominant in the aesthetic values of representation as modernity embraced all spheres of social life.

The idea of a process of de-differentiation in contemporary society is, then, pointing to ways in which a distinct cultural sphere is gradually disappearing. Lash suggests four main components to this emergent cultural paradigm. First that aesthetic objects become models for other sorts of cultural activity such as theoretical and ethical enquiries. Secondly, that cultural objects lose their distinctiveness (what Benjamin famously called their aura in his essay on mass culture: 1970) and become as other forms of consumer production; thirdly, that within the cultural economy it becomes increasingly hard to sustain distinctions between the spheres of production, distribution and consumption; and finally, that the internal relations of what he calls 'the mode of signification' change, summarised in his phrase encapsulating the specific distinction between modernism and postmodernism: 'modernism conceives of representations as being problematic whereas postmodernism problematizes reality' (1990a, p. 13; emphasis in original). Putting this another way we can say that the adequacy of representation is a perennial problem for modern artists, while the adequacy of reality is the problem for postmodernists.

Although Lash does not spell this out, the attraction of his last and most distinctive point is that it chimes so well with our immediate experience of cultural innovation in the twentieth century. At the beginning of the century the arts, in all their various forms, were famously dominated by waves of innovation in which the relationship between the form of representation and its subject-matter became increasingly abstract. Even in those arts in which literal representation was not possible, such as musical composition, innovations fragmented the structure of expression so that it was made 'difficult', and the general audience complained of alienation from these modern forms. Thus was born a source of intellectual despair and confirmation of their worst fears of mass taste (this sense of an elitist distinction from everyday concerns is still the dominant connotation of the cultural modern; the complex interdependencies of modernism, postmodernism and mass culture have been thoughtfully explored in Huyssen 1986; and see also Collins 1989).

In contrast, innovations in postmodern cultural practice seem to involve a turn back to traditions of conventional representation. Most famously, postmodernism in architectural practice has involved a turn away from the aesthetic rigour of high modernism to an heterogeneous stylistic vocabulary. In the latter perspective architects feel free to mix elements taken from different styles without respecting the 'organic unity' of traditions, practices that are held to be a pastiche or superficial by their modernist critics. But although there is less shock of the new, the conventions of representation are frequently used by postmodernists in ways that make our sense of reality feel disturbed or troubled. It is as though normality is cast within the subjugating frame of a dream. This is a type of aesthetic innovation that has been, until the triumph of postmodern practice, most typically associated with the Surrealist movement.

De-differentiation is a technical way of referring to the idea that the languages of representation, themselves becoming more standardised across the globe through the influence of industries of mass entertainment and communication, are increasingly about themselves rather than some thing (the real) which is 'out there'. Issues in realism, as I have said, have dominated aesthetic discourse since the development of a secular culture, especially since the rise of romanticism in the latter half of the eighteenth century. Issues in realism were of particular significance to intellectuals seeking to sustain their authority in cultural matters, largely because the aesthetics of realism provided a framework within which artists could perceive a distinctive social relevance for their work (Chaney 1979, especially Chapter 3; Rosen and Zerner 1984). As modernism became more abstruse and discursive (cf. Wolfe 1975), any pretence at social relevance and/or a vanguard role for aesthetic innovation became patently absurd, to be replaced by strategies of representation which have the same relationship to reality as advertising campaigns (an early attempt to describe this mode of representation is Chaney 1977). In this view Pop Art was the last gasp of modernist hubris and simultaneously the advance-guard of postmodern irony.

Objections will be raised that this account suggests that nobody produces modern abstract art any more, and that artists, whether self-conscious modernists or not, have abandoned claims to social relevance. Both implications are patently false. I will suggest as an alternative that, as in the discussion of nationalism and other cultural identities when I pointed to the co-existence of local cultures within the overarching terrain of mass culture, traditions of modernism will survive and command distinct constituencies within the postmodern cultural paradigm. This approach also allows the possibility that sustaining the cultural form of modernist practice in media such as literature or fine art will be increasingly affected by the marketing practices of advertising and public relations.

I have proposed representation in advertising as a model for cultural practices in which the real becomes problematic. The reason is that advertising is a set of images which are essentially about other images (see the much fuller discussion in Chaney 1993, especially Chapter 5; see also Wernick 1991). Naively, when still dominated by aesthetic realism, advertising was criticised for promoting illusions and misrepresenting needs, functions and uses. As the cultural form of advertising has clearly come to dominate all other cultural forms, it is apparent that advertising discourse does not distort reality but has replaced it. The play of association and reference in the dramatisation of advertising is fundamentally autonomous.

So far I have described the basis of the view that we can detect the emergence of triumphant culturalism as a new way of understanding the relationship of culture and society. The message of triumphant culturalism is both that the nature of representation is changing and, therefore, that the contours of social reality have to be drawn in different ways. We cannot chart the structures of material reality with any confidence, nor presume the primacy of social determination (Stuart Hall and later generations of the Gramscian tradition have signalled their ambivalent acceptance by coining the phrase new times: Hall and Jacques 1989; see also Harris 1992, especially Chapter 9; and Grossberg 1992). The crisis in confidence in social knowledge follows because if we have lost any independent basis for social identity (both as individuals and as groups or institutions), then identity or self-consciousness is possible only through cultural discourses (not all writers on postmodernity accept the logic of this progression: see for example Harvey 1989). And if those discourses are ironic, fragmentary, allusive and articulated through the play of imagery, then all forms of identity will be experienced only as arbitrary, infinitely reflexive projects.

It is of course possible to argue that changes in the social order of post-industrial societies are not so much a paradigmatic change as an intensification of the logic of modernisation. Smart, for example, sees postmodernity as a sort of reflexive consciousness of modernity: 'Postmodernity offers us the possibility of a critical view of modernity. Not the end of modernity, but the possibility of a reconstituted modernity . . . postmodernity re-presents modernity' (1993, p. 116; see also Chapters 2 and 3 of his book for a clear discussion of the prospects for sociology of a radical subversion of social reality). Giddens has also put the theme of reflexivity at the heart of his social theory in his emphasis upon what Smart calls 'the tenuous, negotiated, constantly constituted character of social realities [and] . . . the interminable labour of interpretation that is not only inescapable in social life, but is also constitutive of it' (ibid., p. 63; Giddens 1990). In his recent work Giddens has addressed the implications of this perspective and the way it generates the central importance to accounts of individual identity, gender roles and modes of sexuality of a destabilisation of forms of social knowledge (1991, 1992). He too, however, tends to write of these issues as characteristic of later modernity rather than postmodern society.

The figure most often cited as one of the more apocalyptic voices detecting a dissolution of the social is the French social philosopher Jean Baudrillard (his complex work is admirably reviewed and discussed in Gane 1991a, 1991b). Baudrillard is, in practice, despite a very idiosyncratic conceptual vocabulary, an old-fashioned mass culture theorist. What I mean by this term is that he sees the exponential expansion of networks of mass communication and entertainment as generating so much information that meaning becomes impossible, and representations constitute a hyper-reality in which simulations only represent other simulations (1983a); while the complementary dissolution of structures of social identity generates a mass consciousness and the end of the social (1983b). The traditionalism of this perspective is betrayed by his conviction that it is the ubiquitousness of media imagery that swamps the possibility of critical engagement:

> the media multiply events, 'pushing' the meaning – events no longer have their own space-time; they are immediately captured in universal diffusion, and there they lose their meanings, they lose their references and their time-space so that they are neutralized.
>
> (Baudrillard quoted in Gane 1993, p. 84)

It has frequently been pointed out, and he himself admits, that Baudrillard has been influenced by McLuhan, a theorist of media determinism who briefly enjoyed some celebrity in the 1960s (his best book was published in 1964). Marshall McLuhan was a Catholic romantic who detected in the social impact of new media of mass communication the possibility of new forms of cultural community, which he most famously christened the global village. Baudrillard seems to share some of McLuhan's romanticism except that in his case it leads to a more conventional pessimism that the literalness of media discourse will rob mass culture of myth and illusion: 'But with this faculty of giving reality to the world, then the possible, the imaginary, the illusory all disappear ... A world without any illusory effects will be completely obscene, material, exact, perfect' (quoted in Gane 1993, p. 44).

Rather characteristically Baudrillard values the limitations of cinematic performance for being able to preserve a mythological sense that transcends mundane reality, and thereby makes it supportable. He sees that in America where social mythology has always been particularly bound up with cinematic fables, the structures of social landscapes take on the aura of cinematic perspective: 'In California, particularly, you *live* cinema: you have experienced the desert as cinema, you experience Los Angeles as cinema, the town as a panning shot' (quoted in Gane 1993, p. 34; emphasis is original see also Baudrillard 1988 for a cultural account of experience in America). While writing from a very different perspective, Soja has also picked up on the illusory character of social forms in Los Angeles: 'It [Los Angeles] has in effect been deconstructing the urban into a confusing collage of signs which advertise what are often little more than imaginary communities and outlandish representations of urban locality' (1989, p. 245). It is as if (one of) the most modern cities needs to be seen as rootless representations, as an imagined terrain.

We return now to the main theme of this section – the argument that in the postmodern world the forms of culture no longer represent social reality so much as other forms and images of cultural representation. (I am aware that postmodern theory is more complex and contains more strands than this theme, but I believe that focusing the issues in this way is effective in clarifying contemporary theorising of culture.) I have suggested that this density of cultural imagery – and it is clear that everyday experience is saturated by access to many media of communication and entertainment that can be cheaply and readily appropriated – takes on the character of advertising discourse. (This reminds us of the theme of a lack of depth and superficiality that I think Jameson first used to characterise postmodern culture: 1991; see also Foster 1986, and that has subsequently become a staple theme.) Advertising clearly does not aspire to aesthetic or ethical transcendance; they are commanded by the needs of the here and now so that it makes no sense to imagine advertisements as art-objects.

Of course it is characteristic of the reflexivity of culture that we can and do collect adverts as evidence of a changing consumer culture (see Leiss 1986 for an instance of this approach), and bracket adverts with other consumer objects in a museum of design. But in both cataloguing and collecting we are using adverts much as other fragments of popular culture. These are mass-produced, anonymous, transient mementoes of life-styles. They are ethnographic clues to forms of life not objects that are meaningful in their own right. If we say that individual messages and images are significant only in the context of their discourse, although we may have a personal affection for particular icons of memory and association, then I think we are beginning to say something generally more important about the character of popular culture.

Before pursuing that line of thought further I shall conclude this section with a few further notes on the metaphor of advertising practice for triumphant culture. I have suggested that advertising lacks transcendental aspirations, although that assertion needs to be qualified by a distinction between advertisements connoting images of identity or style of life and their role in selling specific products. The former role is clearly more general and more bound up with the discursive formulation of consumer culture, as Bauman has argued in relation to the this theme: 'Consumerism stands for production, distribution, desiring, obtaining and using, of symbolic goods. *Symbolic* goods: that is very important' (from an interview published in 1992, p. 223; emphasis is original). Advertising discourse transcends the particularities of product identification and market specification by dramatising symbolic representation and thereby feeds into a broader sense of cultural change: 'Postmodernism, then, has to be understood against the background of a long-term process involving the growth of a consumer culture and expansion in the number of specialists and intermediaries engaged in the production and circulation of symbolic goods' (Featherstone 1991, p. 126).

The character of symbolic representation in advertising discourse neatly illustrates the twin themes of this section – that the development of self-referential, functionless, technically sophisticated imagery has been bracketed with the loss of authority of conventional modes of social identity and structures of social order. These themes as different levels of analysis come together in the contemporary importance of life-style as a dramatisation of identity – particularly if we remember that life-styles are (although usually unacknowledged) what are represented in advertising discourse (on life-styles and consumer culture see Shields 1992). They are the presupposition of consumer culture: 'The implication is that we are moving towards a society without fixed status groups in which the adoption of styles of life (manifest in choice of clothes, leisure activities, consumer goods, bodily dispositions) which are fixed to specific groups have been surpassed' (Featherstone 1991, p. 83). Life-style is the language of social identity in postmodern culture, it is a mode of representation that denotes only itself. Infinitely plastic it can be changed, ironicised, discarded in the endless pursuit of an authentic self-hood. Life-styles are therefore forms of cultural creativity for popular experience; they are art-forms for the masses.

VIRTUAL REALITY

In the first section of this chapter I described theoretical developments that have argued for a transformation in the status of culture. Using the old-fashioned terms of the Marxist framework, culture is no longer seen as a superstructure generated by a socio-structural base, but rather as a general term for the sea of discourses and regimes of signification through which we constitute lived experience. As we cannot transcend these constitutive practices lived experience is, effectively, social reality. I have used the general term of postmodernism to label this new paradigm although I would make no claim to have described the breadth of work going on under the postmodern label adequately, or to have considered the complexities of the postmodern perspective. In setting out the distinctiveness of this paradigm I necessarily made some contrasts with a largely implied description of modernism; I shall begin this section, which is to be concerned with aspects of forms of entertainment that exemplify postmodern theory, by making another contrast between modern and postmodern eras.

The nineteenth century was the epoch of revolutions. Whether these were long-term structural changes in the character of social production, such as the Industrial Revolution, or cataclysmic moments of transition into the era of modern politics, such as the French Revolution, or inspired moments of romantic failure, such as the Paris Commune, revolutions punctuated the nineteenth century. It is therefore no surprise to find that bohemian avant-gardes usually saw themselves as revolutionaries. What this meant in practice is that it became part of the accepted duty of the project of social relevance for art, to see itself as in some sense the harbinger of modernity; and it was understood that the full flowering of modernism would be a revolutionary transcendence of the old society into the utopian dawn of emancipation. While it would be absurd to pretend that cultural producers (to use a suitably neutral term), shared a common project and would all have signed up to these dreams, some sense of perceived revolutionary possibility is necessary to understand the plethora of 'isms' that have characterised modernism.

In contrast to a century and a half of social revolutions it is by now commonplace, but possibly premature, to announce the death of socialism. (Any comment would have to begin by asking what you meant by socialism.) But the collapse of the great state centralist powers, allied with a widespread disillusionment with the idea of using state powers as means of social engineering, and allied above all with a fragmentation of the industrial working class and the collapse of theories that have seen it as the engine of social and ethical change, have all combined to make revolution seem (at times) a quaint historical anachronism (was the last revolution, fittingly, the Chinese cultural revolution?). Where revolution is used now it refers to shifts in fashions, life-styles and leisure pursuits. Not only are there no more revolutions, in any of the senses used above, there are no more revolutionaries seeking to capture state power in the service of an ideology of wholescale institutional change (or at least they are an endangered species). Dissidence is expressed through turning away from the centre, through pursuing local autonomy rather than transforming society.

It seems possible then that the revolutionary aspirations of modernism are unravelling in a postmodern dystopia of cynicism, apathy and inertia, although it seems to me that it is too soon to pontificate with any confidence. It may well be that the lack of optimism in contemporary experience is a *fin-de-siècle* blip that will be transformed in a decade or two. It does, however, appear consistent with a loss of belief in revolutionary possibility for there to be a growth in what we have come to call new social movements. These are associations based on beliefs in personal redemption, charismatic faiths and sur-rational beliefs. (I coin the term sur-rational to avoid stigmatising belief in various forms of non-scientistic medical and spiritual therapies as irrational; and to deliberately echo Surrealism.) An almost universal feature of the beliefs of new social movements is that conventional physical accounts of material reality are insufficient, and need to be supplemented by a consciousness that reality is constituted, at least in part, through various forms of rapprochement between human and other forms of animate experience.

I want therefore to describe the ecological consciousness of new social movements as deeply cultural (I am of course picking up here again points I made in the conclusion to Chapter 2). The point about cultural in this context is that although it is strongly concerned with representation, particularly of consciousness, it more directly addresses the meaning of culture as creative or reproduction. In this, the oldest meaning of culture, we use the term to refer to the making of social forms, as in agri-culture; at its deepest, literally the making of community (this idea has been addressed in several innovatory ways in Jenks 1993). These modes of highly reflexive theoretical work are at one end of the post-modern cultural paradigm; at the other are the cultural practices through which we signify the imagination of community in the virtual reality of global culture.

Earlier I quoted Soja describing the proliferation of ways of signifying locality in a city such as Los Angeles. The purpose of his remarks, and my citing them, was to indicate that these signs were in some sense false – they were creating rather than representing a reality. Soja continues on the same theme to describe the city, which contains these imagined communities, as 'a gigantic agglomeration of theme parks' (1989, p. 246), a metaphor which serves two functions. It implies that the residential suburbs of a metropolitan city are like entertainment centres; and that there is a form of entertainment in which alternative realities, which mimic desirable features of the real world, are sustained and are attractive to visitors. I shall now argue that in various ways forms of leisure and entertainment which transcend reality have, at the end of the twentieth century, come so to dominate ways of being in the world in post-industrial societies that they constitute the terms of mundane experience (a thesis that is not incompatible with that of Ritzer 1992).

I can explain this puzzling phrase by taking up a point concerned with the aesthetics of realism I discussed in the previous section. It could be argued that the desire to create forms of entertainment which 'take over' the reader/spectator is not new. The desire to represent a reality so compellingly that the 'audience's' emotions are fully caught up in the narrative goes back at least to the psychological reality of the eighteenth-century novel. Habermas, in the context of a different argument, has pointed out that: 'The reality as illusion that the new genre created received its proper name in English, "fiction": it . . . fashioned for the first time the kind of realism that allowed anyone to enter into the literary action as a substitute for his own' (1989, p. 50).

The point is, however, that this new genre (the novel) dramatised the possibility of a new mode of subjectivity: 'The relations between author, work and public changed. They became intimate mutual relationships between privatized individuals' (ibid.). Individuals could look through fictions into a distinctive way of staging social experience (to see how this way of staging acts was a model for the public life of the nineteenth-century city see Chaney 1993, Chapter 2). There was though a crucial aesthetic distance between the subjectivity of privatised spectator looking through fictions and the perceived/imagined reality. It was the inescapable awareness of this distance that generated self-conscious concern with the devices of representation, a reflexive regress that led in time to representational abstraction in high modernism.

The argument about the virtual or hyper-reality of postmodern entertainment is that aesthetic distance has been eroded. (Eroded is too casual a term, but it is an attempt to summarise the logic of culture production in a mass citizenship; and of course in saying that I am accepting the validity of the crisis for intellectuals in being expected to produce culture for mass audiences. On the problematics of representation, both political and theoretical, in postmodern culture see Hutcheon 1989.) Rather than look through fictions to imagine alternatives, we use fictions to stage everyday life. The paradox is that, as Eco (1986) has argued, in searching for reality we are led to 'the absolute fake' of hyper-reality. We are brought back, as Eco was, to puzzling over the cultural significance of the dramatic realism (hyper-reality) of the theme parks (etc.) mentioned above.

Before directly considering the various ways in which we simulate reality as a form of entertainment, I want to suggest that in large

part our difficulty in finding an appropriate
stems from an implicit (and perhaps inappr/
premiss is based in the revolutionary aspirat'
I discussed above. I suggested then that a .
precursor of 'the new society' was seen (albeit in ﾍ.
way of giving substance to the social relevance of art. 'Iᵢ.
this form of self-consciousness is that authenticity becomes a ceᵢ.
focus of critical concern. I think this is shown in the most frequent
comment of the lay public, which is that modern art is a cheat or a
con because 'anyone' could do it.

Discoveries of hoaxes, or that children or animals have been
taken seriously as cultural producers, are always greeted with
jubilation outside the 'art world'. Accepted members of the community of cultural producers are persistently inspected for evidence
that they mean it, that the work, however strange, can claim the
warrant of authentic endeavour. (In addition to this popular
concern with authenticity, the possibility of inspecting art for social
meaning also constitutes the theoretical framework within which a
sociology or politics of culture becomes possible.)

Authenticity is one of the main frameworks within which modernism has been discussed and evaluated. The more general point in
relation to this chapter is that the critical vocabulary of authenticity
has survived and outlasted the cultural paradigm within which it
was dominant. Lacking the commitment to social relevance in
modernism that gave authenticity its power, in postmodern aesthetics the dimension of authenticity is clearly either superfluous or
at best ambiguous (see also Chambers 1990). When we turn to the
various modes of simulating reality that Rojek has so clearly
described (1993, Chapter 4), we should learn not to react in distaste
at the tawdriness of their fakery. It seems unlikely that their visitors
are wilfully disattending the flaws and joins in the production
processes that so artlessly constitute these places. It is more
economical to suggest that the cultural form provides occasions and
forms of participation that have distinctive aesthetic rewards.

Rojek has made a start on considering what these rewards are
by describing the fatal attractions (a Baudrillardian pun) of the
'landscape of postmodernism' as escape areas (1993, p. 136). He
distinguishes and discusses in some detail four types of escape area.
They are: first, black spots – the commercial development of sites
where the famous or subsequently noteworthy have been associated
with death; secondly, heritage sites – recreations of the past either at

ormance sites or through tableaux; thirdly, literary landscapes ɹich are based on the fictive worlds of famous characters; and, ʋnally, theme parks – centres for leisure which have been given a narrative structure through a theme of a distinctive mode of experience.

Although these areas represent a wide range of social objects, their appeal can be summarised as an opportunity to engage with a form of experience that is outside the boundaries of the everyday (or, as I shall go on to argue, really an intensification of the everyday). As such the place has to be compelling – it has to offer you ways in which you can make the imaginative transition. This may be through your presence at the actual site where something newsworthy occurred, or through the employment of various modes of dramatic artifice extending to mechanical figures who effectively simulate human performance, or multi-sensory props characteristic of the original place (hence the Jorvik Centre in York's famous use of smell). It may seem that these devices emulate authenticity, and thus contradict my argument above, but the devices of representation are based on the principle that 'authenticity and originality are, above all, matters of technique. The staging, design and the context of the preserved object become crucial in establishing its "reality" for us' (Rojek 1993, p. 160).

At the heart of my approach lies the belief that, the aesthetics of representation, whether or not any particular component element is authentic or not, is largely irrelevant to the dramatic impact of participation. Thus, this may be where the Battle of Naseby took place, or it may not as they moved it a few miles to facilitate a new road. But that need not affect your ability to empathise with the existential immediacy of those who once made it an historic place. Indeed, we can go further and say that the thrill of a 'white-knuckle' ride is that it persuades you that this is almost what some comparable experience in reality would be like – except that in your terror you can cling on to the ultimate irony of drama that it is artifice. (But then of course there is the neurotic fear that perhaps the machine is out of control . . .)

To stress the dramaturgy of place does not mean that the imaginative empathy facilitated for the audience is necessarily false. Even at its most ideological the narrative purpose of the place may 'work'. Rojek quotes from an early Disneyland promotion pamphlet that this will be: 'a place for teachers and pupils to discover greater ways of understanding and education . . . Here will be the wonders of Nature and Man for all to see and understand' (1993 p. 169).

Ignoring the benefits your visit will bring to the Disney Corporation, it may be that the representation of education will stimulate critical inquiry. The point is that while it is valuable to deconstruct the cultural form of places such as theme parks (see for example Marin 1984 and Gottdiener 1982), the aesthetics of representation are essentially immune to ideology-critique. (The further implication is that we are led to appreciate the need for a different sort of sociology of popular culture; a thesis also developed but on different grounds in Collins 1989.)

What I have called the dramaturgy of place (the devices and procedures through which a particular simulation is effected) in this section, is a more specific version of the account of tourist places. In the previous chapter I argued that tourists are willing collaborators, or we could say a compliant audience, in the manufacture of places. It is certainly true that Rojek's escape areas tend to be sited at tourist resorts, or to constitute focal attractions for tourists in their own right, but more generally the relevance of tourism is through a common base in what I have called the aesthetics of representation. In contrast to an aesthetics of realism in which fiction frames others' performance in ways that make it believable, in an aesthetics of representation fiction frames social space to create places so that the audience, at least in part, constitute the performance. I recognise that the dramatic resources for simulation are the precondition for performance, but they are completed by their visitors, who enact the drama.

The paradox of a culture of simulation is then that audiences engage with the tangible immediacy of representation. Rather than the fictions of realism these are the fictions of collective life. This further makes sense of Rojek's use of escape: he is not suggesting that there is a widespread movement to flee from reality, but rather to seek reassurance: 'Leisure, one might say, is not the antithesis of daily life but the continuation of it in dramatized or spectacular form' (1993, p. 213). The escape is not to somewhere that is outside normality but to a more self-consciously dramatised performance:

> Mass reproduction, the imitation and 'extension' of nature and history and the procession of dramatized mass spectacle organized by the mass communication industry, produce a social environment in which calculated myth and simulation structure the contours of daily life.
>
> (Rojek 1993, p. 209)

I suggested above that the practice of postmodern forms of leisure and entertainment will be increasingly significant for the terms of everyday experience. I have tried to explain what this means by drawing a contrast between the relationship binding representation and audience in modern aesthetics, and that binding representation and audience in a postmodern culture of simulation. In describing the latter I have used a dramaturgical vocabulary, that is words drawn from how we describe dramatic performances, to talk about tourist places. This may seem puzzling if we assume that dramas are performances of stories enacted on stage, or in films or broadcast. The types of places tourists visit do not usually tell narratives in any conventional way and there is not a stage framed as a separate performance space. I have, however, argued elsewhere in much greater detail (1993, especially Chapter 1) that we do not need to restrict our use of dramatic performance to occasions like theatrical enactments.

All social life can be seen to be patterned in forms of performance. We will obviously want to distinguish between degrees of organisation, the self-conscious stylisation of role-play, the rigidity of distinctions between front and back stages etc. (see MacCannell 1973 for an early discussion of this distinction in relation to tourist settings). It will quickly become very complicated to try to specify all the different types of social drama that make up modern culture, but I am less interested in a typology of dramatic forms than in the irony of performance. Drama adapts space, identity and manner to play with the possibility that everyday constraints can be, however temporarily, suspended. Dramatic performance is therefore necessarily always aware of the fragility of its own artifice. It is pointless to criticise tourist places as inauthentic representations; they have to be considered as their own form of drama. They are a reinvention of spectacle that draws attention both to the invention of place, through the use of space, identity and manner, and to the lack of clear boundaries between those places and everyday worlds.

A notion of spectacular drama has often been used in relation to the artifice of postmodern leisure because it is self-conscious, figurative show. I have argued in relation to the development of modern leisure that although it is patterned by audiences for many different types of activity, what they share in common is a commitment to purchasing entertainment (Chaney 1979). Although tourist places are structured and maintained by many different types of professional, the ever-present cast who perform the place for each other and confirm their mutual normality are the visitors who are also the audience. A culture of theme parks provides entertainment (and instruction) through forms of spectacular performance that are simultaneously tangibly real and utterly false. Evermore elaborate artificial devices are likely to be used to heighten the illusion, but this is, of course, not taking the visitors closer to reality but deeper into the fictions of representation.

The logic of this account is that the values of spectacular artifice will not be confined to places in which the framing of knowledge and representation is deliberately ambiguous. If the structures of experience can be made into a form of play through the arbitrariness of the cultural forms of identity (reminding us again of the play on the streets with gender, ethnicity and other stylistic vocabularies), then it is only reasonable to expect that the discourse of actuality, how we talk about and represent the world shared in common, will also take on the characteristics of spectacle. There are three main dimensions to 'the spectacularisation' of representing reality: the discourse of news takes on spectacular characteristics; the events of news are staged as spectacular shows; and the critical commentary on news is couched in spectacular discourse. I will briefly describe more fully each of these dimensions.

The first is a well-worn theme in mass culture accounts. It can easily be illustrated by the quote I used from Baudrillard in the previous section (see p. 188), that the profusion of news so swamps media audiences that the information becomes meaningless (see also Sennett 1977). One aspect of this critique points to a failure to maintain strict category distinctions in the flow of the media, particularly television. Natural and human disasters are jumbled together with drama presentations, cartoons, advertisements and trivial items of social gossip (see Buck 1992). It becomes increasingly hard to keep a clear sense of what is fiction and what is reality.

This process is accentuated by the second dimension in which attention is directed to the spectacular occasions of public drama (see the fuller discussion in Garber *et al.* 1993). Examples here would be major sports occasions such as the Super Bowl and the Olympics; national ceremonials such as significant dates in Presidential and Royal calendars; other sorts of public dramas such as the visit of a Pope to a country, or an enormous concert staged for famine relief or a major trial; and occasions of national and international emotion such as exploits in space, airline disasters and showbusiness stars' marriage and/or death. It may seem tasteless to jumble these events together as some are clearly staged for the media while others are inadvertent spectacles, such as famine in Africa. They do take on a common character, however, through the ways in which they are staged and articulated as dramas for global audiences.

There is then a process of intimate interdependence between the discourses of actuality in the media and the types of event and occasion to which their attention is drawn; a close relationship that is made closer by the third dimension, which I have called critical commentary. This is not a very good name but it serves to refer to a combination of types of quasi-news such as advertisements, the commentaries of experts, spin doctors and professionals, and the activities of public relations agencies in promoting image items that have a function for their clients if not for public debate (see for example Ericson's (1991) excellent studies of the discourses of crime, law and justice in the media). All these activities work to amplify an impression of hyper-reality in news, news commentaries, talk-shows, discussion formats and so on. In this plethora of commentary we can be seen to be being offered the tangible immediacy of participation while this is continually being subverted in a search for distinctions between authentic and inauthentic elements.

Performances couched in an aesthetics of representation are fundamentally immune to ideology-critique, yet many of the studies cited in the previous paragraphs are critiques of ideologies in the public sphere. It is clearly wrong to say that these critiques have no value in critical enquiry, and yet they seem only marginally relevant to the dramas of public life. Abercrombie has argued that it is difficult to sustain any strong account of ideological domination in popular entertainment: 'The discussion so far has shown that incoherence, diversity and pluralisation characterise all three moments of the ideological process [that is text, setting and effect], making each difficult to secure' (1990, pp. 221–2). He goes on to suggest that in the context of new audiences' sampling and casual rearrangements of programming to suit their own agendas these characteristics will be intensified (although see also Thompson (1990) on ideology and mass communications).

It does not seem surprising that electorates in post-industrial societies increasingly choose political leaders on the grounds of their character rather than their policies. American Presidential candidates go and have gone to enormous lengths to simulate various dimensions of authenticity. The fact that critical commentary has been remarkably unanimous in maintaining that almost without exception they have lacked morally desirable qualities has only intermittently dented the simulation of authenticity. As public figures they have corresponded very well to the features of spectacular drama described in this section.

Of course it could be argued that Presidential candidates are simply engaged in old-fashioned lying. Although they are able to trade on the quest for meaning of postmodern audiences, their deceptions come from an older political tradition. Two problems here are, first, how would you know anyway – is not the question part of the problem?; and, secondly, even when one has been revealed as a liar, for example Richard Nixon, they still seem to be able to command a mass following who trust their integrity. This suggests that authenticity is both sought after and irrelevant – it is the appearance of authenticity that is important.

This is reminiscent of the fictional power of pornography. The audience know that they are not in the presence of people copulating, but they need continual displays of the authenticity of actions (most notoriously the climactic cum-shot). In a recent discussion of the representation of presence in pornography, Falk argues that this aesthetic impulse has spilt out of its initial genre to become the primary rationale of documentary media-events and news simul-casting on CNN (note the possible pun on simultaneous and simulation): 'The elimination of the interpretative and even representational distance aiming at the presentness-effect . . . turns the media event, in the last instance, into a spectacle cancelling the difference between (authentic) presence and (fictional) representation' (1993, p. 35). (Baudrillard, too, has acknowledged the hyper-reality of pornography: 'Obscenity . . . is a monstrous rapprochement of things: there is no longer the distance of the gaze, of play . . . it is the total promiscuity of things, the confusion of orders' quoted in Gane 1993, p. 61.)

The most extreme development of this cultural paradigm are those technological developments in which it is possible to create three-dimensional environments precluding any other sensory input during the course of the performance. Popularly known as virtual reality, the technology is still, to my knowledge, at the stage of a machine clamped to the viewer's head. Not only is the world of representation private to that viewer, its particular form and narrative character is also dependent upon his/her creative interaction. It then carries the logic of industries of entertainment that seek to simulate representations that transcend conventional constraints to the absurd conclusion of enclosure within an alternative reality. It seems to me unsurprising that one of the first uses to which entrepreneurs have sought to put this technology is in the service of the pornographic imagination. (It is equally unsurprising that such a mode of exploitation should also immediately generate a moral panic about the dangers of unbridled representation.)

It will be objected of course that it is grotesque to use the aesthetic stance of the pornography viewer/reader as a guide to the attitudes and values of mass culture audiences. The pornographic audience is deemed a deviant minority, probably sick, at best only an index of cultural pathology. And yet this brings us back to the theme that mass culture in its various forms, now postmodernism, has perennially challenged intellectuals' cultural hegemony because it violates their interpretive and evaluative norms. One of the most consistently puzzling features of popular audiences' behaviour has been their enthusiasm for, almost worship of, cultural stars (in the first part of Lewis 1992 there are some interesting discussions of the dominant view of the pathology of fandom, and alternative productive, more creative, views of fans' discriminations).

Stars represent a form of heroism that is an imaginary fame. Generally (but not necessarily) real people, like theme parks they revel in their artificiality. I describe their fame as imaginary because like public opinion it is a figment of media discourse, in providing both a stage for their performance and a medium for all the ways they are to be talked about and pictured (Gledhill 1991). Perhaps more powerfully than other forms of the aesthetics of representation stars stage mundane experience in their likeness. Stars are icons of identity, the most visible formulae of performance in spectacular drama. It is not therefore surprising that stars are capable of inspiring funerary cults. For those caught up in the cult, the time and place of a star's death will always be significant, with other celebrations of notable dates in the star's biography; at its most extreme believers will accept, in a triumph of transcending reality, that the star has conquered death (or that it was only a simulation of death) and is still able to intervene in human affairs.

In certain features the funerary cults of twentieth-century cultural celebrities, such as James Dean, Marilyn Monroe and, above all, Elvis Presley resemble the cargo cults of village societies brutally thrust into the ambit of modern urbanism. But as with so many other parallels it would be a mistake to see them as pre-modern survivals. They are rather emblematically postmodern. Presupposing the manufacture of culture, the members of such cults celebrate the possibility of dramatic empathy. In their souvenirs and mementoes they are tourists of a life rather than a place but the form of their 'visit' is still to exploit virtual reality to constitute the terms of mundane experience.

POSTMODERN POPULISM

I have described how the cultural turn has generated a triumphant culturalism. What this means can be summarised as a crisis in representation. And yet this crisis has not been over the status and adequacy of a representational repertoire (which can be said to have been the burden of modernism), nor yet over the true character of what is to be or should be represented (there is a persistent strain of indifference to reality in postmodern practice). It is rather that the crisis is expressed through its absence. There is a slick proficiency in postmodern cultural practice, a rather casual confidence that is straining all the time at the edges of conventions about representational forms and genres. I earlier used the analogy of dream imagery and there is that quality of plausibility which is allied to a troubled sense of powerless unease. I have tried to show that the crisis generated when these practices become the dominant paradigm is that we are swamped by representation.

Feeling marooned in what I have called elsewhere a fictive landscape (1993, Chapter 5), generates problems over the possibility of independent criteria of evaluation within cultural discourses of representation. There is then a crisis in postmodern representation (although crisis somehow seems too energetic a word); it is a distinctive form of meaninglessness in which we lack a sense of purpose with which to interpret others' performance.

To illuminate some of the problems I have drawn a contrast between two aesthetic perspectives. One I have called the aesthetics of realism is principally associated with the modernist paradigm. The central evaluative dimension in this perspective is with different forms of authenticity. I have suggested that this dimension is replaced by a corresponding concern with verisimilitude and ingenuity in a perspective I have called the aesthetics of representation. Especially in the previous section I tried to spell out some of the characteristics of this perspective and, less fully, why they might be troubling to intellectuals based in the aesthetics of realism. In this concluding section I will consider some of the implications of this talk of perspectives and paradigms for our more general understanding of culture, in particular popular culture.

To avoid introducing unnecessary complications I have not discussed so far the historical framework of these perspectives. In that realism is associated with modernism and representation with postmodernism, the natural deduction would be that an aesthetics of representation is a more recent development. I now, however, want to suggest that it is not difficult to detect a much longer history to an aesthetics of representation than the later twentieth century. For example, the privileged qualities of postmodernism – parody/ pastiche, depthlessness, allegory, spectacular show, and an ironic celebration of artifice – have all been central to the submerged traditions of popular culture. One only has to think of the traditions of music hall and vaudeville, the fair-ground, the circus and pantomime, the melodramatic theatre and the literatures of crime and romance to find all these qualities clearly displayed.

A possible interpretation of this argument would be that 'post'-modernism has always been misleading. To use that term implies too strongly a sense of rupture, a forcible change in how we commonly apprehend our life-world. If we can trace in the traditions of popular entertainment a distinctive aesthetic stance which is based in the conventions of spectacular drama, then a belief in recent radical change is harder to sustain. This is in part the theme of my previous book (1993) and is why in the title I refer to late modern culture. I tried to show in that book that our ways of representing forms of shared identity to ourselves have, in those societies most fully absorbed in a global mass culture, institutionalised popular aesthetics as dominant forms in the second half of the twentieth century. This is then a later development of the potential of modernity rather than a transformation or transcendence.

I do not reject that thesis. I still believe it to be an important qualification of some of the excited excesses of over-apocalyptic theorising (usually undertaken by people who seem to have very little feel for or experience of popular entertainment). I want now, though, to develop my approach a stage further by suggesting that the contemporary dominance of aesthetics of representation is allied to a more radical sense of a lack of firm grounding in structures of social meaning. The consequence is that the conviction that we have embarked upon a distinctive paradigm is justified. There are three ways in which I believe there is a stronger sense of uncertainty in the grounds of contemporary cultural formations, and I shall discuss each in turn and how they relate to a new aesthetic paradigm.

The first concerns the implied social occasions of participation in different cultural forms. I pointed out earlier that in the first authoritative flowering of the aesthetics of realism, usually associated with the innovation of the novel, this new form was associated with new modes of subjectivity. The realism of the novel was and is dependent upon a psychological empathy of private identification. In contrast, the spectacular forms of popular entertainment have been associated with communal occasions for participation. In general the crowd has been a physical and vibrant presence, an essential constituent of the performance.

These differences are commonly associated with class cultures, with the individualism of bourgeois culture being contrasted with the communal traditions of popular culture. It may seem paradoxical that it is when the working class is losing much of its consciousness as a social and cultural formation that aesthetic traditions associated with its heyday are becoming more pervasive. But I would argue that it is precisely because spectacular forms can now be divorced from class cultures that they can more easily be sanitised into the virtual realities of mass entertainment.

The second way in which there is a greater sense of uncertainty in contemporary culture stems from a crisis in modernist cultural practice. I have mentioned at several points that the pursuit of realistic modes of representation, which were faithful to the dynamics of different perspectives and the processual character of experience, culminated in a radical interrogation of the practice of representation. It is in this context that it was almost natural for people such as Barthes and Foucault to declare the death of the author.

And not only was the narrative (author-itative) voice destabilised, there were associated aesthetic strategies for disrupting the coherence of the representational stance, and for exploring reflexive devices which constantly sought to subvert any security the audience might feel as spectators (Hutcheon 1989). The significant import of these strategies has been to politicise representation, by which I mean to continually privilege issues of power and exclusion in any programme of representation.

One way of putting this second point more sharply is to say that the consequence of politicising representation is to rob culture of any pretensions to an aura of high status. The use of the term aura reminds us of Benjamin's thesis that the politicisation of culture follows from the pressures of what he called mechanical reproduction or what I will call industries of mass distribution (Benjamin 1970). Culture is therefore snatched from the privileged enclaves of intellectual expertise, and made into what the culturalists have unfortunately come to call the site or terrain of contested meanings. The paradox of the transformation of cultural performance through the application of complex technology is that it generates both global cultural corporations and local oppositional strategies of subversion.

This leads to the third aspect of a destabilisation of cultural meanings, which is a theoretical recognition that politicisation generates a double-edged concern. One aspect is a recognition that texts are as significant for what they leave out as for what they include; while the other is that textual analyses cannot be divorced from the conditions under which they are read, watched, listened to etc. in everyday experience. In both aspects it has been overwhelmingly the impact of feminist theorising and analyses, obviously with particular attention to representations and significations of gender, that have refused the common sense of established social knowledge (see the different collections in Gammon and Marshment 1988 and Roman *et al.* 1988). In the introduction to the latter volume the editors focus the politicisation of collective identity by arguing that gender is both constitutive of social relations based on perceived differences between the sexes, and a way of signifying relationships of power.

While these three processes are quite different they all contribute to what I have called a strong sense of a lack of firm grounding in the formation of cultural meanings. Further consequences which I believe to have followed from these processes are both practical and relate to forms of entertainment, and theoretical, concerning our understanding of culture. The first consequence has been a popular reinvigoration of aesthetics of reception in which aspects of traditional cultural forms have been transformed by technological elaboration. The second is a gradual recognition that culture, in our contemporary (cultural) circumstances, refers to a limited discursive domain. (This is a view towards which I have been working throughout this book.) What this means is that culture is a characteristic set of ways of using (and discourse because that denotes ways of understanding) distinctive cultural forms.

Two further aspects of this conceptualisation are that there may be several ways of using the same cultural resources – that is that there are (or may be) a multiplicity of cultures within a common social environment – and that different individuals and groups at different points in their lives will feel caught up in one or several cultures. Clearly these formulations have to be put permissively as we must expect a variety of degrees of cultural homogeneity between different groups, environments, age-grades and structures of identity. In this approach I am taking the traditional emphasis on culture as a form of life and recognising that there is no longer any reason to assume coherence in different forms of life, or that there are consistent distinctions between different forms.

It may be objected that this way of conceptualising culture is so permissive that the object, culture, disappears. This may indeed, in a way, be the price one has to pay; the cost of a recognition that culture in a triumph of reflexivity is an invention of the cultural imagination. The contours of a cultural formation are as continually being invented as the traditions of national identity or the places of tourist landscapes. This does not mean that any particular culture lacks substance or force; rather that it is in a continuous process of negotiation. It, that is culture as a mode of collective identity, is being played out, performed, in all the ways it provides the terms (that is the meanings) for interaction and experience. I believe this to be an analogous approach to Dorothy Smith's recommendation (1988) that we see femininity as a textually mediated discourse. That is that everyday social relations are mobilised around the texts through which codes of femininity are articulated. The idea of mobilisation is to indicate contest, qualification, subversion and transformation as well as acceptance.

I have previously suggested (1993) that culture is more fruitfully understood as a style rather than an entity or formation and the present approach is meant to be consistent with that suggestion. A style is a characteristic mode of performance and can be used in relation both to a set of cultural objects and to an individual or group's way of using those objects. It is an approximate characterisation and can encompass significant exceptions, modifications and developments through time. It seems to me that this idea of a style is faithful to the social phenomena of destabilised identities in postmodern societies. We have several times had to acknowledge the ways in which personal identity is no longer unified or consistent through time in the fragmentations of modernity; and to the extent that all our local cultures are cast within a metropolitan ambit, identity necessarily becomes as much a reflexive project as any other form of cultural imagination (Giddens 1991).

The idea that a culture is a style is clearly consistent with what I suggested (at the end of the first section) is a paradigmatic emphasis on the importance of life-styles. The argument earlier was that life-styles relate to identity in two ways. First, they serve as a means of social placement, identifying elective communities in a world in which there are no longer stable structures of social identity or status. Secondly, they can act as a means of reference for individuals, a point of comparison that permits evaluation and emulation. Life-styles are therefore interpretive frameworks (ways of justifying or making sense of potentially puzzling performances), that facilitate creative adaptation. If culture is always the bridge between individuals and their collective identities, then life-styles are a particular exemplification of an aesthetics of representation (McRobbie, 1991, reviewing her work says that she has always felt that subcultures should be seen as popular aesthetic movements). Life-styles then provide an appropriately ambiguous, for postmodern society, mediation between individuality and community.

It will be objected that this is an excessively voluntaristic view of culture: by this is meant too great an emphasis on the creative powers of individuals, with insufficient attention being paid to the ways in which culture acts to inscribe meanings. It is true that I am more interested in the practice of social life than more abstract entities, so I tend to write from that perspective, but the account of culture offered here is consistent with a political economy of representation. At several points I have set out my use of a concept of cultural form. I also noted in the previous chapter that my use of cultural forms, in particular through the emphasis on the social organisation of production of different cultural activities in this formulation, can be incorporated into a much broader account of the cultural economy of the postmodern world. In so doing one has to begin with contemporary corporate control of industries of representation.

I have suggested that an important difference between earlier spectacular forms of popular entertainment and more contemporary examples has been the application of complex technology (and that the impetus to invest in technological development has stemmed from disruptions in the grounds of cultural hierarchies). The illusions of simulated reality in both communication and entertainment

are now so much more entrancing because of the powerful technological resources available.

These resources also, however, increase the capital investment in
cultural production. In conjunction with the capital to command
complex distribution networks, enormous advertising budgets as
well as the cost of creative personnel, it is easy to see that there
will be pressures of agglomeration in cultural production. There
will also be political-bureaucratic pressures for dominant national
organisations. The history of mass communication has shown that
national state powers have never been content to leave these
industries unregulated, and so the economic and ideological tra-
jectories of future developments will be strongly inflected by
national conventions on relations between the state and media
industries (on recent British experience see Golding 1992).

These factors in conjunction mean that global communication
and entertainment corporations will effectively oligopolise mass
culture (see Curran and Gurevitch 1991, especially Part 1). In areas,
as diverse as fashion, the huge diversity of musical styles, and all the
forms of narrative imagery, there has been a regression towards a
global culture which is now in some quarters being celebrated as a
defining characteristic of the postmodern world. And this of course
provides the medium for American cultural imperialism, which has
outlasted an era of economic dominance.

It seems likely that the corporate culture of international entertainment will be heavily biased in favour of consensualist values.
And precisely because languages of representation are simultaneously signifying relationships of power, it is inevitable that
corporate understanding of consensualist values will be those that
favour established structures of privilege. The simulated world of
international entertainment will take masculine privileges, Chris-
tianity, white culture, American spectacular imagery, the social
forms of post-industrial societies, and economically deregulated
capitalism as the norms of idealised social arrangements.

This is an ideological agenda which will sometimes be pursued
very shrilly and sometimes from an implicit ideological backdrop
to the construction of 'normality'. There will be continual battles
by those excluded or disadvantaged by this agenda to contest its
terms; battles over particular narrative strategies which will be
affected by a large number of specific considerations for each form,
in each national circumstance, and by each cast of personnel (for
studies of two examples see Roddick 1983 on innovations in one

studio in Hollywood in the 1930s, and Feuer *et al.* 1984 on innovations in network television).

At the same time, we also have to recognise that industries of representation are peculiarly dependent on local ethnicities. There are two reasons for this. The first is that global entertainment corporations are continually driven by a search for new product. Popular entertainment may be structured by the reiteration of certain formulas and genres which provide staple narrative forms, and there may be an endless nostalgic regression in re-cycling previous eras and styles, but even so there will be an overwhelming need for novelty in performances, styles and manners. The history of popular music since the development of cheap recordings as a medium of mass entertainment specifically targeted at youth audiences has shown this clearly.

The second reason is that marketing experience has found it impossible to contain mass audiences. It has proved necessary, and indeed more profitable, to differentiate audiences through a multiplicity of 'narrow-casting' or selective marketing strategies. In effect this means attempting to cater to the specificities of local cultural practice (and local should be understood here as both regionally and socio-structurally patterned).

It would be foolish to pretend that relationships between mass cultural marketing organisations and local cultural practice are likely to be predominant, or even ever, harmonious. As I have said frequently, local cultures will be mobilised by an insistence on defining themselves through modifications or in opposition to dominant cultural agendas.

This can be illustrated by the example of the tourist industry where there is a very large number of finely graded distinctions in locale, accommodation, facilities, and so on. In relation to a relatively specific concern with the environment Urry has distinguished a number of modes of tourist practice, and industry strategies to cater for them, which show well that tourism is a form of entertainment whose customers are frequently seeking to transcend the limitations of that cultural form (1992; see also Ryan 1991).

An important dimension of the troubled relationships between cultural industries and local cultures is the widespread conviction amongst the latter that appropriation for mass marketing entails emasculation. Indeed it seems inevitable that adaptation for the exigencies of mass marketing will mean a dilution of representational force into bland consensualism, or insensitive imperialistic imposition on a local culture, or both. In relation to the latter process it is gratifying to discover that it is by no means always successful. At the time of writing it seems that the attempt to transpose the sanitised utopianism of Disneyland to the environs of Paris has been a commercial failure. Contemporary attempts to adapt to local tastes are seen in journalistic commentaries to be increasingly desperate.

This brings us back to the theme of the active audience which, as I said in the opening chapters, has generated a lot of research in recent years. The initial basis of active audience theories was the influence of hermeneutic arguments in aesthetics stressing the open-ended character of any text (Freund 1987). This influence was succeeded by a more important dissatisfaction with theories of ideological determination which necessarily (at some level) pre-scribed meanings for audiences. (Hall has emphasised that a study such as that by Morley, of family television viewing demolishes monolithic accounts of audiences and television: 'What the mapp-ings reveal, in sum, is the fine-grained interrelationships between meaning, pleasure, use and choice': 1986, p. 10). A third impetus to an interest in the creativity of audiences has been the work of those formulating accounts of postmodern society and their stress on the indeterminacy of representation.

I have indicated that I am rather scornful of the idea that it is a discovery that practice of everyday cultural projects is creative. It is a founding principle of my approach that culture is reflexive in the sense that it is displayed and sustained through everyday occasions of its being invoked. To this should be added, however, that cultural formations will vary in the degree of ritualisation that is char-acteristic of them. Under the postmodern cultural paradigm reflex-ivity is accentuated in such a way that the transience of performance becomes almost the only aesthetic moment (and thus once again the crisis over purpose and meaning in postmodern cultural practice). The idea of ritualisation makes this point clearer.

In a relatively homogeneous, small-scale society with an artisanal economy, cultural forms are likely to be highly ritualised. This will be true both in terms of reiterated content and mode of per-formance, and in terms of the relationships between cultural per-formance and the temporal and spatial organisation of the lived world. This is obviously quite different to all the forms of particip-ation in contemporary popular entertainment in which there is an overwhelming stress on individual appropriation of performance. I do not wish to imply by this distinction that ritual is absent from mass culture. There are rich and varied forms of ritualisation (some of which I have discussed in Chaney 1986), at the level both of global cultural organisations and local cultural practice, but in both cases the individual's relationship to ritual performance is quite different from that characteristic of tradition.

The phrase 'individual appropriation' is meant to be a short way of referring to a combination of technological developments which have facilitated individual control over the time and place of performance, and attitudes which have denied any authority to the text as performed. In the former use I am thinking, of among others, video-players, personal stereos and a variety of electronic editing facilities, while in the latter these technical resources are employed to create new texts and modes of performance (see for example Beadle 1993 on sampling in pop music as a way of constituting new 'texts' from previously published materials).

If we add in computer gaming, multiple television channels and transient grazing through programming, it becomes clearer that individual appropriation as local cultural practice is a form of electronic collage. These collages are composed of fragments drawn from personal odysseys through infinite layers of representation in performance, structured perhaps by what Benjamin called profane illuminations – compelling encounters that momentarily transfigure everyday urban reality (Cohen 1993). And this reference is deliberately meant to remind us of the Surrealist prefiguring of the postmodern paradigm.

The point is that theories of the active audience are but a pale shadow of local cultural practice. Lash is, I think, arguing for the same conclusion although in more technical language when he says: 'The devaluation of meaning in postmodern signification is simultaneously the de-differentiation of signifier and signified' (1990a, p. 194). Drawing upon the semiological tradition (an avenue I have deliberately ignored) which has analysed the functions of different types of signs in representation, and employs a fundamental distinction between signifier and signified, Lash is confirmed in his conclusion by the recent growth in interest in pragmatics and speech act theory in linguistics. These theories stress the constitution of meaning in performance and are consistent with the collapse of firm distinctions between signifier and that which is being referred to. The play of signifiers becomes the domain of experience, and meaning is thereby partial, allusive, transient and irredeemably contextualised.

The more we pursue these arguments the more justified we are, I believe, in maintaining that the postmodern cultural paradigm involves a distinctive rendering of an aesthetics of representation. Traditions of performance and aesthetic concern are undoubtedly drawn upon but in ways that transform the implied interdependence of individual and collective identity. It is the hidden but inescapable presupposition of arbitrariness in both terms of this pairing (individual and culture) that makes their presence a persistent topic (this is a personal version of a more commonly proposed thesis of the aestheticisation of everyday life in postmodern culture, or what Lash calls aesthetic reflexivity: 1993; see also Featherstone 1992). In postmodern culture, culture becomes more explicitly the primary referent of representation.

The logic of this account is that, more forcefully than ever before, cultural objects are not meaningful or valuable in what they are but only in what they can be used to do. We come back to the crisis in postmodern representation I described at the beginning of this section, with the appreciation now that an evaluative framework for the purpose of culture can only be addressed through what I have called local cultural practices. These are not confined to audience practices but refer as well to producers and performers. Faced with global cultural corporations and marketing procedures we are all inscribed in what is likely to be a number of local cultures. In the practice of participating in cultural forms we have all acquired the responsibilities of producing and making meanings.

In my previous book I proposed the metaphor of design as a way to capture the interdependence of purpose and meaning (1993, Chapter 5). A design is conventionally an integrative project in which objects and their function are married together. Design provides for a social aesthetics through a concern with both the composition and construction of the object and the integrity of the project which it exemplifies. I hope it is only a small step to transpose the idea of design from the immediate creativity of producing objects to the usually less self-conscious creativity of representational practice. In this broader sense of design we are offered the possibility of a social aesthetics concerned with both representational practice and the projects that practice exemplifies.

I have been laying the groundwork for a suggestion that in lifestyle we have a concept that functions as a form of meta-design: that is an overarching project within which individual cultural practices are given a form of validity. We obviously do not yet have any sort of developed vocabulary with which to spell out the detailed principles of the social aesthetics I am proposing, but we can, even so, glimpse the possibility of contesting the sense of meaninglessness which I mentioned at the beginning of this section.

I have so far been making some preliminary notes on elements in a political economy of culture. It is important to stress that these points do not just concern what we might call cultural goods. These are performances, texts, images, occasions, and places etc. that have been constituted primarily as entertainments and illuminations. As soon as we begin to think about drawing boundaries around these categories it becomes apparent that it is impossible to make firm distinctions between cultural and other sorts of economic good. Increasingly, as all the variants of postmodern theory emphasise, the most mundanely functional goods will represent some form of style and life-world through their image and to that extent be meaningful in social practice in ways that transcend functional utility. One cannot be innocent of the play of signification, and this is why I have referred quite often to representational practice. A cultural economy consists of the social organisation of the production, marketing and consumption of representations and significations.

I have tried to show that cultural industries will exist at many levels of complexity. I mentioned above several types of cultural goods, and it is clear that there will be even greater variety in ways of sustaining them as productive enterprises. These will vary between state or private patronage, dependence on advertising, ticket sales, royalties, and associated economic activities. There will also be an enormous variety in the social forms of audiences. I am thinking here of factors such as duration – the length of time an audience exists as an identifiable social formation; commitment – the importance that members of an audience attach to their shared enthusiasm; self-consciousness – the extent to which audience membership is central to their collective identity; and cultural capital – the forms of sophistication and expertise involved in different modes of appreciation.

It is in the combination of the variables of industrial size and complexity, different marketing practices and what I can summarise as the type of constituency commanded that we can establish the major contrast between global cultural organisations and local cultural practices. Mediating between the different levels and forms of structural organisation are the multiplicity of cultural forms that provide the languages of representation for cultural goods. This is then the institutional framework within which we have come to urgently and insistently negotiate ways of representing forms of shared identity to ourselves, and the interdependencies as well as contrasts of individual and collective identity. I have argued that these ways of representing have institutionalised popular aesthetics – but what does this mean?

One answer lies in the size and significance of global cultural corporations which, in the number of people they employ, the amount of capital they invest, the revenue they generate and the numbers of people whose interests they attract, far outstrip any other corporate sector. To the extent that these corporations are dealing in mass audiences they are constituting popular concerns and to that extent institutionalising popular aesthetics. A second and more significant answer can be derived from the relationships between global culture and local cultural practices. This latter approach has to be based on my previous argument that an aesthetics of representation has been remodelled in the transitions of later modernity, so that a practical aesthetics can be detected in the interplay of tensions in negotiating cultural levels and concerns.

It has to be remembered that the popular has always been con-sidered as being sold short if it is confined to counting heads (Schiach 1989). The popular is the culture of a community or class largely excluded from dominant themes of representation and evaluation (Burke 1992, 1978; Hall 1981). There has always been an ironic consciousness in popular discourse, a consciousness of presence and absence, of exclusion and marginality. In all the ways that the social forms of community and class are being re-staged in precisely those relationships between global and local we can expect the 'tone' of local experience to retain that ironic sense of playful complicity. This is not saying the same as Fiske (1989a) that the popular is displayed only in those moments of struggle and resistance against corporate hegemony. That seems to me to have far too much of the residual romanticism of seeking instances of class war. I am saying, though, that the popular is an inarticulate sense of the arbitrariness of social forms. It is in this sense of ironic transience that postmodernism has institutionalised popular aesthetics.

References

Abercrombie, N. (1990) 'Popular culture and ideological effects', in N. Abercrombie, S. Lash and B.S. Turner (eds): *Dominant Ideologies*, Unwin Hyman, London.

Adam, B. (1990) *Time and Social Theory*, Polity Press, Cambridge.

Adorno, T. (1991) *The Culture Industry: Selected essays on mass culture*, Routledge, ed. J. Bernstein, London.

Agnew, J.A. (1993) 'Representing space: space, scale and culture in social science', in Duncan and Ley (1993).

Agnew, J.A. and Duncan, J. (1989) *The Power of Place: Bringing together geographical and sociological imaginations*, Unwin Hyman, Boston.

Albrecht, M.C., Barnett, J.H. and Griff, M. (eds) (1970) *The Sociology of Art and Literature: A reader*, Duckworth, London.

Albrow, M. and King, E. (eds) (1990) *Globalization, Knowledge and Society*, Sage, London.

Anderson, B. (1983) *Imagined Communities: Reflections on the origin and spread of nationalism*, Verso Books, London.

Ang, I. (1985) *Watching 'Dallas': Soap operas and the melodramatic imagination*, Methuen, London.

Appadurai, A. (1990) 'Disjuncture and difference in the global cultural economy', *Public Culture* 2(5).

Archer, M. (1988) *Culture and Agency: The place of culture in social theory*, Cambridge University Press, Cambridge.

Ardener, S. (ed.) (1981) *Women and Space: Ground rules and social maps*, Croom Helm, London.

Avery, R.K. and Eason, D. (eds) (1991) *Critical Perspectives on Media and Society*, Guilford Press, New York.

Bakhtin, M.M. (1969) *Rabelais and His World*, MIT Press, Cambridge Mass.

Balio, T. (ed.) (1990) *Hollywood in the Age of Television*, Unwin Hyman, Boston.

Barr, C. (1980) *Ealing Studios*, Cameron and Tayleur, London.

Barrett, M., Corrigan, P., Kuhn, A. and Wolff, J. (eds) (1979a) *Ideology and Cultural Production*, Croom Helm, London.

—— (1979b) 'Representation and cultural production', ibid.

Barth, G. (1980) *City People: The rise of modern city culture in nineteenth century America*, Oxford University Press, New York.

Barthes, R. (1977) 'The Death of the Author', in S. Heath (ed.) *Image-Music-Text*, Fontana Books, London.

Bathrick, S.K. (1990) 'The Female Colossus: The body as facade and threshold', in Gaines and Herzog (1990).

Baudrillard, J. (1983a) *Simulations*, Semiotext(e), New York.

—— (1983b) *In the Shadow of the Silent Majorities*, Semiotext(e), New York.

—— (1988) *America*, Verso Books, London.

Bauman, Z. (1989) *Modernity and the Holocaust*, Polity Press, Cambridge.

—— (1990) *Legislators and Interpreters: On modernity, postmodernity and intellectuals*, Polity Press, Cambridge.

—— (1992) Intimations of Postmodernity Routledge, London.

Baxandall, M. (1972) *Painting and Experience in Fifteenth Century Italy: A primer in the social history of pictorial style*, Oxford University Press, London.

Beadle, J.J. (1993) *Will Pop Eat Itself? Pop music in the sound-bite era*, Faber and Faber, London.

Beck, U. (1992) *The Risk Society*, Sage, London.

Becker, H.S. (1982) *Art Worlds*, University of California Press, Berkeley.

Bell, D. (1976) *Cultural Contradictions of Capitalism*, Heinemann, London.

Benjamin, W. (1970) 'The work of art in the age of mechanical reproduction', in *Illuminations*, Cape, London.

—— (1973) *Charles Baudelaire*, New Left Books, London.

Bennett, T. (1986a) 'Introduction: popular culture and "the turn to Gramsci"' in Bennett *et al.* (1986).

—— (1986b) 'The politics of the "popular" and popular culture', in Bennett *et al.* (1986).

—— (ed.) (1990) *Popular Fiction: Technology, ideology, production, reading*, Routledge, London.

Bennett, T., and Woollacott, J. (1987) *James Bond and Beyond: Fiction, ideology and social process*, Macmillan, London.

Bennett, T., Martin, G., Mercer, C. and Woollacott, J. (eds) (1981) *Culture, Ideology and Social Process*, Batsford, London.

Bennett, T., Mercer, C., and Woollacott, J. (eds) (1986) *Popular Culture and Social Relations*, Open University Press, Milton Keynes.

Berger, A.A. (1992) *Popular Culture Genres: Theories and texts*, Sage, London.

Berger, J. (1973) *Ways of Seeing*, BBC Books, London.

Berger, P.L. and Luckmann, T. (1967) *The Social Construction of Reality*, Allen Lane, London.

Berman, M. (1983) '*All That Is Solid Melts Into Air*',: *The experience, of modernity*, Verso Books, London.

—— (1992) 'Why modernism still matters', in Lash and Friedman (1992).

Bernstein, B. (1971) *Class, Codes and Control*, Routledge and Kegan Paul, London.

Best, S. and Kellner, D. (1991) *Postmodern Theory and Critical Interrogations*, Macmillan, London.

Bhaba, H.K. (ed.) (1990) *Nation and Narration*, Routledge, London.

Billington, R. *et al.* (1991) *Culture and Society: A sociology of culture*, Macmillan, London.

Bonner, F., Goodman, L., Allen, R., Janes, L. and King, C. (eds) (1992) *Imagining Women: Cultural representations and gender*, Polity Press, Cambridge.

Bourdieu, P. (1977) *Outline of a Theory of Practice*, Cambridge University Press, Cambridge.

—— (1984) *Distinction: A social critique of the judgement of taste*, Routledge and Kegan Paul, London.

—— (1991) *Language and Symbolic Power*, Polity Press, Cambridge.

Bourdieu, P. and Passeron, J-C. (1990) *Reproduction in Education, Society and Culture*,2nd edn, Sage, London.

Bowlby, R. (1985) *Just Looking: Consumer culture in Dreiser, Gissing and Zola*, Methuen, London.

Boyes, G. (1993) *The Imagined Village: Culture, ideology and the English folksong revival*, Manchester University Press, Manchester.

Braden, S. (1978) *Artists and People*, Routledge and Kegan Paul, London.

Brake, M. (1985) *Comparative Youth Culture: The sociology of youth culture and youth subcultures in America, Britain and Canada*, Routledge, London.

Brennan, T. (ed.) (1989) *Between Feminism and Psychoanalysis*, Routledge, London.

Brewer, J. and Porter, R. (eds) (1992) *Consumption and the World of Goods*, Routledge, London.

Brown, M.E. (ed.) (1989) *Television and Women's Culture: The politics of the popular*, Sage. London.

Buck, P.A. (1992) 'Crisis as spectacle: tabloid news and the politics of outrage', in M. Reboy and B. Dagenais (eds) *Media Crisis and Democracy*, Sage, London.

Buck-Morss, S. (1989) *The Dialectics of Seeing: Walter Benjamin and the Arcades project*, MIT Press, Cambridge, Mass.

Burke, P. (1978) *Popular Culture in Early Modern Europe*, Temple Smith, London.

—— (1992) 'We, the people: popular culture and popular identity in modern Europe', in Lash and Friedman (1992).

Burns, E. and Burns, T. (eds) (1973) *Sociology of Literature and Drama*, Penguin Books, London.

Burns, T. (1977a) *The BBC: Public institution and private world*, Macmillan, London.

—— (1977b) 'The organisation of public opinion', in Curran *et al.* (1977).

Button, G. (ed.) (1991) *Ethnomethodology and the Human Sciences*, Cambridge University Press, Cambridge.

Calhoun, C. (ed.) (1992) *Habermas and the Public Sphere*, MIT Press, Cambridge, Mass.

—— (1993) 'Postmodernism as pseudo-history', *Theory, Culture and Society*, 10(1).

Callinicos, A. (1989) *Against Postmodernism: A Marxist critique*, Polity Press, Cambridge.

Carey, J.W. (ed.) (1988) *Media Myths and Narratives: Television and the press*, Sage, London.

Carey John (1992) *The Intellectuals and the Masses: Pride and prejudice among the literary intelligentsia 1880–1939*, Faber and Faber, London.

Carter, E. (1984) 'Alice in the Consumer Wonderland', in McRobbie and Nava (1984).

Chafee, L. (1993) 'Dramaturgical politics: the culture and ritual of demonstrations in Argentina', *Media,Culture and Society*, 15(1).

Chambers, I. (1985) *Urban Rhythms: Pop music and popular culture*, Macmillan, London.

—— (1990) *Border Dialogues: Journeys in Postmodernity*, Routledge, London.

Chanan, M. (1979) *The Dream that Kicks: The prehistory and early years of cinema in Britain*, Routledge and Kegan Paul, London.

Chaney, D. (1972) *Processes of Mass Communication*, Macmillan, London.

—— (1977) 'Fictions in mass entertainment', in J. Curran *et al.* (1977).

—— (1979) *Fictions and Ceremonies: Representations of popular experience*, Edward Arnold, London.

—— (1983a) 'A symbolic mirror of ourselves', *Media, Culture and Society*, 5(2).

—— (1983b) 'The department store as cultural form', *Theory, Culture and Society*, 1(3).

—— (1986) 'The symbolic form of ritual in mass communication', in Golding *et al.* (1986).

—— (1988) 'Photographic truths', *Social Discourse/Discours Social*, 1(3): 397–422.

—— (1990) 'Subtopia in Gateshead: the MetroCentre as cultural form', *Theory, Culture and Society*, 7(4).

—— (1993) *Fictions of Collective Life: Public drama in late modern culture*, Routledge, London.

Clark, J. *et al.* (1990) *Anthony Giddens: Consensus and controversy*, Falmer Press. London.

Clarke, J. and Critcher, C. (1985) *The Devil Makes Work: Leisure in capitalist Britain*, Macmillan, London.

Clarke, J., Critcher, C. and Johnson, R. (eds) (1979) *Working Class Culture: Studies in history and theory*, Hutchinson, London.

Clifford, J. and Marcus, G.E. (eds) (1986) *Writing Culture: The poetics and politics of ethnography*, a California University Press, Berkeley.

Clover, C.J. (1992) *Men, Women and Chainsaws: Gender in the modern horror film*, British Film Institute, London.

Cohen, A.P. (ed.) (1986) *Symbolising Boundaries: Identity and diversity in British cultures*, Manchester University Press, Manchester.

Cohen, M. (1993) *Profane Illumination: Walter Benjamin and the Paris of Surrealist revolution*, University of California Press, Berkeley.

Cohen, S. (1985) *Visions of Social Control*, Polity Press, Cambridge.

—— (1987) *Folk Devils and Moral Panics: The Creation of Mods and Rockers*, 3rd edn, Basil Blackwell, Oxford.

Cohen, S. and Taylor, L. (1974) *Psychological Survival*, Penguin Books, London.

Cohen, S. and Young, J. (eds) (1971) *Images of Deviance*, Penguin Books, London.

Collins, J. (1989) *Uncommon Cultures: Popular culture and postmodernism*, Routledge, London.

Collins, R., Curran, J., Garnham, N., Scannell, P., Schlesinger, P. and Sparks, C. (eds) (1986) *Media, Culture and Society: A critical reader*, Sage, London.

Colls, R. (1977) *The Collier's Rant*, Croom Helm, London.

Connor, S. (1991) *Postmodernist Culture: An introduction to theories of the contemporary*, Basil Blackwell, Oxford.

Corner, J. (1986) 'Codes and cultural analysis', in Collins *et al.* (1986).

—— (ed.) (1991) *Popular Television in Britain: Studies in cultural history*, British Film Institute, London.

Corrigan, P. (1979) *Schooling the Smash Street Kids*, Macmillan, London.

Couvares, F.G. (1984) *The Remaking of Pittsburgh: Class and culture in an industrialising city 1877–1919*, State University of New York Press, Albany, NY.

Crane, D. (1992) *The Production of Culture: Media and the urban arts*, Sage, London.

Crapanzo, V. (1992) *Hermes' Dilemma and Hamlet's Desire: On the epistemology of interpretation*, Harvard University Press, Cambridge, Mass.

Cumberbatch, G. and Howitt, D. (1989) *A Measure of Uncertainty: The effects of mass media*, John Libbey, London.

Cunningham, H. (1980) *Leisure in the Industrial Revolution*, Croom Helm, London.

Curran, J. and Gurevitch, M. (eds) (1991) *Mass Media and Society*, Edward Arnold, London.

Curran, J. and Seaton, J. (1992) *Power without Responsibility: The press and broadcasting in Britain*, 4th edn, Fontana, London.

Curran, J., Gurevitch, M. and Woollacott, J. (eds) (1977) *Mass Communication and Society*, Edward Arnold, London.

Curran, J., Smith, A. and Wingate, P. (eds) (1987) *Impacts and Influences*, Methuen, London.

Dahlgren, R. and Sparks, C. (eds) (1991) *Communication and Citizenship*, Routledge, London.

Daniels, S. (1993) *Fields of Vision: Landscape imagery and national identity in England and the United States*, Polity Press, Cambridge.

Daniels, S. and Cosgrove, D. (1993) 'Spectacle and text: landscape metaphors in cultural geography', in Duncan and Ley (1993).

Darnton, R. (1984) *The Great Cat Massacre and Other Episodes in French Cultural History*, Basic Books, New York.

Davidoff, L. and Hall, C. (1987) *Family Fortunes: Men and women of the English middle class 1780–1850*, Hutchinson, London.

Davis, F. (1992) *Fashion, Culture, and Identity*, University of Chicago Press, London.

Davis, H. and Walton, P. (eds) (1983) *Language, Image and Media*, Basil Blackwell, Oxford.

Dayan, D. and E. Katz (1987) 'Performing media events', in Curran *et al.* (1987).

—— (1988) 'Articulating consensus: the ritual and rhetoric of media events', in J.C. Alexander (ed.) *Durkheimian Sociology: Cultural studies*, Cambridge University Press, Cambridge.

Denning, M. (1987) *Mechanic Accents: Dime novels and working class culture in America*, Verso, London.

Denzin, N.K. (1992) *Symbolic Interactionism and Cultural Studies: The politics of interpretation*, Basil Blackwell, Oxford.

Dodd, P. and Colls, R. (eds) (1985)*The Idea of Englishness: National, identity in arts, politics and society 1880–1920*, Croom Helm, London.

Donajgrodski, J.P. (ed.) (1982) *Social Conflict in Nineteenth Century Britain*, Croom Helm, London.

Downes, D. and Rock, P. (1988) *Understanding Deviance*, 2nd edn, Clarendon Press, Oxford.

Duncan, J. and Ley, D. (eds) (1993) *Place/Culture/Representation*, Routledge, London.

Dundes, A. (1977) 'Jokes and covert language attitudes', *Language in Society*, 6(2).

Dunning, E. and Rojek, C. (eds) (1992) *Sport and Leisure in the Civilising Process: Critique and counter-critique*, Macmillan, London.

Dyer, R. (1987) *Heavenly Bodies: Film stars and society*, Macmillan, London.

Eco, U. (1986) *Faith in Fakes: Travels in hyperreality*, Secker and Warburg, London.

Eisenstein, E.L. (1993) *The Printing Revolution in Early Modern Europe*, Cambridge University Press, Cambridge.

Eldridge, J. (ed.) (1993) *Getting the Message: News, truth and power*, Routledge, London.

Elias, N. (1978) *The Civilising Process Vol.1: The History of Manners*, Basil Blackwell, Oxford.

—— (1982) *The Civilising Process Vol. 2: State Formation and Civilization*, Basil Blackwell, Oxford.

Elias, N. and Dunning, E. (1986) *The Quest for Excitement: Sociological essays on sport and leisure*, Basil Blackwell, Oxford.

Elliott, P.R.C. (1972); *The Making of a Television Series*, Constable, London.

Ellis, J. (1982) *Visible Fictions: Cinema, television and video*, Routledge, London.

Enzensberger, H.M. (1970) 'Constituents of a theory of the media', *New Left Review*, 64.

Ericson, R.V., Banarek, P.M., and Chan, J.B.L. (1991) *Representing Order: Crime, law and justice in news media* Open University Press, Milton Keynes.

Espinosa, P. (1982) 'The audience in the text: ethnographic observations of a Hollywood story conference', *Media, Culture and Society*, 4(1).

Evans, R. (1982) *The Fabrication of Virtue: English prison architecture 1750–1840*, Cambridge University Press, Cambridge.

Ewen, S. (1988) *All Consuming Images: The politics of style in contemporary culture*, Basic Books, New York.

Falk, P. (1993) 'The representation of presence: outlining the anti-aesthetics of pornography', *Theory, Culture and Society*, 10(2).

Farrar, Hyde A. (1990) *An American Vision: Far western landscape and national culture 1820–1920*, New York University Press, New York.

Featherstone, M. (ed.) (1990) *Global Culture: Nationalism, globalization and modernity*, Sage, London.

—— (1991) *Consumer Culture and Postmodernism*, Sage, London.

—— (1992) 'Postmodernism and the aestheticization of everyday life', in Lash and Friedman (1992).

Featherstone, M., Hepworth, M. and Turner, B.S. (eds) (1991) *The Body: Social process and cultural theory*, Sage, London.

Ferguson, M. (1982) *Forever Feminine: Women's magazines and the cult of femininity*, Heinemann, London.

—— (ed.) (1990) *Public Communication – the New Imperatives*, Sage, London.

Feuer, J., Kerr, P. and Vahimayi, T. (eds) (1984) *MTM: "Quality Television"*, British Film Institute, London.

Finkelstein, J. (1991) *The Fashioned Self*, Polity Press, Cambridge.

Finlay, M. (1990) *The Potential of Modern Discourse: Musil, Peirce and perturbation*, Indiana University Press, Bloomington.

Fishman, M. (1980) *Manufacturing the News*, Texas University Press, Austin.

Fiske, J. (1989a) *Understanding Popular Culture*, Unwin Hyman, London.

—— (1989b) *Reading Popular Culture*, Unwin Hyman, London.

Foster, H. (ed.) (1986) *Post Modern Culture*, Pluto Press, London.

Foucault, M. (1976) *The Birth of the Clinic: An archaeology of medical perception*, Tavistock Press, London.

—— (1977) *Discipline and Punish: The birth of the prison*, Allen Lane, London.

—— (1986) 'What is an author?', in Rabinow (1986).

Frankenberg, R. (ed.) (1992) *Time, Health and Medicine*, Sage, London.

Franklin, S. *et al.* (1992) 'Feminism and cultural studies: pasts, presents and futures', in P. Scannell *et al.* (1992).

Freund, E. (1987) *The Return of the Reader: Reader-response criticism*, Methuen, London.

Frisby, D. (1985) *Fragments of Modernity: Theories of modernity in the, work of Simmel, Kracauer and Benjamin*, Polity Press, Cambridge.

Frith, S. (1983) *Sound Effects: Youth, leisure and the politics of* rock Constable, London.

Frith, S. and Horne, H. (1987) *Art into Pop*, Methuen, London.

Gaines, J. (1990) 'Introduction: fabricating the female body', in Gaines and Herzog (1990).

Gaines, J. and Herzog, C. (eds) (1990) *Fabrications: Costume and the female body*, Routledge, London.

Gallagher, C. and Laquer, T. (eds) (1987) *The Making of the Modern Body: Sexuality and society in the nineteenth century*, University of California Press, Berkeley.

Gallop, J. (1982) *Feminism and Psychoanalysis: The daughter's seduction*, Macmillan, London.

Gammon, L. and Marshment, M. (eds) (1988) *The Female Gaze*, Verso Books, London.

Gane, M. (1991a) *Baudrillard: Critical and fatal theory*, Routledge, London.

—— (1991b) *Baudrillard's Bestiary: Baudrillard and culture*, Routledge, London.

—— (ed.) (1993) *Baudrillard Live: Selected interviews*, Routledge, London.

Gans, H. (1974) *Popular Culture and High Culture*, Basic Books, New York.

Garber, M., Matlock, J. and Walkowitz, R.L. (eds) (1993) *Media Spectacles*, Routledge, London.

Garnham, N. (1986) 'The media and the public sphere', in Golding *et al.* (1986).

Geertz, C. (1973) *The Interpretation of Cultures*, Hutchinson, London.

—— (1983) *Local Knowledge: Further essays in interpretive, anthropology*, Basic Books, New York.

Gellner, E. (1983) *Nations and Nationalism*, Basil Blackwell, Oxford.

Geraghty, C. (1991) *Women and Soap Opera*, Polity Press, Cambridge.

—— (1992) 'British soaps in the 1980s', in Strinati and Wagg (1992).

Giddens, A. (1984) *The Constitution of Society: Outline of the theory of structuration*, Polity Press, Cambridge.

—— (1990) *The Consequences of Modernity*, Polity Press, Cambridge.

—— (1991) *On Modernity and Self-Identity: Self and society in the late modern age*, Polity Press, Cambridge.

—— (1992) *Transformation of Intimacy: Love, sexuality and eroticism in modern societies*, Polity Press, Cambridge.

—— (1993) 'Introduction', to Werlen (1993).

Gilroy, P. (1987) *There Ain't No Black in the Union Jack*, Hutchinson, London.

Girouard, M. (1985) *Cities and People: A social and architectural*, history Yale University Press, New Haven, Conn.

Giroux, H., Simon, R. and contributors (1989) *Popular Culture, Schooling and Everyday Life*, Bergin and Garvey, Mass.

Gitlin, T. (1978) 'Media sociology: the dominant paradigm', *Theory and Society*, 6(3).

Glasgow University Media Group (1976) *Bad News*, Routledge, London.

—— (1982) *More Bad News*, Routledge, London.

Gledhill, C. (ed.) (1987) *Home Is Where The Heart Is: Studies in melodrama and the women's film*, British Film Institute, London.

—— (ed.) (1991) *Stardom: Industry of desire*, Routledge, London.

Goffman, E. (1968) *Asylums: Essays on the social situation of mental patients and other inmates*, Penguin Books, London.

—— (1977) *Gender Advertisements*, GMacmillan, London.

—— (1981) *Forms of Talk*, Basil Blackwell, Oxford.

Golby, J.M. and Purdue, A.W. (1984) *The Civilization of the Crowd: Popular culture in England 1750–1900*, Batsford, London.

Golding, P. (1992) 'Communicating capitalism: resisting and re-structuring state ideology – the case of Thatcherism', *Media, Culture and Society*, 14(4).

Golding, P. and Murdock, G. (1991) 'Culture, communications and political economy', in Curran and Gurevitch (1991).

Golding, P., Murdock, G. and Schlesinger, P. (eds) (1986) *Communicating, Politics: Mass communications and the political process*, Leicester University Press, Leicester.

Gottdiener, M. (1982) 'Disneyland: a utopian urban space', *Urban Life*, 2(2).

Gouldner, A.W. (1976) *The Dialectic of Ideology and Technology: The origins, gammar, and future of ideology*, Seabury Press, New York.

Gregory, D. (1989) 'Presences and absences: time–space relations and structuration theory', in D. Held and J.B. Thompson (eds) *Social Theory of Modern Societies: Anthony Giddens and his critics*, Cambridge University Press, Cambridge.

Grossberg, L. (1986) 'On postmodernism and articulation: an interview with Stuart Hall', *Journal of Communication Inquiry*, 10(2).

—— (1992) *We Gotta Get Out of This Place: Popular, culture and popular conservatism*, Routledge, London.

Grossberg, L, Nelson, C. and Treichler, P. (eds) (1992) *Cultural Studies*, Routledge, London.

Guttman, A. (1978) *From Ritual to Record: The nature of modern sports*, Columbia University Press, New York.

—— (1986) *Sports Spectators*, Columbia University Press, New York.

Habermas, J. (1989) *The Structural Transformation of the Public Sphere*, Poliy Press, Cambridge.

Hall, S. (1972) 'The determinations of news photographs', *Working Papers in Cultural Studies*, No. 3.

—— (1980) 'Cultural studies: two paradigms', *Media, Culture and Society*, 2(1).

—— (1981) 'Notes on deconstructing "the popular"' in R. Samuel (ed.) *People's History and Socialist Theory*, Routledge and Kegan Paul, London.

—— (1986) 'Introduction', to D. Morley *Family Television: Cultural power and domestic leisure*, Comedia, London.

—— (1991) 'The local and the global: globalization and ethnicity'; and 'Old and new identities, old and new ethnicities', in King (1991b).

Hall, S. and Jacques, M. (eds) (1989) *New Times*, Lawrence and Wishart, London.

Hall, S. and Jefferson, T. (eds) (1976) *Resistance through Rituals*, Hutchinson, London.

Hall, S. and Whannel, P. (1964) *The Popular Arts*, Hutchinson, London.

Hargreaves, D. (1967) *Social Relations in a Secondary School*, Routledge and Kegan Paul, London.

Hall, S., Critcher, C., Jefferson, T., Clarke, J. and Roberts, B. (1978) *Policing the Crisis: Mugging, the state and law and order*, Macmillan, London.

Hall, S., Hobson, D., Lowe, A. and Willis, P. (eds) (1980) *Culture, Media, Language*, Hutchinson, London.

Hargreaves, D. *et al.* (1975) *Deviance in Classrooms*, Routledge and Kegan Paul, London.

Hargreaves, J. (1986) *Sport, Power and Culture: A social and historical analysis of popular sports in Britain*, Polity Press, Cambridge.
Harris, D. (1992) *From Class Struggle to the Politics of Pleasure: The effects of Gramscianism on cultural studies*, Routledge, London.
Harrison, M. (1988) *Crowds and History: Mass Phenomena in English Towns 1790–1835*, Cambridge University Press, Cambridge.
Harvey, D. (1989) *The Condition of Postmodernity*, Basil Blackwell, Oxford.
Hawkes, T. (1977) *Structuralism and Semiotics*, Methuen, London.
Hebdige, D. (1979) *Subculture: The meaning of style*, Methuen, London.
—— (1988) *Hiding in the Light: On images and things*, Routledge, London.
—— (1992) 'Digging for Britain: an excavation in seven parts', in Strinati and Wagg (1992).
Henderson, L. (1993) 'Justify our love: Madonna and the politics of queer sex', in Schwichtenberg (1993).
Hewison, R. (1987) *The Heritage Industry: Britain in a climate of decline*, Methuen, London.
Hobsbawm, E. (1990) *Nations and Nationalism since 1780: Programme, myth, reality*, Cambridge University Press, Cambridge.
Hobsbawm, E. and Ranger, T. (eds) (1983) *The Invention of Tradition*, Cambridge University Press, Cambridge.
Hobson, D. (1982) *'Crossroads': The drama of a soap opera*, Methuen, London.
Hoggart, R. (1957) *The Uses of Literacy*, Chatto and Windus, London.
Holt, R. (1989) *Sport and the British: A modern history*, Clarendon Press, Oxford.
Horkheimer, M. and Adorno, T.W. (1972) 'The culture industry', in *Dialectic of Enlightenment*, Herder and Herder, New York.
Hunt, L. (ed.) (1989a) *The New Cultural History*, University of California Press, Berkeley.
—— (1989b) 'Introduction: history, culture and text', ibid.
Hutcheon, L. (1989) *Politics of Postmodernism*, Routledge, London.
Huyssen, A. (1986) *After the Great Divide: Modernism, mass culture, postmodernism*, Indiana University Press, Bloomington.
Inglis, F. (1988) *Popular Culture and Political Power*, St Martin's Press, New York.
Jackson, P. (1992) *Maps of Meaning*, Routledge, London.
Jackson Lears, T.J. (1985) 'The concept of cultural hegemony: problems and possibilities', *American Historical Review*, 90(3).
Jameson, F. (1991) *Postmodernism, or the Cultural Logic of Late Capitalism*, Verso Books, London.
Jay, M. (1973) *The Dialectical Imagination: A history of the Frankfurt School and the Institute of Social Research, 1923–1950*, Heinemann, London.
Jenkins, H. (1992) *Textual Poachers: Television fans and participatory culture*, Routledge, London.
Jenks, C. (ed.) (1993) *Cultural Reproduction*, Routledge, London.
Johnston, R.J. (1991) *A Question of Place: Exploring the practice of human geography*, Basil Blackwell, Oxford.
Kappeler, S. (1986) *The Pornography of Representation*, Polity Press, Cambridge.

Karp, I. and Lavine, S. (eds) (1991) *Exhibiting Cultures: The poetics and politics of museum display*, Smithsonian Institute, Washington, DC.

Karp, I., Kreamer, C.M. and Lavine, S.D. (eds) (1992) *Museums and Communities: The politics of public culture*, Smithsonian Institute, Washington, DC.

Katz, C. and Monk, J. (eds) (1993) *Full Circles: Geographies of women over the life-course*, Routledge, London.

Katz, E. and Lazarsfeld, P. (1956) *Personal Influence*, Free Press, Glencoe, Illinois.

Keith, M. and Pile, S. (eds) (1993) *Place and the Politics of Identity*, Routledge, London.

Kendrick, W. (1987) *The Secret Museum: Pornography in modern culture*, Viking, New York.

Kern, S. (1983) *The Culture of Time and Space, 1880–1918*, Harvard University Press, Cambridge Mass.

King, A.D. (1991a) 'Introduction', in King (1991b).

—— (ed.) (1991b) *Culture, Globalisation and the World System*, Macmillan, London.

Korr, C.P. (1990) 'A different kind of success: West Ham United and the creation of tradition and community', in R. Holt (ed.) *Sport and the Working Class in Modern Britain*, Manchester University Press, Manchester.

Kristeva, J. (1993) *Nations without Nationalism*, Columbia University Press, New York.

Kuhn, A. (1985) *The Power of the Image: Essays on representation and sexuality*, Routledge and Kegan Paul, London.

Kuhn, T. (1970) *The Structure of Scientific Revolutions*, Chicago University Press, Chicago.

LaCapra, D. and Kaplan, S.L. (eds) (1982) *Modern European Intellectual History: Reappraisals and new perspectives*, Cornell University Press, New York.

Laing, S. (1986) *Representations of Working Class Life 1957–1964*, Macmillan, London.

Lash, S. (1988) 'Discourse or figure? Postmodernism as a regime of signification', *Theory, Culture and Society*, 7 (2–3).

—— (1990a) *Sociology of Postmodernism*, Routledge, London.

—— (1990b) 'Learning from Leipzig – or politics in the semiotic society *Theory, Culture and Society*, 7(4).

—— (1993) 'Reflexive modernization: the aesthetic dimension', *Theory, Culture and Society*, 10(1).

Lash, S. and Friedman, J. (eds) (1992) *Modernity and Identity*, Basil Blackwell, Oxford.

Leiss, W., Kline, S. and Jhally, S. (1986) *Social Communication in Advertising*, Methuen, London.

Le Mahieu, D.L. (1988) *A Culture for Democracy: Mass communication and the cultivated mind in Britain between the wars*, Clarendon Press, Oxford.

Levine, L.W. (1988) *Highbrow/Lowbrow: The emergence of cultural hierarchy in America*, Harvard University Press, Cambridge, Mass.

Lewis, L.A. (ed.) (1992) *The Adoring Audience: Fan culture and the popular media*, Routledge, London.

Long, E. (1991) 'Feminism and cultural studies', in Avery and Eason (1991).

Lull, J. (1990) *Inside Family Viewing: Ethnographic research on television's audience*, Routledge, London.

—— (ed.) (1992) *Popular Music and Communication*, 2nd edn, Sage, London.

Lury, C. (1992) 'Popular culture and the mass media', in R. Bocock and K. Thompson (eds) *Social and Cultural Forms of Modernity*, Polity Press, Cambridge.

MacAloon, J.J. (1981) *This Great Symbol: Pierre de Coubertin and the origins of the modern Olympic Games*, University of Chicago Press, Chicago.

MacCannell, D. (1973) 'Staged authenticity: arrangements of social space in tourist settings', *American Sociological Review*, 79 (5).

—— (1977) *The Tourist: A new theory of the leisure class*, Macmillan, London.

—— (1992) *Empty Meeting Grounds: The tourist papers*, Routledge, London.

McGregor, G. and White, R.S. (eds) (1986) *The Art of Listening: The creative hearer in language, literature and popular culture*, Croom Helm, London.

McGuigan, J. (1992) *Cultural Populism*, Routledge, London.

McLuhan, M. (1964) *Understanding Media*, Routledge and Kegan Paul, London.

McQuail, D. (1987) *Mass Communication Theory: An introduction*, 2nd edn, Sage, London.

McRobbie, A. (ed.) (1989) *Zoot Suits and Second-Hand Dresses*, Macmillan, London.

—— (1991) *Feminism and Youth Culture: From 'Jackie' to 'Just Seventeen'*, Macmillan, London.

McRobbie, A. and Nava, M. (eds) (1984) *Gender and Generation*, Macmillan, London.

Malcolmson, R.W. (1973) *Popular Recreations in English Society 1700–1850*, Cambridge University Press, Cambridge.

Mandziuk, R.M. (1993) 'Feminist politics and postmodern seductions: Madonna and the struggle for postmodern articulation', in Schwichtenberg (1993).

Manning, P. (1992) *Erving Goffman and Modern Sociology*, Polity Press, Cambridge.

Marcus, G. (1989) *Lipstick Traces: A secret history of the twentieth century*, Secker and Warburg, London.

Marin, L. (1984) *Utopics: Spatial play*, Humanities Press, Atlantic Highlands, NJ.

Martin, B. (1981) *A Sociology of Contemporary Cultural Change*, Basil Blackwell, Oxford.

May, L. (1980) *Screening out the Past: The birth of mass culture and the motion picture industry*, Oxford University Press, New York.

Melly, G. (1970) *Revolt into Style: The pop arts in Britain*, Allen Lane, London.

Mercer, C. (1986) 'Complicit pleasures', in Bennett *et al.* (1986).

Merelman, R.M. (1984) *Making Something of Ourselves: On culture and politics in the United States*, University of California Press, Berkeley.

Meyrowitz, J. (1985) *No Sense of Place: The impact of electronic media on social behavior*, Oxford University Press, New York.

Middleton, D. and Edwards, D. (eds) (1990) *Collective Remembering*, Sage, London.

Miller, M.B. (1981) *The Bon Marché: Bourgeois culture and the department store, 1869–1920*, Princeton University Press, New Jersey.

Mills, C. (1993) 'Myths and meanings of gentrification', in Duncan and Ley (1993).

Minihan, J. (1977) *The Nationalisation of Culture: The development of state subsidies to the arts in Great Britain*, Hamish Hamilton, London.

Modleski, T. (1984) *Loving with a Vengeance: Mass-produced fantasies for women*, Methuen, London.

Morley, D. (1992) *Television, Audiences and Cultural Studies*, Routledge, London.

Morley, D. and Robins, K. (1989) 'Spaces of identity: communication technologies and the reconfiguration of Europe', *Screen*, 20(4).

—— (1990) 'No place like *Heimat*', *New Formations*, 12.

—— (1992) 'Techno-Orientalism', *New Formations*, 16.

Morris, M. (1988) 'Things to do with shopping centres', in S. Sheridan (ed.) *Grafts: Feminist cultural criticism*, Verso Books, London.

Murdock, G. (1993) *The Battle for Television: Private pleasures and public goods*, Macmillan, London.

Naremore, J. and Brantlinger, P. (eds) (1991) *Modernity and Mass Culture*, Indiana University Press, Bloomington.

Nava, M. (1992) *Changing Cultures: Feminism, youth and consumerism*, Sage, London.

Neale, S. (1985) *Cinema and Technology: Image, sound and colour*, Macmillan, London.

Negrin, L. (1993) 'On the museum's ruins: a critical appraisal', *Theory Culture and Society*, 10(1).

Negus, K. (1993) *Producing Pop: Culture and conflict in the popular music industry*, Edward Arnold, London.

Nicholson, L. (ed.) (1990) *Feminism/Postmodernism*, Routledge, London.

Nochimson, M. (1992) *No End to Her: Soap opera and the female subject*, University of California Press, Berkeley.

Olszewska, A. and Roberts, K. (eds) (1989) *Leisure and Life-Style: A comparative analysis of free time*, Sage, London.

Orwell, G. (1954) *Nineteen Eighty-Four*, Penguin Books, London.

—— (1970) *The Road to Wigan Pier*, Penguin Books, London.

Palmer, J. (1991) *Potboilers: Methods, concepts and case studies in popular fiction*, Routledge, London.

Patton, C. (1993) 'Embodying subaltern memory: kinesthesia and the problematics of gender and race', in Schwichtenberg (1993).

Pearson, G. (1983) *Hooligan: A history of respectable fears*, Macmillan, London.

Pearson, N. (1982) *The State and the Visual Arts*, Open University Press, Milton Keynes.

Peters, E. (1985) *Torture*, Basil Blackwell, Oxford.

Peterson, R. (ed.) (1976) *The Production of Culture*, Sage, London.

Pieterse, J. Nederveen (1992) *White on Black: Images of Africa and Blacks in Western popular culture*, Yale University Press, New Haven.

Plant, S. (1992) *The Most Radical Gesture: The Situationist International in a postmodern age*, Routledge, London.

Polsky, N. (1967) *Hustlers, Beats and Others*, Penguin Books, London.

Porter, R. (ed.) (1992) *Myths of the English*, Polity Press, Cambridge.

Press, A. (1991) *Women Watching Television*, University of Pennsylvania Press, Philadelphia.

Pugh, S. (ed.) (1990) *Reading Landscape: Country – city – capital*, Manchester University Press, Manchester.

Rabinow, P. (ed.) (1986) *The Foucault Reader*, Penguin Books, London.

Radway, J. (1987): *Reading the Romance: Women, patriarchy and popular culture*, Verso, London.

Real, M.R. (1977) *Mass-Mediated Culture*, Prentice-Hall, New Jersey.

Reid, D.A. (1976) 'The decline of Saint Monday 1766–1876', *Past and Present*, 71.

Ritzer, G. (1992) *The McDonaldization of Society: An investigation into the changing character of contemporary social life*, Sage, London.

Roddick, N. (1983) *A New Deal in Entertainment: Warner Brothers in the 1930s*, British Film Institute, London.

Rojek, C. (1985) *Capitalism and Leisure Theory*, Tavistock, London.

—— (ed.) (1988) *Leisure for Leisure*, Macmillan, London.

—— (1993) *Ways of Escape: Modern transformations in leisure, and travel*, Macmillan, London.

Roman, L.G. *et al.* (eds) (1988) *Becoming Feminine: The politics of popular culture*, Falmer Press, London.

Rosaldo, R. (1993) *Culture and Truth: The remaking of social analysis*, Routledge, London.

Rosen, C. and Zerner, H. (1984) *Romanticism and Realism: The mythology of nineteenth century art*, Faber and Faber, London.

Rosenberg, B. and White, D. (1957) *Mass Culture*, Free Press, New York.

Ross, A. (1989) *No Respect: Intellectuals and popular culture* , Routledge, London.

Rowe, W. and Schelling, V. (1991) *Memory and Modernity: Popular culture in Latin America*, Verso Books, London.

Ryan, C. (1991) *Recreational Tourism: A social science perspective*, Routledge, London.

Samuel, R. (ed.) (1989) *Patriotism: The making and unmaking of British*, National Identity.

Vol. I: *History and Politics*;

Vol. II: *Minorities and Outsiders*;

Vol. III: *National Fictions*, Routledge, London.

Samuel, R. and Thompson, P. (1990) 'Introduction', in (eds) *The Myths We Live By*, Routledge, London.

Scannell, P. (1992) Public service broadcasting and modern public life in Scannell *et al.* (1992).

Scannell, P., Schlesinger, P. and Sparks, C. (eds) (1992) *Culture and Power: A Media, Culture and Society reader*, Sage, London.

Schapiro, M. (1973) *Words and Pictures: On the literal and the symbolic in the illustration of a text*, Mouton, The Hague.

Schiach, M. (1989) *Discourse on Popular Culture*, Polity Press, Cambridge.

Schiller, H.I. (1976) *Communication and Cultural Domination*, International Arts and Sciences Press, New York.

—— (1992) *Mass Communication and American Empire*, 2nd edn, Westview Press, Oxford.

Schlesinger, P. (1978) *Putting 'Reality' Together: BBC News*, Constable, London.

—— (1991) 'Media, the political order and national identity', *Media, Culture and Society*, 13(3).

Schudson, M. (1987) 'The new validation of popular culture: sense and sentimentality in academia', *Critical Studies in Mass Communications*, 4(1).

—— (1989) 'The sociology of news production', *Media, Culture and Society*, 11(3).

—— (1993) *Advertising: The Uneasy Persuasion. Its dubious impact on American society*, Routledge, London.

Schudson, M. and Mukerji, C. (eds) (1991) *Re-thinking Popular Culture*, California University Press, Berkeley .

Schulze, L., Barton White, A. and Brown, J.D. (1993) 'A sacred monster in her prime: audience construction of Madonna as low-other', in Schwichtenberg (1993).

Schwarzbach, F.S. (1982) 'Terra incognita – an image of the city in English literature 1820–1855', in P. Dodd (ed.) *The Art of Travel*, Cass, London.

Schwichtenberg, C. (ed.) (1993) *The Madonna Connection:, Representational politics, subcultural identities and cultural theory*, Westview Press, Oxford.

Segal, A. (1970) 'Censorship, social control and socialization', *British Journal of Sociology*, 21(1).

Sennett, R. (1977) *The Fall of Public Man*, Knopf, New York.

Shanks, M. and Tilley, C. (1987) *Reconstructing Archaeology: Theory and practice*, Cambridge University Press, Cambridge.

Shields, R. (1991) *Places on the Margin: Alternative geographies of modernity*, Routledge, London.

—— (ed.) (1992) *Lifestyle Shopping: The subject of consumption*, Routledge, London.

Short, J.R. (1991) *Imagined Country: Society, culture and environment*, Routledge, London.

Silverman, E.K. (1990) 'Clifford Geertz: towards a more "thick" understanding?', in C. Tilley (ed.) *Reading Material Culture*, Basil Blackwell, Oxford.

Silverstone, R. (1985) *Framing Science: The making of a BBC documentary*, British Film Institute, London.

Sinfield, A. (1992) *Faultlines: Cultural materialism and the politics of dissident reading*, Clarendon Paperbacks, Oxford.

Siskind, J. (1991) 'The invention of Thanksgiving: A ritual of American nationality', *Critique of Anthropology*, 11(2).

Sklar, R. (1978) *Movie-Made America: A cultural history of American movies*, Chappell, London.

Smart, B. (1993) *Postmodernity*, Routledge, London.

Smith, A.D. (1988) 'The myth of the "modern nation" and the myth of nations', *Ethnic and Racial Studies*, 11(1).

—— (1989) 'The origins of nations', *Ethnic and Racial Studies*, 12(3).

—— (1991) *National Identity*, Penguin, London.

Smith, D.E. (1988) 'Femininity as discourse', in Roman *et al.* (1988).

Snyder, R.W. (1986) 'The voice of the city: vaudeville and the formation of mass culture in New York neighbourhoods, 1880–1930', PhD thesis, New York University.

Soja, E. (1989) *Postmodern Geographies*, Verso Books, London.

Sparks, R. (1992) *Television and the Drama of Crime: Moral tales and the place of crime in public life*, Open University Press, Milton Keynes.

Stallybrass, P. and White, A. (1986) *The Politics and Poetics of Transgression*, Methuen, London.

Stedman Jones, G. (1983) *Languages of Class: Studies in English working class history, 1832–1982*, Cambridge University Press, Cambridge.

Stilgoe, J.R. (1988) *Borderland: Origins of the American suburb 1820–1939*, Yale University Press, New Haven.

Storch, R.D. (ed.) (1982) *Popular Culture and Custom in Nineteenth Century England*, Croom Helm, London.

Stott, W. (1973) *Documentary Expression and Thirties America*, Oxford University Press, New York.

Sturrock, J. (1979) *Structuralism and Since: From Lévi-Strauss to Derrida*, Methuen, London.

Strinati, D. and Wagg, S. (eds) (1992) *Come on Down? Popular media, culture in post-war Britain*, Routledge, London.

Suleiman, S.R. (ed.) (1985) *The Female Body in Western Culture: Contemporary perspectives*, Harvard University Press, London.

Synott, A. (1993) *The Body Social: Symbolism, self and society* , Routledge, London.

Tagg, J. (1988) *The Burden of Representation: Essays on photographies and histories*, Macmillan, London.

Tatum, S. (1982) *Inventing Billy the Kid: Visions of the outlaw in America 1881–1981*, University of New Mexico Press, Albuquerque.

Taylor, I. and Taylor, L. (1973) *Politics and Deviance*, Penguin Books, London.

Tester, K. (1991) *Animals and Society: The humanity of animal rights*, Routledge, London.

—— (1992) *Civil Society*, Routledge, London.

Thomas, K. (1983) *Man and the Natural World: Changing attitudes in England, 1500–1800*, Allen Lane, London.

Thompson, E.P. (1963) *The Making of the English Working Class*, Victor Gollancz, London.

—— (1967) 'Time, work-discipline and industrial capitalism', *Past and Present*, 38.

—— (1971) 'The moral economy of the English crowd', in the Eighteenth Century *Past and Present*, 50.

—— (1993) *Customs in Common*, Penguin Books, London.

Thompson, J.B. (1990) *Ideology and Modern Culture: Critical social theory in the era of mass communication*, Polity Press, Cambridge.

Tomlinson, A. (ed.) (1990) *Consumption, Identity and Style*, Routledge, London.

Tonkin, E. (1992) *Narrating Our Pasts: The social construction of oral history*, Cambridge University Press, Cambridge.

Tracey, M. and Morrison, D. (1979) *Whitehouse*, Macmillan, London.

Tuchman, G. (ed.) (1974) *The Television Establishment: Programming for power and profit*, Prentice-Hall, Englewood Cliff, New Jersey.

—— (1978) *Making News*, Free Press, New York.

Tuchman, G., Daniels, A.K. and Benet, J. (eds) (1978) *Hearth and Home: Images of women in the mass media*, Oxford University Press, New York.

Tudor, A. (1989) *Monsters and Mad Scientists: A cultural history of the horror movie*, Basil Blackwell, Oxford.

Tulloch, J. (1990) *Television Drama: Agency, audience and myth*, Routledge, London.

Turner, B.S. (1984) *The Body and Society: Explorations in Social Theory*, Basil Blackwell, Oxford.

—— (1992a) *Regulating Bodies: Essays in medical sociology*, Routledge, London.

—— (1992b) 'Ideology and utopia in the formation of an intelligentsia: reflections on the English cultural conduit', *Theory, Culture and Society*, 9(1).

Turner, G. (1990) *British Cultural Studies: An introduction*, Unwin Hyman, London.

Urry, J. (1988) 'Cultural change and contemporary holiday-making', *Theory, Culture and Society*, 5(1).

—— (1990) *The Tourist Gaze: Leisure and travel in contemporary societies*, Sage, London.

—— (1991) 'Time and space in Giddens' social theory', in C. Bryan and D. Jary (eds) *Giddens' Theory of Structuration: A critical appreciation*, Routledge, London.

—— (1992) 'The tourist gaze and the "Environment"', *Theory, Culture and Society*, 9(3).

Van Dijk, T.A. (1991) *Racism and the Press*, Routledge, London.

Wagner, R. (1981) *The Invention of Culture*, Chicago University Press, Chicago.

Warner, M. (1985) *Monuments and Maidens: The allegory of the female form*, Weidenfeld and Nicolson, London.

Warner, S.B. Jr. (1983) 'The management of multiple urban images', in D.

Fraser and A. Sutcliffe (eds) *The Pursuit of Urban History*, Edward Arnold, London.

Warnke, M. (1993) *The Court Artist: On the ancestry of the modern artist*, Cambridge University Press, Cambridge.

Warren, S. (1993) 'This heaven gives me migraines: The problems and promise of landscapes of leisure', in Duncan and Ley (1993).

Weedon, C. (1987) *Feminist Practice and Poststructuralist Theory*, Basil Blackwell, Oxford.

Wenner, L.A. (ed.) (1989) *Media, Sports and Society*, Sage, London.

Werlen, B. (1993) *Society, Action and Space*, Routledge, London.

Wernick, A. (1991) *Promotional Culture: Advertising, ideology and symbolic expression*, Sage, London.

Williams, J. (1991) 'Having an away day: English football supporters and the hooligan debate', in J. Williams and S. Wagg (eds) *British Football and Social Change*, Leicester University Press, Leicester.

Williams, R. (1958) *Culture and Society 1780–1950*, Chatto and Windus, London.

—— (1961) *The Long Revolution*, Chatto and Windus, London.

—— (1973) *The Country and the City*, Chatto and Windus, London.

—— (1974) *Television: Technology and cultural form*, Fontana, London.

—— (1976) *Keywords: A vocabulary of culture and society*, Fontana, London.

—— (1977) *Marxism and Literature*, Oxford University Press, Oxford.

Williams, R.H. (1982) *Dream Worlds: Mass consumption in late nineteenth century France*, University of California Press, Berkeley.

Williamson, J. (1978) *Decoding Advertisements: Ideology and meaning in advertising*, Marion Boyar, London.

Willis, P. (1977) *Learning to Labour: How working-class kids get working-class jobs*, Saxon House, Farnborough.

—— (1978) *Profane Culture*, Routledge and Kegan Paul, London.

—— (1990) *Common Culture: Symbolic work at play in the symbolic cultures of the young*, Open University Press, Milton Keynes.

Winship, J. (1987) *Inside Women's Magazines*, Pandora, London.

Wolfe, T. (1975) *The Painted Word*, Farrar, Strauss and Giroux, New York

Wolff, J. (1980) *The Social Production of Art*, Macmillan, London.

—— (1990) *Feminine Sentences: Essays on women and culture*, Polity Press, Cambridge.

Wolff, K.H. (ed.) (1950) *The Sociology of Georg Simmel*, University of Chicago Press, Chicago.

Women's Studies Group (1978) *Women Take Issue: Aspects of women's subordination*, Hutchinson, London.

Wright, W. (1975) *Sixguns and Society: A structural study of the western*, University of California Press, Berkeley.

Yeo, S. and Yeo, E. (eds) (1981) *Popular Culture and Class Conflict 1590–1914*, Harvester Press, Brighton.

Young, E.D.K. (1986) 'Where the daffodils blow: elements of communal imagery in a northern suburb', in A.P. Cohen (1986).

Young, M. (1988) *The Metronomic Society: Natural rhythms and human timetables*, Harvard University Press, Cambridge, Mass.

Zaller, J.R. (1992) *The Nature and Origins of Mass Opinion*, Cambridge University Press, Cambridge.

Zemon Davis, N. (1975) *Society and Culture in Early Modern France*, Stanford University Press, California.

Zukin, S. (1992) 'Postmodern urban landscapes: mapping culture and power', in Lash and Friedman (1992).

Zurcher, L.A. and Kirkpatrick, R.G. (1976) *Citizens for Decency: Anti-pornography crusades as status defense*, Texas University Press, Austin.

Name index

Abercrombie, N. 75, 200
Adam, B. 102, 147
Adorno, T.W. 14
Agnew, J.A. 146, 148
Albrecht, M.C. *et al.* 18, 19
Albrow, M. 126
Althusser, L. 21, 32, 33
Anderson, B. 29, 101, 108
Ang, I. 35
Annals, 56, 57
Appadurai, A. 149
Archer, 139
Ardener, S. 152
Arnold, 11
Arts Council, 61
Avery, R.K. 16, 28

Bakhtin, M.M. 39
Balio, T. 54
Barr, C. 54
Barrett, M. *et al.* 20
Barth, G. 53
Barthes, R. 46, 205
Bathricks, K. 68
Baudrillard, J. 17, 25, 188, 189, 199, 201
Bauman, Z. 8, 9, 92, 129, 183, 190
Baxandall, M. 45
Beadle, J.J. 212
Beck, U. 31, 137
Becker, H.S. 18
Bell, D. 15
Benjamin, W. 14, 27, 51, 170, 185, 206, 212

Bennett, T. 48, 77
Berger, A.A. 28
Berger, G. 68
Berger, P.L. 84
Berman, M. 86
Bernstein, B. 60
Best, S. 182
Bhaba, H.K. 29
Billington, R. 10
Birmingham Centre for Contemporary Cultural Studies 21, 38, 39, 81
Blake, W. 11
Bonner, F. *et al.* 33, 120, 124
Bonnie and Clyde, 37
Bourdieu, P. 31, 65, 69, 112, 119, 156, 157
Bowdler, Dr. 117
Bowie, D. 73
Bowlby, R. 160,
Boyes, G. 15
Braden, S. 61
Brake, M. 39, 80
Brantlinger, P. 16
Brennan, T. 70
Brewer, J. 76
British Film Institue, 60
British Sociological Association 20
Brown, M.E. 33, 82
Brookside, 84
Buck, P.A. 199
Buck-Morss, S. 51, 170
Burke, P. 117, 136, 215
Burns, T. 107

Subject index

abstract art 186
abstraction 22
academia 16
activists 121
actuality 199–200
advertising 75,186; character of 190; replacing reality 187
adverts, ethnographic clues to forms of life 190,
aesthetics 118; popular 215; practical 215; of realism 194, 203–4; of representation 196–7, 200, 203–4, 213
aesthetic, autonomy 19; innovation 186; paradigm, new 205
aestheticisation of everyday life 82
aesthetes 130
affiliations 129
agrarian society 86
AIDS 129
alienation 185
America 16; mythologist 134, 189; North 15, 53, 55, 106, 111, 127
American: cultural imprialism 209; Presidential candidates 200; rural poverty, studies of 14; sociology 18
analysis 20, 80, 149; hegemonic 155; intellectual 23; linguistic 23; of popular culture, 92; structural and ethnographic, of representation 70; textual 206
analytic 22

anarchy 116; of images 120
anonymity 96; of mass society 14; of urban life 174
anthropological 16
anthropologist 9; cultural 56, 87
anthropology 40; of ourselves 14
appearance 164, 173
apocalyptic 14
appropriation 76
arbitrariness 213
arcades 170
archaeology 40
architecture, as organisation of space 149
art 9, 19
artefacts 19
articulation 23
artificial, self-consciously 149
artifice 196; of postmodern leisure 198; spectacular 199
artists 18, 26, 151, 186
audience 31, 35, 54, 75–6, 113, 117, 143; a broader conception of consumer culture 82; abstract collectivities 27; active 35–6, 53, 82, 85, 211–12; behaviour 81; creativity of 211; mass 67–8, 85, 158, 210; socially segregated 12
authenticity 12, 97, 145; central focus of critical concern 195; simulation of 201; superfluous, 195
author 49; death of 205
authorising the customer 177